The Spirit and the Song

Theology, Religion, and Pop Culture

Series Editor: Matthew Brake

The *Theology, Religion, and Pop Culture* series examines the intersection of theology, religion, and popular culture, including, but not limited to television, movies, sequential art, and genre fiction. In a world plagued by rampant polarization of every kind and the decline of religious literacy in the public square, *Theology, Religion, and Pop Culture* is uniquely poised to educate and entertain a diverse audience utilizing one of the few things society at large still holds in common: love for popular culture.

Select titles in the series

The Spirit and the Song: Pneumatological Reflections on Popular Music,
  edited by Chris E. W. Green and Steven Félix-Jäger
Post-Christian Religion in Popular Culture: Theology through Exegesis,
  by Andrew D. Thrasher
Nazi Occultism, Jewish Mysticism, and Christian Theology in the Video Game Series Wolfenstein, by Frank G. Bosman
The Last of Us and Theology: Violence, Ethics, Redemption?, edited by Peter Admirand
Fantasy, Theology, and the Imagination, edited by Andrew D. Thrasher and
  Austin M. Freeman, with Fotini Toso
Theology and Wes Craven, edited by David K. Goodin
Theology and the DC Universe, edited by Gabriel Mckee and Roshan Abraham
Theology and Star Trek, edited by Shaun C. Brown and Amanda MacInnis Hackney
The Spirit and the Screen: Pneumatological Reflections on Contemporary Cinema, edited by Chris E. W. Green and Steven Félix-Jäger
Theology and the Avett Brothers, edited by Alex Sosler
Bob Dylan and the Spheres of Existence, by Christopher B. Barnett

The Spirit and the Song

Pneumatological Reflections on Popular Music

Edited by
Chris E. W. Green
Steven Félix-Jäger

LEXINGTON BOOKS/FORTRESS ACADEMIC
Lanham • Boulder • New York • London

Published by Lexington Books/Fortress Academic
Lexington Books is an imprint of The Rowman & Littlefield Publishing Group, Inc.
4501 Forbes Boulevard, Suite 200, Lanham, Maryland 20706
www.rowman.com

86-90 Paul Street, London EC2A 4NE, United Kingdom

Copyright © 2024 by The Rowman & Littlefield Publishing Group, Inc.

All rights reserved. No part of this book may be reproduced in any form or by any electronic or mechanical means, including information storage and retrieval systems, without written permission from the publisher, except by a reviewer who may quote passages in a review.

British Library Cataloguing in Publication Information Available

Library of Congress Cataloging-in-Publication Data

Names: Green, Chris E. W., editor. | Félix-Jäger, Steven, editor.
Title: The spirit and the song: pneumatological reflections on popular music / edited by Chris E. W. Green, Steven Félix-Jäger.
Description: Lanham : Lexington Books/Fortress Academic, 2024. | Series: Theology, religion, and pop culture | Includes bibliographical references and index. | Summary: "This book considers how music can transport listeners beyond themselves. Both music and the Spirit operate between languages and cultures, between desires and longings, between the visible and invisible, and between the deep and near. Thus, the Spirit, through music, unites and gathers communities, revealing new Possibilities"— Provided by publisher.
Identifiers: LCCN 2024023771 (print) | LCCN 2024023772 (ebook) | ISBN 9781978716384 (cloth) | ISBN 9781978716391 (epub)
Subjects: LCSH: Popular music—Religious aspects—Christianity. | Spirit.
Classification: LCC ML3921.2 .S63 2024 (print) | LCC ML3921.2 (ebook) | DDC 781.1/2—dc23/eng/20240529
LC record available at https://lccn.loc.gov/2024023771
LC ebook record available at https://lccn.loc.gov/2024023772

Contents

Introduction: Music Makes the World New   1
Chris E. W. Green

PART I: MUSIC, AFFECT, AND THE SPIRIT   7

1 Thus Sings the Lord: The Spirit, the Body, and the Sacramental Nature of Singing   9
Chris E. W. Green

2 The Sacred Song: How Divine Creativity Is Revealed in the Physics and Metaphysics of Music   23
Edwin Rodríguez-Gungor

3 We Feel Fire When It's Hot: Affect and Manipulation in Music   39
Steven Félix-Jäger

4 "Everything Means Nothing to Me": The Spirit of Wisdom within Qoheleth, Kierkegaard's *Either/Or*, and the Elliott Smith Songbook   53
Sophia A. Magallanes-Tsang

PART II: MUSIC AS CULTURAL EXPRESSION   67

5 The Spirit-Haunted Lyrics of Jason Isbell   69
Amber Benson

6 The Spirit in Neoclassical, Wordless Music   87
Marc Byrd and Aaron Gabriel Ross

7 Spiritual Longing in the Music of Jimi Hendrix   103
Blaine Charette

8	"The Answer, My Friend": A Pneumatological Reading of Bob Dylan's "Blowin' in the Wind" *Jeffrey S. Lamp*	115
9	Rivers Underneath: The Spirit in Underground Music *Jeremy Hunt*	129

PART III: MUSIC IN CHRISTIAN WORSHIP AND WITNESS — 141

10	"There Is a Cloud": The Holy Spirit in Contemporary Worship Songs *Shannan K. Baker*	143
11	When the Spirit Moves: Black Gospel Music as an Embodied Witness *Jennifer Thigpenn*	159
12	"Oh Happy Day": The Migration and Reclamation of the Soul of Pentecostal Faith *Kimberly Ervin Alexander*	173
13	Global Spirit and Globalizing Spirits: Worship Song's Role in Turkish Liturgical Identity *Jeremy Perigo*	197
14	"We Were All Vibing the Same Way": Luthercostality in South Brazil *Marcell Silva Steuernagel*	215

Conclusion: The Classic Fade Out — 231
Steven Félix-Jäger

Index — 237

About the Editors and Contributors — 241

Introduction
Music Makes the World New
Chris E. W. Green

For old-time Pentecostal preaching, the story from Acts 16 of Paul and Silas singing in the Philippian jail held a kind of primal significance:

> At midnight Paul and Silas prayed, and sang praises unto God: and the prisoners heard them. And suddenly there was a great earthquake, so that the foundations of the prison were shaken: and immediately all the doors were opened, and every one's bands were loosed. (Acts 16:25-26 KJV)

Preachers delighted in joining this image of fettered saints singing praises at the darkest hour with the story of David soothing Saul with his songs (1 Sam. 16:14-23) and the story of the priestly choir leading King Jehoshaphat's warriors into victory (2 Chron. 20:21-23). These stories were laced with quotes from the Psalms, including especially Ps 100:1: "Make a joyful noise unto the Lord . . . come before his presence with singing" (Ps. 100:1 KJV). Taken together, these texts were heard to announce a call: believers are bound to sing because singing is essentially and inevitably liberating and triumphant. Thus, music and singing are the heart of the work of the church, a vital means of bringing the Spirit's healing power and the beauty of Christ's holiness to bear in the world—even when the singers and musicians are not especially skilled, even when the songs are not especially noteworthy or refined.

Such a vision of music and singing is not exclusively Pentecostal or charismatic, of course, although it does perhaps take unique shape in those movements. All Christians sing to God and share a delight in the gifts of music. But the Pentecostal/charismatic emphasis on the power of the Spirit at work in song perhaps draws attention to something too easily forgotten: singing and the Spirit are intimately, inseparably bound up together. This is why Paul urges the Ephesians not to be debauched with wine but to be "filled with the

Spirit, *as you sing* psalms and hymns and spiritual songs to one another, singing and making melody to the Lord in your hearts, giving thanks to God the Father at all times and for everything in the name of our Lord Jesus Christ" (Eph. 5:18-20). You see the point: singing—sung prayer, in particular—takes us right into the event that is God, the source, guide, and goal of all reality. Thus, as the Psalms endlessly remind us, nothing is more fitting or necessary than for us to sing—both our sorrows and our praise.

THE HEART IS MADE FOR SINGING

As a frame for the various themes raised by the contributions that make up this collection, let me say a few words about the peculiar connection between music, the Spirit, and human being-in-experience. First and foremost, it has to be admitted that music, precisely because it belongs to Spirit and to human being, is the least thinkable art, the hardest art to theologize about. Danielle Anne Lynch has said that music "suspends the boundary between the human subject and the divine subject, and in this way allows for experience of the transcendence of God."[1] And, she suggests, that same power of suspension also overcomes or unfastens the boundary between soul and body, and the body and the natural world, as well as between neighbors and strangers, even enemies—all graces of the Spirit who draws all things toward oneness.

We know something of this from our own experiences of singing, do we not? Caught up in the song, we find we are taken up into a kind of unmaking and remaking of the world. As Nick Cave has said, music's furtive sanctity finds ways past the walls of our suffering, our layered defense mechanisms, to touch something good, something true, "the sacred essence."[2]

> I think music, out of all that we can do, at least artistically, is the great indicator that something else is going on, something unexplained, because it allows us to experience genuine moments of transcendence . . . I think there is more going on than we can see or understand, and we need to find a way to lean into the mystery of things—the impossibility of things—and recognise the evident value in doing that, and summon the courage it requires to not always shrink back into the known mind . . . Many people will, of course, disagree, although I tend to think most musicians have more time for these spiritual considerations, because when they make music, when they lose themselves in music, fall deep inside it, they encounter such strong intimations of the divine. Of all things, music can lift us closer to the sacred.[3]

Given that what Lynch and Cave are saying is true, it would be a mistake to speak of music as a conduit or means of religious experience and spiritual expression. We must say instead that music is a kind of sacramental communion with reality at its most mysterious and most "impossible." To put it in less explicitly theological terms, the experience of transcendence in song and singing makes us feel something of the improbable coming-together of things, the surprising harmonic and rhythmic convergences of reality as it is meant to be—an experience which makes us come more fully alive ourselves, drawing out of us a fresh fullness of being.

Thanks to its ineffability and "impossibility," music both transgresses and transcends the limitations of language, reaching otherwise unreachable depths and breadths. Music, at least at its depths, is the least thinkable art and the hardest art to theologize about. Insofar as it is true to itself, it lifts us up. And yet, in that same way and at the same time, it also grounds us, enlarging us by fixing our attention on *this* sound, *this* moment. Music perceives the inner essence of our reality as a whole just because it receives so fully and gladly, like a perfect mirror, some particular and peculiar good.

Music gets to the heart of the matter, we might say, just because it gets to the heart of matter itself. Indeed, it is not insignificant that reality itself, physically as well as metaphysically, is musical or song-like. Jean-Louis Chrétien reveals this secret in his stunning reflections on silence in painting:

> Silent music is the very music of silence, silence as music. From the very fact of its being music, it gives a singular density to silence. If we were to look upon musicians playing through a pane of glass so thick that it prevented us from hearing what they were playing, this would not be a music of silence, but rather a forbidden music, a frustrating music that would exasperate our desire to hear. But all of the songs of angels or of men, all of the pictorial concerts, performed solo or by groups, which traverse the many centuries of painting, give us silence to hear. We are deprived of nothing; on the contrary, we are filled.[4]

Jacques Attali has remarked that music is more than an object of study; it is instead, he says, "a way of perceiving the world," a mode of understanding.[5] Somehow, music sensitizes us to what is real, making us more keenly aware of what is happening in and around us. Although we can, of course, use music to dull our senses or deaden our imagination—there are "escapist" songs as surely as there are escapist stories—the moment we taste the transcendent in a song, the moment we feel something of the true, the good, the beautiful, we cannot help but be reawakened to the painful wonder of things.

Music not only perceives the world; it *precedes* it. As Jenson rightly notes, "the world presents itself not only as a congeries of sights but also and indeed first as a congeries of sounds."[6] We do not, he reminds us, have any "instant defenses for our ears" as we do for our eyes. Our ears are designed to "channel sound in willy-nilly." Thus, music—in a way unlike painting, sculpture, architecture, or even poetry read aloud—is a relief from the sound of noise.

By singing or listening to a song, "we replace the buzz in our ears with rhythms and melodies and harmonies." In the making of music, then, human beings are *re*making the world and, in some significant sense, *saving* it. And that is as true of a half-remembered ditty crooned or hummed while doing laundry as it is of a majestic orchestral performance.

THE SPIRIT OF SONG, THE SONG WHO IS SPIRIT

Theologians have to ask why it is that the beauty of music tells us the truth and shows us the good. They must also have something to say about how God makes this to be so. Anthony Baker, riffing on Hans Urs von Balthasar's claim that the truth is symphonic, suggests we might think of Jesus as "the true music of the world" and the Holy Spirit as the one who makes that music happen—sometimes also in and through the worship of the people of God. In this model, Christ, as the new and renewing "score" of creation written by the Father, is played by the church as an orchestra under the guidance of the Spirit.[7]

The Father's truth is not, Baker argues, "a completed score," one the church possesses as a product it can use as it likes, but is instead a living reality discovered or encountered in "the action of playing it back to God the way it was written."

> By performing the divine symphony, all the instruments of creation discover why they have been assembled together. Initially they stand or sit next to one another as strangers, in mutual contradiction. Suddenly, as the music begins, they realize how they are integrated. Not in unison, but what is far more beautiful—in symphony.[8]

What Baker says here is not to be taken simply as a high-brow metaphor for our relation to God and to one another in God. The symphonic is not merely an analogy of being; it is, as I have been arguing, experientially and existentially true as well—and in the most direct ways. The human being is the singing animal because she is animated by the Breath of the God who makes the Word sing. If we fail to grasp that truth, we cannot really understand anything about our condition or calling at all.

CONCLUSION

Jeremy Begbie asks us to take seriously the fact that music, "so often thought to be at best half-articulate and at worst corrupting," actually holds special power "to help us discover, understand and expound theological truth, to the advantage of theology and the deepening of our knowledge of God."[9] The reverse is also true: the experience of God and the study of theology, which necessarily includes reflection on our experience, can deepen our understanding of music.

The essays in this volume attempt in various ways to come to grips with these and other truths about the song and the Spirit, seeking to find a broader and deeper understanding of the manifold connections between music, prayer, faith, language, experience, and theology. However it comes to us, music, inasmuch as it is true to itself, acts creatively and redemptively on us—sometimes gently, sometimes forcefully, but always for good. The conviction that guides this volume is that music can act on us in these ways because it acts directly on the heart so that the heart opens in response, coming alive in the encounter.

The heart is made for singing, and music sung from the heart makes the world new. To confess in faith the third article of the creed is to see that the spirit of song is nothing other than the movement of the Spirit who is our very life and longing. It should not then surprise us that, as Karl Rahner says, the heart that's alive thinks of God—and sings.[10]

NOTES

1. Danielle Anne Lynch, "Approaches to Music in Modern Theology," PhD thesis (Leeds, UK: University of Leeds, 2015), 7.
2. Nick Cave and Séan O'Hagan, *Faith, Hope, and Carnage* (New York: Farrar, Straus and Giroux, 2022), 24.
3. Cave and O'Hagan, *Faith, Hope, and Carnage*, 28–30.
4. Jean-Louis Chrétien, *Hand to Hand: Listening to the Work of Art* (New York: Fordham University Press, 2003), 21.
5. Jacques Attali, *Noise: The Political Economy of Music* (Minneapolis: University of Minnesota Press, 1985), 4.
6. Robert W. Jenson, "Christ as Culture 2: Christ as Art," *International Journal of Systematic Theology* 6.1 (2004), 69–76 (72).
7. Anthony D. Baker, "Fiddling with the Melody: Illuminating von Balthasar's Symphony of Truth," *The Other Journal* 15 (Fall 2009); available online: https://theotherjournal.com/2009/05/fiddling-with-the-melody-illuminating-von-balthasars-symphony-of-truth/.
8. Baker, "Fiddling with the Melody," n.p.
9. Jeremy S. Begbie, *Theology, Music and Time* (Cambridge: Cambridge University Press, 2004), 8.
10. Karl Rahner, *The Great Church Year* (New York: Crossroads, 1993), 93–94.

BIBLIOGRAPHY

Attali, Jacques. *Noise: The Political Economy of Music*. Minneapolis: University of Minnesota Press, 1985.

Baker, Anthony. "Fiddling with the Melody: Illuminating von Balthasar's Symphony of Truth." *The Other Journal* 15 (Fall 2009): n.p.; available online: https://theotherjournal.com/2009/05/fiddling-with-the-melody-illuminating-von-balthasars-symphony-of-truth/.

Begbie, Jeremy S. *Theology, Music and Time*. Cambridge: Cambridge University Press, 2004.

Cave, Nick and Séan O'Hagan. *Faith, Hope, and Carnage*. New York: Farrar, Straus and Giroux, 2022.

Chrétien, Jean-Louis. *Hand to Hand: Listening to the Work of Art*. New York: Fordham University Press, 2003.

Jenson, Robert W. "Christ as Culture: Christ as Art." *International Journal of Systematic Theology* 6.1 (2004): 69–76.

Lynch, Danielle Anne. "Approaches to Music in Modern Theology." PhD thesis. Leeds, UK: University of Leeds, 2015.

Rahner, Karl. *The Great Church Year*. New York: Crossroads, 1993.

Part I
MUSIC, AFFECT, AND THE SPIRIT

Chapter 1

Thus Sings the Lord

The Spirit, the Body, and the Sacramental Nature of Singing

Chris E. W. Green

SINGING BEYOND SONG

"I'll Fly Away," page 333 in the so-called Red-Back Hymnal, was a staple of the sweaty Pentecostalism of my youth.[1] Over the years, as my theological horizons broadened, I came to regard the song as both artless and heterodox, trading in a cheap and corrosive otherworldliness wholly at odds with the Gospel. Eventually, however, I realized our singing actually subverted the song's seemingly escapist message.[2] We would not have thought of it in such terms, of course, but our singing, at its best, restored us to our bodies and made us one body in common praise, grounding us in shared gladness and longing, intertwining our spirits with our voices, and bonding us in ways too mysterious and complex for words. For a long time, I had thought, not without reason, that the song was unworthy of our singing. Yet I have come to appreciate more and more how at times our singing both saved us and saved the song itself, both awakening and awakened by a deeper magic.

Eamon Duffy's *The Stripping of the Altars,* a controversial, ground-breaking exploration of religious life in late medieval and early modern England, sheds light on a similarly enigmatic reality. Pre-Reformation English spirituality was, by his account, vibrant, diverse, and deeply engaging—for laity as well as clergy. Contrary, then, to the prevailing narrative that emerged after the Elizabethan establishment, Catholic spirituality in England wove a rich tapestry of rites and practices, offering solace and guidance even to those unfamiliar with Latin and without access to the Roman Canon.

Virginia Reinburg furthers Duffy's argument, showing how worshipers knew what was happening and how to participate "because it was conducted in a ritual language of gestures and symbols they knew from secular life."[3] Ironically, it was the royally enforced shift to the vernacular that rendered congregants passive in worship, the liturgy having become strange precisely because it was suddenly too familiar.

My "I'll Fly Away" realization taught me something like the same lesson Duffy and Reinburg demonstrated in their studies. There is a wisdom, a mystical way of being and knowing, that transcends altogether the analytical, rational, and discursive, revealing itself perhaps more than anywhere else in the act of singing, the most saturated phenomenon.[4] For that reason, singing not only can but cannot help but transcend songs, especially in the context of liturgical worship, because of the sacramental nature of singing.

With all that in mind, I set forth in the following pages a brief theology of singing as sacramental, incorporating insights from both Jewish and Christian traditions, including the Pentecostal movement in which I was raised, attempting to show something of what it means for singing to be mysterious, how it is integral to Christian identity, and why it opens out naturally onto mystical experience.

"O FOR A THOUSAND TONGUES"

We sang other songs in our Pentecostal church, our voices accompanied by claps and stomps as well as piano, organ, guitars, drums, and tambourines. We sang songs from the Red-Back—"Leaning on the Everlasting Arms" (p. 359); "The Old Rugged Cross" (p. 305); "Power in the Blood" (p. 390); "Just a Little Talk with Jesus" (p. 92); "He Set Me Free" (p. 235)—and others not in the songbook, like Carl Boberg's "How Great Thou Art"; T.O. Chisholm's "Great is Thy Faithfulness"; Thomas Dorsey's "The Lord Will Make a Way Somehow"; Claude Ely's "Send Down That Rain," "Ain't No Grave," and "You've Got to Move"; Jack Hayford's "Majesty"; Andre Crouch's "Through it All," "Can't Nobody Do Me Like Jesus," and "The Blood Will Never Lost Its Power," as well as other songs written by artists whose names are lost to history. We loved the stories behind the hymns as much as we loved the hymns themselves.

Not all of our songs were songs, properly speaking; some were simple choruses or tunes. We took 1 Cor. 14:15, Eph. 5:18-19, Col. 3:16 very seriously, understanding ourselves as heirs and compatriots of the saints and prophets. We imagined our voices mingling with the voices of Zechariah, Mary, Simeon, David, Asaph, Miriam, Paul, and Silas. We saw ourselves not only delighting God and wooing backsliders but also, like Jehoshaphat's army of Levites, driving back the forces of the evil one. We felt we were practicing for the heavenly choir, and we wanted nothing more than for others to join us in the singing.

Almost always, we sang with one voice. What Grant Wacker observed in his study of early Pentecostalism held true for us as well: "Musical harmony induced social harmony . . . as singing required a concerted action of many in a common and manifestly pleasurable endeavor."[5] Later, I learned what Bonhoeffer had said about the virtues of singing in unison. And although I am sure no one in our congregation had heard of him, much less read his *Life Together,* we would have agreed wholeheartedly with the sentiment of his reasoning:

> The essence of all congregational singing on this earth is the purity of unison singing—untouched by the unrelated motives of musical excess—the clarity unclouded by the dark desire to lend musicality an autonomy of its own apart from the words; it is the simplicity and unpretentiousness, the humanness and warmth, of this style of singing. Of course, this truth is only gradually and by patient practice disclosed to our oversophisticated ears. Whether or not a community achieves proper unison singing is a question of its spiritual discernment. This is singing from the heart, singing to the Lord, singing the Word; this is singing in unity.[6]

Here, we were honoring our Wesleyan-holiness inheritance and following (again, unknowingly) John Wesley's guidelines for singing. Although he laid out seven, our practice most fully embodied his third, fourth, and seventh instructions:

> III. Sing *All*. See that you join with the congregation as frequently as you can. Let not a slight degree of weakness or weariness hinder you. If it is a cross to you, take it up and you will find a blessing.
>
> IV. Sing *lustily* and with good courage. Beware of singing as if you were half dead, or half asleep; but lift up your voice with strength. Be no more afraid of your voice now, nor more ashamed of its being heard, than when you sung the songs of Satan.
>
> VII. Above all sing spiritually. Have an eye to God in every word you sing. Aim at pleasing him more than yourself, or any other creature. In order to this attend strictly to the sense of what you sing, and see that your heart is not carried away with the sound, but offered to God continually; so shall your singing be such as the Lord will approve of here, and reward when he cometh in the clouds of heaven.[7]

Ours was a radically sectarian vision. We not only spoke of ourselves as more truly Christian than others, but we also felt that superiority, a superiority that expressed itself in frequent and harsh judgment against our neighbors—especially our Roman Catholic and liberal Protestant neighbors. Sometimes, however, despite our foremost intentions and ambitions, we found ourselves inadvertently caught up in an ecumenical chorus—thanks to the wisdom of God embedded in the grace of singing.

TO SING IS TO ASCEND AS ONE

Sister Kathleen Harmon, liturgical theologian and director of music for the Institute for Liturgical Ministry in Dayton, Ohio, highlights the peculiar grace of singing, what it is that sets it apart from speaking. Speaking, she says, "sets up confrontational differences between the speaker and the hearer," while singing, at least in its liturgical form, conforms individuals in a single shared identity. To speak, interlocutors face off against each other. To sing, "they face the same direction."[8]

When words and music come together in a shared song, liturgical participation is effectively catalyzed, Harmon argues, transforming separate individuals into a corporate partnership and manifesting the deeper unity that underlies all things.[9] And this coming together happens in ways that enact the integration and enlargement of the self, not its abrogation or effacement.

Elicited or incited by the sung liturgy, the self's fullness comes in "a progressive expansion of self-awareness from self-alone to self-in-community to self-in-community-in-Christ."[10] Thus, congregational liturgical singing uniquely and preeminently "facilitates our entrance into the cosmic horizon that is Body of Christ enacting the paschal mystery."[11] As she elaborates:

> Communal singing is, then, perhaps the surest way to prevent liturgical celebration from becoming privatized, because it builds and binds the Body of Christ in ways both conscious and unconscious. Through singing, the sound waves generated by many voices overlap and intertwine, and what enters the body and stirs the soul of each individual is the multivalent vibration of many individuals becoming the one Body of Christ. Through their singing, assembly members make a gift of self to one another that becomes gift of all to God and to the world.[12]

In his epoch-making *Star of Redemption,* Franz Rosenzweig argued that liturgical singing, because it is animated by love for the neighbor, becomes an overwhelming force, pulling present-day believers in their gatherings into "the immense unison" of the future eternally redeemed community.[13] For him, as Steven Kepnes explains,

Communal prayer is a concentration of this power through the coming together of the community of believers. Since the love that the community concentrates has its origin in God's love for the human, when this love is concentrated it has the coercive power of God who originated it.[14]

Rabbi Abraham Joshua Heschel, one of the best-known and most widely read twentieth-century Jewish theologians, insists, however, that such compelling power comes to bear only as the congregation follows the lead of the cantor and rises to meet its task—during the liturgy and after it:

Are only the seraphim endowed with a sense for the glory? "The heavens declare the glory of God." How do they declare it? How do they reveal it? "There is no speech, there are no words, neither is their voice heard." The heavens have no voice; the glory is inaudible. And it is the task of man to reveal what is concealed; to be the voice of the glory, to sing its silence, to utter, so to speak, what is in the heart of all things. The glory is here—invisible and silent. Man is the voice; his task is to be the song. The cosmos is a congregation in need of a Cantor.[15]

In Jewish theology, therefore, as well as Christian theology, music is heavenly and transcendent precisely because it is earthly and immanentizing. It uplifts as it grounds. Like Jacob's ladder, it is not only heavenly and earthly but heavenly-and-earthly, not merely connecting or bridging heaven to earth but making them one. The *niggun* is "a path to God, a 'song of ascension.'"[16] Thus, Rabbi Kalonymus Kalman Shapira, Rebbe of the Warsaw ghetto, instructed his followers that their songs would lift them to the heavens like ladders as they sang with "a heart broken open" by the joys of obedience. He promised that as their song rose toward God, them standing on their toes like the angels, they would suddenly find themselves borne up, the whole of their lives rising and converging in the music:

Take a musical phrase, turn your face to the wall, or simply close your eyes and remind yourself that you stand in the presence of God. With your heart breaking open, you are here to pour out your soul to God with music and melody, emerging from the depths of your heart. Inevitably, you will begin to feel the emergence of your spirit in great joy and delight. At first it was you singing to your soul, to wake her up, but slowly you will feel your soul singing her own song . . . Through the sound of music, your soul pierces upward toward the heights. In heaven, it is as if your soul were seized by its sob and drawn out by its tongue. Its heart, guts and all its inner being emerge with its tune, and rise upon the path of notes. Your soul's ascents, falls, and all its peregrinations are engraved upon its melody, the movement of the melody is carved into your soul's voice. The tune comes together, and it lifts up your soul with its guts to pour it forth and bring it close to God.[17]

This lifting-up could be done, he said, even apart from the gathering, even when all that remains in the soul are groans and sighs:

> You do not need to be in a community to sing this way. Even when you are at home, any time you feel capable, you can sing as described above. And you do not need to scream and shout. There is music made even with a whisper or a breath that can still be heard in heaven.[18]

Rabbi Shapira's insights, rooted deeply in Hasidic wisdom, resonate with what I regard as the best of my own Pentecostal experience in my youth, not least because it shows how the work of the congregation and the responsibility of the individual are finally one and the same.

TO SING IS TO DESCEND ALONE FOR THE MANY

The moral philosopher Stanley Cavell, renowned for his work in ethics, aesthetics, and the mysteries of ordinary language, describes the guiding ambition of Romanticism as a longing for the hope of a just community—"not the overcoming of our isolation, but the sharing of that isolation; not to save the world out of love, but to save love for the world, until it is responsive again."[19] Thus, insofar as they are uprooted from religious faith, music and singing cannot quite be wholeheartedly intercessory, settling instead for holding space for the longed-for advent of intercession. Spiritual singing, however, singing that remains devoted to religion, aspires both to the sharing and the overcoming of isolation. It attempts both to save the world in love and to save love for the world, not only in the church's gathering but also in the hearts of individual believers as they suffer the thrownness of life.

Catherine Doherty, the Catholic activist and spiritual writer, at the height of the Death of God movement, found herself moved to intercessory singing, becoming one in that singing with the Mother of Sorrows:

> I thought of Mary holding his body. She knew, though it might have been a mystery to her also, that he would rise from the dead. I knew he would too. But they kept throwing the dead Christ into my lap, and I kept singing lullabies to him because I knew he wasn't dead. I knew he was only sleeping in the hearts of those people. I sang him a Russian lullaby:
>
>> Sleep, beloved child of mine. Sleep,
>> little mite. Sleep while there is time.
>> Very soon, very soon, you will be called
>> into battle, and before you know it, you
>> will grow up. I will have to embroider

your saddle with silver and with wool.
But not yet. Sleep, little child. Sleep,
little mite, before life will call you to its battle.

I sang thus to him in my heart the same lullaby my mother sang to me, though nobody heard me singing.[20]

All to say, we not only sing with others, facing the same direction (as Harmon suggested); we also sing for and over them—even, when necessary, *against* them. So, if singing is harmonizing, it is also combative. If it leads us up as one, it also leads us out for the many.

SINGING TELLS THE TRUTH AHEAD OF TIME

In a 2006 lecture to the Hymn Society of Great Britain and Ireland, Rowan Williams, then the Archbishop of Canterbury, argued that singing is, in a very real sense, "deeper" than speaking, not only historically but also existentially. Challenging the common assumption prevalent in both religious and societal contexts that human communication is essentially about "saying things," transmitting messages by using words as tools to make inner realities outwardly available, Williams contends that communication is not and has never been solely confined to spoken words, positing that our Neanderthal ancestors might have engaged more in singing than in conversation and discourse.[21]

Although he might resist the use of the word, Williams' argument makes it clear that the church's singing is necessarily *mystical*, because it is a transcendent and transfiguring communion that is, as he says, "actually not too far away from being a kind of sacrament."[22] As we sing, we discover most fully "the integrity of spirit and body," the reciprocity and mutuality we are meant to have in ourselves and with one another before God. And it is precisely for this reason, Williams concludes, that when we sing, "we say something about the nature of the universe in Christ."[23]

Denys Turner, in a famous lecture, argued that music is "prototypically Eucharistic."[24] Arguably, he does not go far enough, however. Certainly not, if what Albert Blackwell, himself a theologian and a musician, says about the deepest reality of music is true: "Dwelling at music's heart is a sacramental potency, awaiting only appropriate times and places for its actualisation, for manifesting the holy and for expressing our experiences of the holy."[25] What is sacramental potency if not creation's capacity for the infinite? A capacity music bears because we, the creatures who make music, bear it. Thus, in every sacramental moment, the infinite and the finite become together the realization of what St. Paul calls "new creation," a transfigured and transfiguring reality in which God is all in all, filling all things with the theandric energy of Christ.

What are we saying, though, when we say singing is sacramental? How are we to speak about it so that the statement is not misleading, vacuous, or banal? We need more than the conventional definitions. We cannot label it a means of grace because that suggests singing is a delivery mechanism for something other than itself—something simply divine, as opposed to human, or at least entirely spiritual. It also does not help to say singing is an outward sign of an inner reality because precisely what makes a sacrament a sacrament is the sign and signified being one. So, when we say singing is sacramental, we do not mean it facilitates the experience of God (although, as Blackwell says, it does manifest the holy); we mean our singing happens in and as the communion of the Holy Trinity, so that (whether we have any feeling of it or not) we mystically experience God's experience of God. An astounding claim, of course, but are not all the Gospel's claims astounding?

If in Christ the seen and unseen have been made one and all things drawn up into the uncreated life of God, then all phenomena may be—and in time must be—saturated just as he himself is. Singing, in its own way, tells the truth ahead of time. And singers are allowed, at times, to know it. As Catherine Pickstock says, "To believe the evidence of our ears is . . . to deny nihilism. Moreover, it is to believe in transcendence. More, it is to believe in the healing of time, and, therefore, sacramentally to receive the incarnation of God in his time, his passion and resurrection."[26]

But again: what does it mean to say we experience God's experience of God? In what sense do we receive the incarnation and the healing of time? It does not mean that when we sing, we always feel all the good that is happening, or even that all we feel is good. That is not true even in the context of the church's worship at its purest. It is a claim of *faith*, not sight; a seeing of what cannot be seen. We experience God's experience of God just in the sense that Jesus takes what we are doing personally, acts in our acting. He is singing; therefore, we can sing. As St. Augustine argues in his *Confessions* and *Enarrationes*, it is at the Eucharist that we discover ourselves as Christ's body, and in the praying of the Psalms that we find ourselves speaking in his voice. To sing the Psalms, therefore, is "to make our own voice the voice of the Body of Christ in worship."[27] For that reason, our singing takes on dimensions that exceed anything we can intend or even desire.

Is this true of all singing? Is it always true of the church's singing? No and no. Even when it is true, it cannot be fully felt or understood, for the same reasons that not every meal is communion and what we receive at the table is not dependent on what anyone comprehends or perceives. Still, the praise of the saints and the witness of the prophets tell us there is an inexhaustible goodness that attends our singing, an infinite creativity present for us whether we are present to it or not.

Hence, a theology of singing can and must take seriously human experience, "the evidence of our ears," wherever it comes and to whomever it comes, and learn to read that testimony in the light of what the Gospel declares to be true of us and our relation to the God of the Gospel, revealed in what happened to Jesus of Nazareth.

I WILL KEEP ON SINGING

Although singing sometimes surpasses and subverts the musical and lyrical merit of a song, a song's uprightness and worth does matter, because the essence of singing, its peculiar glory, emerges only in the alignment and resonance of soul, spirit, and body, person to person, with the song and the singing.

Phenomenologically speaking, as singers come into agreement with themselves and with one another, they realize together, with a sweet and joyous pang, the beauty, goodness, and truth of what they are singing and how the experience of transcendence calls forth their own harmony, setting them in rhythm. Theologically speaking, they can know this and can give themselves so completely to the singing because the Spirit shines and burns in the coming-together of creatures, the communion that is the life of the Son to the Father's delight. Hence, in Paul Evdokimov's words, the most powerful testimony to the Christian faith and the greatest evangelization of the world is found in the liturgical hymn, the Doxology, "which rises from the depths of the earth, in which moves the powerful breath of the Paraclete who alone converts and heals."[28]

In the light of the liturgy, creaturely existence is seen to be essentially and ultimately musical, moving toward the final brilliant fullness of creation in which every creature sings (in every sense of that word). This, at least, is the vision of the Fathers. For them, as Evdokimov explains, the Christian life is oriented by the liturgy to the God who is also neighbor:

> "I go forward singing to you," St John Climacus cries joyously. The same cheerfulness radiates from the winged words of St Gregory of Nazianzus: "Your glory, O Christ, is man, whom you have stationed in this world like an angel, a crier of your splendor; it is for you that I live, for you that I speak; I have become a living oblation to you—the one talent that is left of all my possessions." In the same vein, St Gregory Palamas writes, "Illumined, man reaches the eternal heights . . . and already here on earth he has become a complete miracle. Even without being in heaven, he emulates the untiring singers of hymns; like another angel of God on earth, he leads the entire created family to God."[29]

Olivier Clément, in his *Roots of Christian Mysticism,* sums up this doxastic wisdom, showing how humans become criers of God's splendor, complete miracles, just as their prayers become songs and their songs become prayers:

> Dionysius the Areopagite celebrated the "sympathy" that holds all creation together and transforms its contradictions into living tensions. Here is the Trinitarian fabric once again. Every creature, however lowly in itself, yet expresses an infinite intelligence. Humanity must be united with every creature in order to make the praise of its tongue-tied nature to be heard. For "prayer like a sigh has always resided in the mystery and essential nature of creation" (Basil Rozanov, *The Apocalypse of our Time*). The person of prayer understands that "everything is praying, every creature is singing the glory of God."[30]

The music of my youth was rarely, if ever sublime, even at its best. We did not experience and could not have performed anything like what my wife Julie and I heard at Evensong in St. Paul's, London. We did not and could not have philosophized about our worship, at least not with anything like the subtlety and profundity of a St. Gregory or a Dionysius. The elaborate, the speculative, the majestic—such modes were not in our repertoire. But we *did* know the transcendent intimately. We were sometimes carried up into the glorious, our spirits ascending with the music. Other times, the glorious seemed to fall on us suddenly, leaving us in a weighty quiet.

According to *Musicam Sacram,* Vatican II's ecumenical instructions on liturgical music, although splendor is sometimes desirable and fitting, "the true solemnity of liturgical worship depends less on a more ornate form of singing and a more magnificent ceremonial than on its worthy and religious celebration, which takes into account the integrity of the liturgical celebration itself."[31] Whatever our music lacked, our hearts strove to make up for—an effort whose beauty remained unaltered and undeterred by our untrained voices and the simplicity of our thoughts. What we would have called "anointed" singing stirred the deep wells of our hearts, drew us down toward silence or groans, and moved our bodies to dancing. Simple as the songs may have been, musically and lyrically, there was, at least at times, the move of God in our singing of them. We knew that to be true because the singing "took us somewhere."[32] And that, I believe, is a testament to the Spirit's resourcefulness and the inherently sacramental and mystical nature of singing at its truest, as well as to our desire for God and the infectious joys of shared worship.

POSTSCRIPT

Once, at the end of one of his eschatology lectures, Robert Jenson asked an organist to finish the talk for him by playing a Bach triple fugue.[33] In that same spirit, I am inviting you, after having read this chapter, to do something similar: find and listen to Aretha Franklin's "I'll Fly Away," and ask yourself why this song, of all songs, would be so fitting at a funeral and how, with its undeniable shortcomings, it can be made—by singing, by the way it is sung—into something so human, so divine.

NOTES

1. For an overview of the history of the hymnal and its contents, see: https://redbackhymnal.com/.

2. I should have asked myself why so many artists like Andy Griffith, Johnny Cash, Kenny Rogers, Kanye West, Steve Goodman, and Gillian Welch and Alison Krauss have recorded the song, and how it is that these various versions can be so different from one another—some playful and campy, others sad, still others transcendent.

3. Virginia Reinburg, "Liturgy and Laity in Late Medieval and Reformation France," *The Sixteenth Century Journal* 23.3 (Autumn 1992): pp. 526–547 (p. 529).

4. Jean-Luc Marion, *The Essential Writings* (New York: Fordham University Press, 2013), p. 142.

5. Grant Wacker, *Heaven Below: Early Pentecostals and American Culture* (Cambridge, MA: Harvard University Press, 2003), p. 96.

6. Dietrich Bonhoeffer, *Life Together* (Dietrich Bonhoeffer Works—Reader Edition; Minneapolis: Fortress Press, 2015), p. 40.

7. Martin V. Clarke, "John Wesley's 'Directions for Singing': Methodist Hymnody as an Expression of Methodist Beliefs in Thought and Practice," *Methodist History* 47:4 (July 2009): pp. 196–209 (p. 196).

8. Kathleen Harmon, *The Mystery We Celebrate, the Song We Sing: A Theology of Liturgical Music* (Collegeville, MN: Liturgical Press, 2008), p. 29.

9. As Harmon (*The Mystery We Celebrate, the Song We Sing*, p. 46) puts it, "The experience of music—both its production and its reception—induces a sense of collective identity. Immersed in the music's unfolding tensions and releases, harmonizations and rhythms, we face a common horizon. And in the borderless sharing that results, we discover that we are that horizon, that the vision, which beckons in front, is the reality planted within, our essential oneness with one another and with all that exists."

10. Harmon, *The Mystery We Celebrate, the Song We Sing*, p. 68.

11. Harmon, *The Mystery We Celebrate, the Song We Sing*, p. 68.

12. Harmon, *The Mystery We Celebrate, the Song We Sing*, p. 68.

13. Franz Rosenzweig, *The Star of Redemption* (Madison, WI: University of Wisconsin Press, 2005), p. 271.

14. Steven Kepnes, *Jewish Liturgical Reasoning* (Oxford: Oxford University Press, 2007), p. 119.

15. Abraham Joshua Heschel, "The Vocation of the Cantor"; available online: https://www.hebrewcollege.edu/wp-content/uploads/2018/11/Heschel-The-Vocation-of-the-Cantor.pdf.

16. Rabbi Zalman Schachter-Shalomi and Joel Segel, *Davening: A Guide to Meaningful Jewish Prayer* (Woodstock, VT: Jewish Lights, 2012), p. 57.
17. Rabbi Kalonymus Kalman Shapira, *Bnei Machshava Tova* 18; available online: https://www.sefaria.org/Bnei_Machshava_Tova%2C_Principles_and_Advice.18?lang=en.
18. Rabbi Shapira, *Bnei Machshava Tova* 18.
19. Stanley Cavell, *Must We Mean What We Say* (Cambridge: Cambridge University Press, 2015), p. 212.
20. Catherine Doherty, *Fragments of My Life: A Memoir* (Combermere, ON: Madonna House Publishing, 2007), p. 190.
21. Rowan Williams, "What Are We Saying by Singing?" (October 2006); available online: https://hymnsocietygbi.org.uk/2006/10/treasure-no-72-what-are-we-saying-by-singing/.
22. Williams, "What Are We Saying by Singing?"
23. Williams, "What Are We Saying by Singing?"
24. Denys Turner, *Faith, Reason, and the Existence of God* (Cambridge: Cambridge University Press, 2008).
25. Albert L. Blackwell, *The Sacred in Music* (Louisville: Westminster John Knox Press, 1999), p. 28.
26. Catherine Pickstock, "Music: Soul, City, and Cosmos after Augustine," in *Radical Orthodoxy: A New Theology;* John Milbank, Catherine Pickstock and Graham Ward, eds., (London: Routledge, 1999), pp. 243–277 (p. 269).
27. Rowan Williams, "Augustine and the Psalms," *Interpretation: A Journal of Bible and Theology* 58.1 (2004): 17–27 (17).
28. Paul Evdokimov, *The Sacrament of Love*: *The Nuptial Mystery in the Light of the Orthodox Tradition* (Crestwood, NY: St Vladimir's Seminary Press, 1995), p. 63.
29. Evdokimov, *The Sacrament of Love*, pp. 262–263.
30. Olivier Clément, *The Roots of Christian Mysticism* (New York: New York City Press, 2005), p. 216.
31. *Musicam Sacram* 11; available online: https://www.vatican.va/archive/hist_councils/ii_vatican_council/documents/vat-ii_instr_19670305_musicam-sacram_en.html.
32. Thanks to Mark Chironna for giving me this phrase.
33. Robert W. Jenson, "The Great Transformation," in *The Last Things: Biblical and Theological Perspectives on Eschatology;* Carl E. Braaten and Robert W. Jenson, eds. (Grand Rapids: Eerdmans 2002), pp. 33–42 (p. 42).

BIBLIOGRAPHY

Blackwell, Albert L. *The Sacred in Music*. Louisville: Westminster John Knox Press, 1999.

Bonhoeffer, Dietrich. *Life Together*. Dietrich Bonhoeffer Works—Reader Edition. Minneapolis: Fortress Press, 2015.

Cavell, Stanley. *Must We Mean What We Say*. Cambridge: Cambridge University Press, 2015.

Clarke, Martin V. "John Wesley's 'Directions for Singing': Methodist Hymnody as an Expression of Methodist Beliefs in Thought and Practice." *Methodist History* 47, no. 4 (July 2009): 196–209.

Clément, Olivier. *The Roots of Christian Mysticism.* New York: New York City Press, 2005.

Doherty, Catherine. *Fragments of My Life: A Memoir.* Combermere, ON: Madonna House Publishing, 2007.

Evdokimov, Paul. *The Sacrament of Love: The Nuptial Mystery in the Light of the Orthodox Tradition.* Crestwood, NY: St Vladimir's Seminary Press, 1995.

Harmon, Kathleen. *The Mystery We Celebrate, the Song We Sing: A Theology of Liturgical Music.* Collegeville, MN: Liturgical Press, 2008.

Heschel, Abraham Joshua. "The Vocation of the Cantor." Available online: https://www.hebrewcollege.edu/wp-content/uploads/2018/11/Heschel-The-Vocation-of-the-Cantor.pdf.

Jenson, Robert W. "The Great Transformation." In *The Last Things: Biblical and Theological Perspectives on Eschatology,* edited by Carl E. Braaten and Robert W. Jenson. Grand Rapids: Eerdmans, 2002.

Pickstock, Catherine. "Music: Soul, City, and Cosmos after Augustine." In *Radical Orthodoxy: A New Theology,* edited by John Milbank, Catherine Pickstock and Graham Ward (pp. 243–277). London: Routledge, 1999.

Kepnes, Steven. *Jewish Liturgical Reasoning.* Oxford: Oxford University Press, 2007.

Musicam Sacram 11; available online: https://www.vatican.va/archive/hist_councils/ii_vatican_council/documents/vat-ii_instr_19670305_musicam-sacram_en.html.

Reinburg, Virginia. "Liturgy and Laity in Late Medieval and Reformation France." *The Sixteenth Century Journal* 23, no. 3 (Autumn 1992): 526–547.

Rosenzweig, Franz. *The Star of Redemption.* Madison, WI: University of Wisconsin Press, 2005.

Schachter-Shalomi, Rabbi Zalman and Joel Segel. *Davening: A Guide to Meaningful Jewish Prayer.* Woodstock, VT: Jewish Lights, 2012.

Shapira, Rabbi Kalonymus Kalman. *Bnei Machshava Tova* 18. Available online: https://www.sefaria.org/Bnei_Machshava_Tova%2C_Principles_and_Advice.18?lang=en

Turner, Denys. *Faith, Reason, and the Existence of God.* Cambridge: Cambridge University Press, 2008.

Wacker, Grant. *Heaven Below: Early Pentecostals and American Culture.* Cambridge, MA: Harvard University Press, 2003.

Williams, Rowan. "Augustine and the Psalms." *Interpretation: A Journal of Bible and Theology* 58, no. 1 (2004): 17–27.

———. "What Are We Saying by Singing?" October 2006. Available online: https://hymnsocietygbi.org.uk/2006/10/treasure-no-72-what-are-we-saying-by-singing/.

Chapter 2

The Sacred Song

How Divine Creativity Is Revealed in the Physics and Metaphysics of Music

Edwin Rodríguez-Gungor

The prophets claim that God is "singing" (Zeph. 3:17). In this chapter, I suggest that music is the essence of creation and that the work of God, as we can conceive it, is really that of a *song*.[1] The term *music* comes from the Greek word for "muse" or "muses," which signals the origin of music as being in the divine. If true, then where music is, the Spirit is. We all know that music has the power to shift things, to change the atmosphere, and to break through barriers, but there is reason to believe that everything that *is,* is music. In what follows, I am not suggesting music is a vehicle God uses, nor am I using it as an anthropomorphic description of how God is in the world. I am claiming that somehow music *is* God being present in the world—ontologically.[2] It is an assertion that the metaphysical is known to us through the rudimentary, musical structure of matter and that all matter is God actively singing a *sacred song*. Hence, when we experience matter, we are experiencing God's sustained melody.

IN THE BEGINNING ... GOD

When we read the first verse of the sacred text: "In the beginning, God," it seems one could claim that *God* is the central point of the narrative—not just God's doings. That would mean that the descriptions of *what* happened in creation are less important than the *Who* that was there: God. The bit we should not miss is that God existed before anything else and is responsible for everything that came to be, period. Consequently, our theologizing about *how* God made things is at best an aside.

By choosing not to ground our faith in the how or when of creation, we can only ground it in God the creator. This is the axiomatic truth that must shape us. The Apostles' Creed says it crisply: "We believe in God, creator of heaven and earth." Nothing else needs to be claimed by the people of God for us to remain faithful to the faith. If that is true, then one can dare to imagine the theological implications of all kinds of various possible how's and when's?

For the purpose of this chapter, let's consider theistic evolution and look at the story of music through that lens. Science tells us that the earliest life forms on Earth (i.e., microscopic organisms that left signals of their presence in rocks) appeared around 3.7 billion years ago. About 480 million years ago, insects appeared. Apparently, God loves insects because there are over two million species of them (there are some three hundred thousand species of beetles alone!). Reptiles began to appear about 315 million years ago. Hominids, who precede us, Homo Sapiens, didn't appear until some four million years ago. Homo Sapiens didn't show up until a mere 300,000 years ago. Though no Christian would argue against the idea that human beings are the crown of God's creation and that God intentionally created us to be in God's likeness and image, God appears to have been happy to have the world he created with lots and lots of bugs, plants, birds, fish, and reptiles without one single human being around expressing any religious practice. In a very real way, we are the new kids on the block.

Then, there is the discussion about the beginning of the beginning—which is where our story about music starts. Let's talk about music through the optics of this long, evolutionary process. It begins with a *bang*—a Big Bang.

THE BIG BANG

We begin with one of those interesting stories where the scientists involved discover something they were not looking for. In the spring of 1964, two radio astronomers, Arno Penzias and Robert Wilson, began refitting a very sophisticated 20-foot radio antenna for their work in astronomy.[3] It was an antenna that was originally developed by Bell Labs to receive transmissions from the first communications satellite ever put into earth's orbit. As Penzias and Wilson began using the antenna, it was picking up signals from many sources. After analyzing and tweaking their measurements to remove spurious contributions from other signals, the antenna still detected a weak signal that kept showing up no matter which direction it pointed. This is strange because signals always reflect the Doppler effect—where the crests of a wave get denser in the direction the wave originates and sparser in the opposite. The Doppler effect is a constant observed in both sound and light waves. When we hear an approaching ambulance siren, it appears to be at a higher pitch than after it passes and distances from us—then the pitch lowers. The same is true of the lights on the ambulance. The light of an approaching ambulance is bluer when it approaches and redder when it gets further away (though light shifts are more indiscernible to our eyes).[4] In Penzias' and Wilson's case, no matter what they tried, they could not get rid of the ambient noise. Confusingly, the noise didn't seem to be coming from anywhere in particular, but from *everywhere* at once.

After trying to refit the antenna for months to eliminate that background sound, Penzias frustratingly discussed the problem with a researcher from MIT, Bernard Burke. Burke shared with him a theory by Robert Dicke and James Peebles, both working at Princeton, about "a black body radiation that is filling the Universe."[5] Penzias and Wilson scooped the idea up as the explanation of the phenomenon they had been observing. In May 1965, a paper by Penzias and Wilson in the *Astrophysical Journal* announced what was later to be called the *cosmic microwave background* (CMB). In 1978, Arno Penzias and Robert Wilson received the Nobel Prize in Physics for their discovery of CMB radiation. Amedeo Balbi wrote of their discovery, "This feeble microwave radiation, that cosmologists call cosmic microwave background (or CMB) is the fossil 'signal' from the very first moments of the Universe."[6]

A signal from the first moment of the universe? What kind of signal was it?

Researchers later discovered that CMB radiation contained waves that looked exactly like acoustic waves—like music.[7] When describing CMB in more detail, Babli says, "Exploring the first moments of the universe, cosmologists then had a startling revelation: the primeval plasma was crossed by waves similar to those produced by sounds in the air-ripples propagating in space, a rich choir accompanying cosmic evolution . . . the cosmic orchestra."[8] He contends that the evidence shows that something had "acted as a conductor for the cosmic orchestra, producing synchronized acoustic oscillations which resulted in a regular pattern of peaks and troughs in the spectrum."[9]

Cosmologists immediately examined the data gathered by Penzias and Wilson and realized that these waves were propagating all through the primordial universe. Though they had ceased billions of years before, these waves left a trace of their existence imprinted within the structure of the CMB, like a fossil of a plant or animal whose body was imprinted in sedimentary rock. In the past few decades, cosmologists have been combing the CMB data to find what information is hiding in their pattern and how that data can be interpreted. Elena Mannes adds, "Cosmology has contributed fascinating evidence regarding the relationship between musical sound and the birth of the universe."[10]

All of this suggests that the cry of the infant universe was a *song*—perhaps a Voice? When scientists use the language of music/song, it does not carry the same meaning as it does for those who think theologically. When theologians hear of a "conductor for the cosmic orchestra," we think capital "C" Conductor—or of an intelligent, Creator-God. Though we think in very different directions, theologians can still gain insight from scientific discovery—from those who investigate the first book of God. For instance, the physicists tell us that the initial "music" in creation wasn't a kind that could be heard by human ears—it was more like a song of light. We theologues can muse: Perhaps a song expressed by a being of light? Sound waves and light waves are similar in that they both have amplitude, wavelength, speed, and frequency. Obviously, light waves are much faster than sound waves, but they are still waves. The significance of the discovery of CMB is that it undergirds the claim that the universe was, at one moment in time, very simple. Though the complexities of the universe emerge quickly, the presence of CMB shows that the entire cosmos once went through a single phase—a moment of birth; a Big Bang (or sound).[11] A question that begs to be answered for us theists: *Is creation itself God singing?* Could the "Let there be . . ." in the Genesis narrative be the first song God sung? If so, then all creation is music, and the creator is the first *singer*.

WAVES, FREQUENCIES, AND NUMBERS

Everything that exists, right down to the basic atom and its constituents (i.e., a central nucleus, protons, neutrons, and electrons), carries a constant oscillatory mechanism that propels it into a wave. One can easily create a wave by handing one end of a rope to a friend and moving both ends up and down. All waves carry a mathematical description that is characterized by a *frequency*. A frequency is the number of oscillations a wave passes through any fixed point during a period (frequency is also related to *rhythm*, a critical component of music). Science demonstrates that *everything* is in motion (as a wave) at one frequency or another—every atom, every star, every planet, every solid object, every blade of grass, and every living cell in every living creature is moving (though often imperceptible to the naked eye) at some frequency.

These frequencies are analogous to numbers. In the ancient world, Pythagoras made the amazing discovery that one could replicate all the notes in the musical scale by dividing a string by the sequence of integer numbers. Balbi writes,

> The existence of mathematical relations among musical tones is a direct consequence of the undulatory nature of sound. Each sound originates from a

vibration propagating through a medium, usually the air, by means of acoustic waves. If we could observe the passage of an acoustic wave through the air we would see the molecules moving back and forth along the direction of propagation of the wave.[12]

Pythagoras came to believe that all he saw was somehow the coincidence of waves and mathematics. He arrived at a statement by which he is still remembered: "All things are number."[13] In this vein, the inventor of calculus, Gottfried Wilhelm Von Leibniz, famously quipped, "Music is the pleasure the human soul experiences from counting without being aware that it is counting."[14] Pythagoras was so committed to the link between numbers and all of the cosmos that he went on to develop a system of mathematical and wave relations—a full cosmology—between the heavens and the earth.[15]

In medieval philosophy, the concept of the existence of musical harmonies intrinsic to the spacing between planets was under consideration. In the 1700s, Johannes Kepler wrote a piece entitled *Hamonices Mundi* (written in Latin) to discuss the "harmonies" he found in physical phenomena.[16] This is often referred to as the "music of the spheres." Kepler's central thesis of the *Harmonices Mundi* was to demonstrate the existence of a connection between planetary motion and the numerical relations of musical intervals, giving a scientific foundation to the idea that there really was a *music of the spheres*.[17] He claimed each planet in motion around the Sun produces a definite sound. Kepler knew that orbits were elliptical and not perfectly circular and thought the planets emitted notes that modulated slightly along the way. He theorized that Venus produced a major sixth note and that the Earth produced a minor sixth note. He concludes, "The Earth sings Mi, Fa, Mi"[18] Kepler would be delighted that cosmologists of the twenty-first century are continuing to adopt musical metaphors to explain the universe around us.

Could it be that creation itself is music—the song of God? C. S. Lewis and J. R. R. Tolkien highlight how music and song were central to the creative processes of the worlds within their respective mythologies. In Lewis' *The Magician's Nephew*, Narnia is born through Aslan's powerful song. Aslan sings the land, plants, animals, and other creatures into existence within the Narnian universe. In Tolkien's Middle-earth story, music plays an essential role. In *The Silmarillion*, the supreme deity, Eru Ilúvatar, creates the Ainur (angelic beings) who participate in a grand musical composition called the "Ainulindalë." This divine symphony is what lays down the foundation of Arda (the world), shaping its history and destiny. But I am suggesting more than this—more than the notion that music is the controlling metaphor for *how* God created. I am suggesting that music is the primary metaphor for understanding the metaphysics of our physical universe. In other words, music is not merely a fine analogy for how God is with us or a nice means to experiencing the divine presence; it is a manifestation of that presence.[19]

The prophet Zephaniah claims that God is continually "singing" (Zeph. 3:17), which is to say that creation is being preserved by God's voice. Everything in the universe, from the tiniest quark to the largest star to the largest expanse of dark matter, is in motion—a motion that's sustained by God. God continues to sing to ensure that "all things hold together" (Col. 1:17). It might seem that in saying "God continues to sing," I have confused my categories, the metaphorical for the ontological, lapsing out of theology into poetry. But I am trying to make a point with this phrasing, one which is essential to the core concern of this chapter. Following Abraham Heschel,[20] I am arguing that such anthropological language is sometimes the only way to challenge idolatrous *conceptions* of God, which are hard to overturn. When we think "scientifically," we tend to conceptualize God as a maker and a manager—not an artist. What I am attempting to do in this chapter is argue that God's work is art, that God is truly singing, and that we come up against this reality both physically and metaphysically, both through the use of reason and through the use of faith. Thus, I am not confusing categories but testifying to my conviction that our categories are themselves confusing because they leave us with the wrong impressions about God, ourselves, and this world God has given us.

EXITUS-REDITUS

The pattern of thought that defines most of Thomas Aquinas' *Summa* is his construct of *exitus-reditus*—the idea that everything that is (both seen and unseen) comes from the Trinity-God (*exitus*) and, as a result, everything returns—or boomerangs—back to God (*reditus*). If creation is song and all that exists continues to be song (by virtue of its waveform motion), it can be argued that the continual vibration of all matter is that which ultimately goes back to God. A text from Romans infers this: "For from Him, and through Him [*exitus*], and to Him [*reditus*] are all things. To Him be the glory forever" (Rom. 11:36).[21] Perhaps this is the origination of what we understand to be worship.

This would make sense of the claim in the Revelation that "every created thing" is giving God praise, honor, and glory (Rev. 5:13). Psalm 148 speaks of praise that comes from spiritual beings, like angels; inanimate beings, such as the sun, moon, stars, water, sky, oceans, lightning, hail, snow, clouds, winds, mountains, hills, and trees; and animate creatures: sea creatures, cattle, wild animals, birds, and humans (old and young). Psalm 8 speaks of the cries of infants being an unconscious praise that God uses as a stronghold against evil (Ps. 8:2). Job states, "Ask the beasts, and they will teach you; the birds of the heavens, and they will tell you; or the bushes of the earth, and they will teach you; and the fish of the sea will declare to you" the praises of God (Job 12:7-8 *ESV*). Isaiah tells us that "the mountains and the hills burst into song" and that "all the trees of the field clap their hands" (Isa. 55:12). Jesus spoke of stones "crying out" in praise (Lk. 19:40). A. A. Anderson (in his commentary on Ps. 148) insists that biblical passages that refer to the worship of all creation (animate and inanimate) are not simple poetic fancies. He argues: "It may be slightly odd to think of the varied metrological phenomena as praising God, yet it may not be too much of a rationalization to say that the creature or created phenomenon renders the highest praise to its creator by fulfilling the task for which it was created."[22]

As creation (seen and unseen) issues forth from God (*exitus*), music is there. Understood physically and scientifically following the dictates of reason, it is vibration, sound, music, song, time, and rhythm. Columbia physicist Brian Green asserts, "[E]very object on earth vibrates, our bones do too."[23] But when we think theologically about what physicists call "vibration," we understand metaphysically and theologically, by faith, that the vibrations themselves are *really* the return of worship to God (*reditus*) by the inanimate and animate creation. Karl Barth adds concerning human beings, "Man is only a late-comer slipping shamefacedly into creation's choir in heaven and earth, which has never ceased its praise."[24] The created order fulfills the arc of *exitus-reditus* simply by being itself. God delights in this and continues to sing a sustaining song over it.

WHAT TIME IS IT?

Another significant indication of creation being the song of God is that the frequencies embedded in all music are a direct function of time. The physical reality, of course, can be recognized as God's song only by faith. But science does recognize that it is truly song. And that fact, I believe, is pregnant with meaning in exactly the sense that Rom. 1:20 suggests. As such, it is arguable that the waves of creation, the music of the cosmos, form what we understand as the space-time continuum. That would suggest that the whole dimension of created things is subject to the construct of time precisely because it exists in the domain of timed phrases (i.e., the frequencies of waves). Thinking about time in this way helps one imagine how God is outside of time. As the creator who sings the creation, God would not be subject to the laws of creation—God is non-wave, non-motion, the prime mover (using Aristotle's limited morphology). God, as pure actuality, would not be subject to wave motion or time.

The dominating construct of time from the frequencies of creation's song may also help us to understand the rhythms related to our biological cycles and rhythms. We humans carry many built-in clocks. These "clocks" govern the way we walk, run, dance, our heartbeat, respiratory rate, digestion, sleep, and so on. Chronobiology is the science that focuses on the natural rhythms in the human body that occur over a twenty-four-hour cycle (i.e., a circadian rhythm). The concept of *entrainment* explores how environmental oscillations impact our circadian rhythms. Entrainment works on us to adapt to the various rhythmic shifts that occur around us (e.g., the rotation of the earth). The concept of entrainment leads to the theory of *coupled oscillators*.[25] Simply stated, this is the impact caused by the song of creation that moves things into synchrony.

There is a famous story of Dutch physicist Christiaan Huygens, who invented the pendulum clock in 1656, that captures the notion of coupled oscillation. Huygens made the odd discovery that, when he put two clock pendulums that were swinging at different rates together, they eventually began swinging in perfect synchrony. Then, when he moved the two clocks to separate walls, they lost step with each other. Mannes claims, "[Coupled oscillators] are found all over the natural world both within the same organism and between organisms—for example, crickets that chirp in unison. When the oscillators are nonidentical, a strong coupling force can overcome the differences in natural frequency."[26] It is reasonable to suggest that these coupling forces are further evidence of the dominating construct of time and open the discussion of how music synchronizes and brings us together in church and in society. Returning to Mannes:

> Researchers are very intrigued by the idea that music can actually synchronize people's brain states. When we go to a concert—be it rock or classical—part of what makes it enjoyable and special is that it's a shared experience. And it's not just that our physical bodies are present in the same space. We're all entraining to the beat. So do our brains synchronize in other ways, too? Can music put a community—a society—of brains into the same state? Logic says yes.[27]

Insofar as the research is right and music synchronizes people's brains at rock concerts, is it possible that the song of God is working to entrain the universe to be on the same frequency as Godself?[28] Could this be how God is moving creation into perfection and holiness? We may not be used to thinking of the *physical* universe as anything more than a "stage" for God's act; it may, therefore, seem strange for us to hear that the Spirit may be using material realities in ways that bear spiritual effects. But should it be strange? Surely not if we believe in the sacraments! Or if we take seriously the stories of Jesus healing the sick by touching and being touched by them. Or, to cut to the heart of the matter, if we take the incarnation itself at all seriously.

THE ARC OF SYNCHRONICITY

If God's song functions as a coupled oscillator to bring us into synchronization, why is so much out of sync? Let me suggest two reasons. First, in the beginning, God's song-initiated creation is described as "formless and empty" (Gen. 1:2). Matter appears, but it was in *chaos*.[29] In this nascent stage, even the bonds between electrons and nuclei were not formed. This is when "matter becomes a mixture of positively charged ions and electrons."[30] Physicists call this a "plasma." On this view, things were not created "in sync," though they were moving toward that.

God's ongoing singing strengthened synchronicity as atoms bonded, stars and planets appeared, and the universe expanded. Remarkably, most atoms in the universe (about 99.9 percent) are very light—either hydrogen or helium.[31] Complex and heavy atoms like calcium and metals exist, but we only know of them on this planet. Balbi notes:

> It is really strange, when we consider the matter we experience in our everyday life. All metals, like iron, gold, copper; most of the atoms in the crust of our planets, like calcium and silicon; those in our own body, like carbon; those in the Earth's atmosphere, like oxygen and nitrogen; all these kinds of atoms are but a small percentage of the atomic elements in the Universe.[32]

God's voice advanced matter from simple to complex, caused the dawning of primitive life, and eventually brought the appearance of hominids and Homo Sapiens. This developmental process of synchronization continues because creation is still happening. To this day, stars continue to be born.[33] So, it might be argued that the first reason for the lack of synchronicity in the universe is the fact that creation is still unfinished and still being entrained.

The other reason that there is a lack of synchronicity and unity is that something happened along the way that pulled the song God was singing from harmony into dissonance. Dissonance is more noise than music—like a person screaming, a siren blaring, a horn honking, or an alarm blasting. This is where sound pushes against other sounds, vexing and putting all those around on edge. Theologians call it *sin*.[34] The dawning of evil turned the frequency we had become via God's song into a frequency of dissonance. St. Maximus wrote, "The devil, man's tempter from the beginning, had separated [humankind] in his will from God, and had separated men from each other."[35] In contrast to that separation, Henri De Lubac wrote,

God is working continually in the world to the effect that all should come together into unity, by this sin which is the work of man, "the one nature was shattered into a thousand pieces" and humanity which ought to constitute a harmonious whole, in which "mine" and "thine" would be no contradiction, is turned into a multitude of individuals, as numerous as the sands of the seashore, all of whom show violently discordant inclinations.[36]

God's response to sin? He wrote a *new song* that delivers us from dissonance and entrains us to God's intended frequency—the physical and the metaphysical, the material and the immaterial, working together in the Spirit's wisdom. Again, I know this may sound like a poetic way of saying God acted or spoke redemptively, but those notions are no less anthropomorphic! I believe we should take the psalmist seriously when he says God has "put a new song in my mouth" (Ps. 40:3). Revelation 5 speaks of God putting a new song into creation, which was praise for the appearance of Jesus Christ. The appearing of Jesus in the world was really and truly, in the fullest sense, the creative song of God to free humankind from the devil, sin, and death, and to bring the hope of life in a world that is still yet to come.

CREATION AS FREQUENCY

Speaking of coupled oscillators brings us back to *frequencies*. Remember, *everything* that exists is in motion (as a wave) at one frequency or another—every atom, every star, every planet, every solid object, every blade of grass, every living cell in every living creature. I think this must also include the created, unseen world of angels, demons, and all heavenly "things" (Heb. 8:5). It is arguable that the unseen things are "unseen" precisely because they are moving at a frequency that makes them that way.

What if God being the creator means that things become what God sings them to be? Matter becomes matter. Life becomes life wherever that song is directed. This song, which is in itself immaterial and infinite, both grants to all things, seen and unseen, their reality and draws those very things back toward their ultimate beginning in the God who is uncreated and beyond being. When God claims, "Behold, I am making all things new" (Rev. 21:5), maybe he makes things new by singing those things in a new frequency. Miracles appear because a miracle song is sung and it transforms what *is* into a new frequency—a new reality, a new creation. Consider the resurrected body of Jesus that could move through walls, appear, and disappear. Could it be that his new, resurrected body was tuned to a different frequency than the one all of us are tuned to? Perhaps our future resurrected bodies will carry that frequency, and we will be as he *is*.

Is a prophetic word first a prophetic song heard by the prophets? Or when "the Spirit of the Lord suddenly took Philip away" after baptizing the Ethiopian traveler in Acts 8, was God singing over Phillip in a different frequency that caused him to end up in Azotus? And then there is the unique song that becomes you and me. God, as the "Father of spirits" (Heb. 12:9), sings a unique song for each of us to be formed into who we are (Ps. 139). Evidence of God's ongoing creation is the birth of every human being who is "fearfully and wonderfully made" (v. 14). This is where the full weight of Zeph. 3:17 is felt for us as individuals: "The LORD your God in your midst, The Mighty One, will save; He will rejoice over you with gladness, He will quiet you with His love, He will rejoice over you with singing."[37] Each one of us is a God song—a dream of God sung true. Jenson has argued that we must not reject the way Scripture speaks of God.[38] If we dismiss it all as anthropomorphic, we end up losing touch with the truth of God's *personal* relation to us, and without *that*, we can understand nothing of God, ourselves, or the world. Nothing is more personal than singing, and, as I have tried to show, that reality is present (in multiple ways) not only in our hearts and minds but also in our bodies, and not only in us and to us but in the non-human creation in ways we are only now beginning to understand. That, to me, is a reminder that our philosophies and theologies, both secular and sacred, have put asunder things that belong together.

Is it possible that the way the Spirit primarily speaks, leads, and works in our lives is through the manifold dimensions of song, which come to us in the music of the material world as well as in the music human beings create? What if music is not, as Steven Pinker suggests, "auditory cheesecake," or a simple pleasurable offshoot of our linguistic capacity?[39] This points to a truth we all know intuitively—not all communication happens through words. In fact, Albert Mehrabian's research in communication showed that 38 percent of any message is communicated through tone of voice, 55 percent through body language, with only 7 percent of the communication happening through words.[40]

Perhaps God's "still, small voice" is musical rather than being jammed primarily with words. Words may come, but are they always necessary? The famous dictum usually ascribed to St. Francis of Assisi comes to mind: "Always preach the gospel, and, if necessary, use words." What if God only needs to use words occasionally? Here is an example of a wordless encounter:

> I remember the night, and almost the very spot on the hill-top, where my soul opened out, as it were, into the infinite, and there was a rushing together of the two worlds, the inner and the outer. It was deep calling unto deep—the deep that my own struggle had opened up within being answered by the unfathomable deep without, reaching beyond the stars. I stood alone with Him who had made me,

and all the beauty of the world . . . The perfect stillness of the night was thrilled by a more solemn silence. The darkness held a presence that was all the more felt because it was not seen. I could not any more have doubted that *He* was there than that I was. Indeed, I felt myself to be, if possible, the less real of the two. (168)

The evidence shows there is a communicative power embedded in music, even without words. Making music is believed to have preceded rational speech as a way to communicate—a kind of "pre-talk" through sounds of laughter, joy, groans of pain, or ecstasy. Mannes claims,

[M]usic is in fact encoded in our bodies and brains. The fact that music seems to trigger our emotions in a way that nothing else does suggests to many scientists that it has an important place in the natural world and that it has something to do with the evolution of our species.[41]

We know that Neanderthals made flutes of mammoth bones—some 35,000 years ago. These flutes provide compelling evidence that human beings of the Stone Age had a musical culture.[42] We modern Homo sapiens are sure that words are the most precious communication we possess. But in creation, it appears that words follow the music, both in the order of being and in the order of knowing. Anthropologists believe the appearance of music in the lives of hominids was very early, millions of years before the use of language. Mannes asserts:

We humans know instinctively that music has primal power. Historians and anthropologists have yet to discover a culture without music. Music predates agriculture—and perhaps even language. The foundations of music have been traced as far back as existence itself, to the birth of our universe.[43]

Cellist Michael Fitzpatrick says music taps into "the natural pulse rates of the way our blood flows, the way our heart beats, the way our brain waves flow . . . it can calm the mind, relax the body, and free the emotions."[44] The opera singer Irene Gubrud asserts, "In one sense we are music. Our bodies are a symphony."[45]

What these artists and scientists have discovered in their own ways is already known to Christians through the scriptures. Paul urges us to "be filled with the Spirit" and to speak "to one another with psalms, hymns, and songs from the Spirit." We are, he insists, to "sing and make music from your heart to the Lord" (Eph. 5:18-19). It appears that the Spirit is still waiting and watching for God's song over us like he was in Gen. 1:2 as he was "hovering over the waters."

There seems to be no end to the songs God sings. Even at the return of Jesus, the prophecies say there will be a new heaven and a new earth (Rev.

21). And Paul reminds us that God has in store for us "what no eye has seen, what no ear has heard, and what no human mind has conceived." These are "the things God has prepared for those who love him" (1 Cor. 2:9). All that God has done from creation and all that God will do until the end of time comes to us as music in manifold ways, physical and spiritual. In speaking of the eschaton, Jensen claims, "The end is music."[46]

NOTES

1. In this writing, I am using "song" and "music" synonymously.

2. I do recognize that both the metaphysical and the physical are created, so in that sense, neither is univocally true of God's being, which is uncreated (this is not a claim to pantheism). What lies beyond reality in the uncreated life of God as Creator and how God "sings" rests solely in mystery and is beyond human knowing, but I am asserting that the biblical claim that God is singing is more than mere analogy or anthropomorphism.

3. Amedeo Balbi, *The Music of the Big Bang: The Cosmic Microwave Background and the New Cosmology* (Astronomers' Universe) (Kindle Locations 519–89). Kindle Edition.

4. For a fuller explanation of the Doppler effect, see Balbi, *The Music of the Big Bang*, Loc. 408–14).

5. Balbi, *The Music of the Big Bang*, Loc. 585.

6. Balbi, *The Music of the Big Bang*, Loc. 519.

7. Balbi, *The Music of the Big Bang*, Loc. 58.

8. Balbi, *The Music of the Big Bang*, Loc. 1107.

9. Balbi, *The Music of the Big Bang*, Loc. 1471.

10. Elena Mannes, *The Power of Music: Pioneering Discoveries in the New Science of Song* (New York: Bloomsbury, 2011), *Introduction*.

11. Balbi, *The Music of the Big Bang*, Loc. 621.

12. Balbi, *The Music of the Big Bang*, Loc. 1038.

13. Huffman, Carl. "The Role of Number in Philolaus Philosophy." *Phronesis*, vol. 33, no. 1, 1988, pp. 1–30 (3). *JSTOR*, http://www.jstor.org/stable/4182291. Accessed 29 Dec. 2023.

14. Quoted in Mannes, *The Power of Music,* 3.

15. Constantine J. Vamvacas, *The Founders of Western Thought—The Presocratics: A diachronic parallelism between Presocratic Thought and Philosophy and History of Science* (New York: Springer, 2009).

16. An English translation of Kepler's *Harmonice Mundi* is available as: Johannes Kepler with E. J. Aiton, A. M. Duncan, and J. V. Field, trans., *The Harmony of the World* (Philadelphia: American Philosophical Society, 1997).

17. The *Hamonices Mundi* also relates Kepler's discovery of the *third law of planetary motion.*

18. Kepler, *The Harmony of the World,* Book V, Chapter 6, 440.

19. Again, this is not a claim for pantheism, but perhaps a nod to pan*en*theism. To put a sharper point on it, I believe the metaphysical is made known to us through music in a way that rumors the incarnation. In the incarnation, all things (that is, the entire creation, seen and unseen) are drawn together into the personal life of Jesus who is God, the Son. It is because of the incarnation that the sacramental is possible—where God is present in sacramental actions. Music, then, if not a sacrament is sacramental in that God's self is tucked away in it. It should not shock us that many miss God's presence in this way. One need only recall the story where Jacob exclaimed, "The Lord is certainly in this place, and I did not know it!" (Gn 28:16).

20. Abraham J. Heschel, *The Prophets* (New York: Harper Perennial, 2001), 271–76.

21. All scripture references are in the *NASB* unless otherwise stated.

22. A. A. Anderson, *The Book of Psalms*, 2 vol. (London: Oliphants, 1972), *ii*, p. 950.

23. Elena Mannes, *The Power of Music: Pioneering Discoveries in the New Science of Song* (New York: Bloomsbury, 2011), p. 13.

24. Karl Barth, *Church Dogmatics,* Vol II: "The Doctrine of God," Pt 1, CD II.1§31 (London: T&T Clark, 1957), 648.

25. Steven Strogatz and Ian Stewart, "Coupled Oscillators and Biological Synchronization," *Scientific American*, December 1993, 102–17.

26. Mannes, *The Power of Music*, 20.

27. Mannes, *The Power of Music*, 38–39.

28. The notion of coupled oscillation seems appropriate as an apologetic for why the people of God should gather for prayer, praise, singing, and sacrament, where we can be entrained to God's song and be synchronized as a community.

29. We don't know what happened in the unseen world, but there was also some kind of chaos that is reflected in the fall of angels. See Lk 10:18.

30. Balbi. *The Music of the Big Bang*, Loc. 379–81.

31. Balbi. *The Music of the Big Bang*, Loc. 458.

32. Balbi, *The Music of the Big Bang,* Loc. 461–64.

33. From NASA's website: https://www.nasa.gov/universe/where-are-new-stars-born-nasas-webb-telescope-will-investigate/#:~:text=When%20it%20comes%20to%20making,up%20to%20100%20times%20greater (Accessed 11/05/23).

34. Sin or "evil" for St. Augustine is an expression of the principle of privation, which holds that evil itself does not have any positive existence or substance but is rather the paling or disordering of the good God had created. The emerging synchronization was pushed back into *chaos*—this is *anti-*creation. Evil, then, is seen as a corruption or deprivation of the good naturally present from God's singing.

35. Henri De Lubac, *Catholicism, Christ and the Common Destiny of Man* (San Francisco: Ignatius Press, 1988), 35.

36. De Lubac, *Catholicism, Christ and the Common Destiny of Man,* 34.

37. *NKJV.*

38. Robert W. Jenson, *Systematic Theology*, 1 (New York: Oxford University Press, 1997), 222.

39. Steven Pinker, *How the Mind Works* (New York: W. W. Norton, 1997).
40. Albert Mehrabian, *Silent Messages: Implicit Communication of Emotions and Attitudes,* 2nd ed. (Belmont: Wadsworth, 1981).
41. Mannes, *The Power of Music,* 5.
42. Mannes, *The Power of Music,* 101.
43. Mannes, *The Power of Music, Introduction.*
44. Mannes, *The Power of Music,* 14.
45. Mannes, *The Power of Music.*
46. Robert W. Jensen shows that music is a controlling metaphor for Christian thought. He explains that the narrative that is true of God is one that "goes in waves, and it's waves overlap and intersect in indefinitely many ways . . . with interactions between hyperbar levels of the music." He holds that music is narratival (following Jeremy Begbie), expressing all the tensions and resolutions of God's work in the world and in his total history with us. See idem, *"Ipse Pater Non Est Impassibilis," Divine Impassibility and the Mystery of Human Suffering,* James F. Keating and Thomas Joseph Whited, O. P., eds. (Grand Rapids, MI: William B. Eerdmans Publishing Company, 2009), 121. Robert W. Jenson, *Systematic Theology,* 2 (New York: Oxford University Press, 1999), 369.

BIBLIOGRAPHY

Anderson, A. A. *The Book of Psalms,* Vol. 2. London: Oliphants, 1972.
Balbi, Amedeo. *The Music of the Big Bang: The Cosmic Microwave Background and the New Cosmology.* Astronomers' Universe. Kindle Edition.
Barth, Karl. *Church Dogmatics,* Vol II: "The Doctrine of God," Pt 1, CD II.1§31. London: T&T Clark, 1957.
Jensen, Robert W. "Ipse Pater Non Est Impassibilis." In *Divine Impassibility and the Mystery of Human Suffering,* edited by James F. Keating and Thomas Joseph Whited. Grand Rapids: Eerdmans, 2009.
———. *Systematic Theology,* 2. New York: Oxford University Press, 1999.
Kepler, Johannes. *The Harmony of the World.* E. J. Aiton, A. M. Duncan, and J. V. Field, trans. Philadelphia: American Philosophical Society, 1997.
Lubac, Henri De. *Catholicism, Christ and the Common Destiny of Man.* San Francisco: Ignatius Press, 1988.
Mannes, Elena. *The Power of Music: Pioneering Discoveries in the New Science of Song.* New York: Bloomsbury, 2011.
Mehrabian, Albert. *Silent Messages: Implicit Communication of Emotions and Attitudes,* 2nd edition. Belmont: Wadsworth, 1981.
NASA's website: https://www.nasa.gov/universe/where-are-new-stars-born-nasas-webb-telescope-willinvestigate/#:~:text=When%20it%20comes%20to%20making,up%20to%20100%20times%20greater (Accessed 11/05/23).
Pinker, Steven. *How the Mind Works.* New York: W. W. Norton, 1997.

Strogatz, Steven, and Ian Stewart. "Coupled Oscillators and Biological Synchronization." *Scientific American* 269, no. 6 (December 1993): 102–17.

Vamvacas, Constantine J. *The Founders of Western Thought—The Presocratics: A Diachronic Parallelism Between Presocratic Thought and Philosophy and History of Science.* New York: Springer, 2009.

Chapter 3

We Feel Fire When It's Hot

Affect and Manipulation in Music

Steven Félix-Jäger

I have been deeply touched by popular music on many occasions, but two instances stand out. The first time I ever heard Muse's "Resistance," I was struck in a way I hadn't experienced before. At the time, Muse, a British alternative rock band, was one of my favorite bands, and I was stoked to see they came out with a whole album thematically based on George Orwell's *Nineteen Eighty-Four*—one of my favorite works of fiction. I decided to listen to the album all the way through. The first song, "Uprising," was just as I expected—a hard-hitting alternative rock song with soaring vocals that matched the theme of rising anger toward governmental establishments. Then came track 2: "Resistance." It started subtly with a somber, minor-key melody played on the piano, followed by an atmospheric tom beat. Matt Bellamy sang the first verse with his typical grandiose legato when, all of a sudden, at around the 1:30 mark, the pre-chorus shifted abruptly to a cheery funk beat in major key. The pre-chorus repeated twice before seamlessly returning to a heavier version of the verse motif for the chorus. The dramatic, almost theatrical variations in the song affected my emotions significantly. I experienced tension, intensity, surprise, relief, and then joy.

While listening to Muse, which surprised me by *subverting* my expectations, I can also recall a moment when a song gave me great satisfaction by *meeting* my expectations. One night while painting (I'm also a visual artist), I was listening to a playlist of newly released Christian worship music. This was the first time I ever heard Bethel Music's "It Is Well" led by Kristene DiMarco. It's a beautifully arranged, slow-tempo, contemplative worship song. The majority of the song is just DiMarco singing along to a simple piano accompaniment. Thematically, the song reflects a deep sense of confidence in God's faithfulness and goodness, even in the midst of trials and challenges. There were subtle references, both musically and lyrically, to the

1873 hymn "It Is Well With My Soul" by Horatio Spafford. The song played modestly for three minutes, when suddenly the cymbals began to swell and, to my delight, DiMarco tagged Spafford's hymn! The band played the hymn for another two minutes, building dynamically the entire time. The live crowd was singing the hymn loudly and in unison, DiMarco filled spaces with powerful commands and ad libs until the band resolved back to a down chorus with just DiMarco and the piano. I was so struck by the power of this song that I sat back in my chair, in a sort of trance, for several minutes after it ended. The song did exactly what I wanted it to do, and in the end, it evoked in me a range of emotions, from vulnerability and introspection to moments of strength and empowerment.

These two examples contrast in several ways. One song was secular, and the other was sacred (a worship song). One song surprised me, and the other did exactly what I hoped for. Both of these songs, however, moved me deeply. Both sent shivers down my spine. Both of these songs created an emotional landscape that resonated with my deepest feelings. Both songs felt timeless, as if they transcended the moment and connected with something universal. Listening to them, I felt fully present in the moment, processing emotions that were difficult to articulate in words. After listening to the songs, I was left lingering in my thoughts. Both of these examples demonstrate that music is an incredibly affective (and effectively incredible) art form.

Because music moves us so deeply in ways we can hardly understand or bring adequately to speech, we might find ourselves wondering if it, in some way, controls us or is used to control us. Perhaps we grow uncomfortable with the idea that something external to us holds some sort of power over us. Some of these fears, however, are based on the faulty notion that we are, and ought to be, impenetrable. Rather, we are affected by external things all the time, whether we're aware of it or not. Therefore, instead of denying the fact that we are susceptible to external influences, we should learn to distinguish when they are neutral, helpful, or harmful. Throughout this chapter, I'd like to discuss the extent to which music can affect us and determine how it can be used to manipulate people. So we will elaborate on two points: (1) Music is affective by nature, but affect does not mean manipulation, and (2) the use of an affective art form like music involves ethical responsibility. We will begin this chapter by disentangling the terms affect, persuasion, and manipulation. We will see that the conversation about music and manipulation is muddled in part by equivocations. Finally, as a sort of case study, we will look at contemporary worship music to determine if some criticisms that worship music is manipulative are valid. We will explore the use of music in Christian worship and how the Spirit is understood to be at work in worship. We'll see that significant to this conversation is the integrity of the worship leader that's leading the congregants spiritually while utilizing the highly affective medium of music. Thus, this chapter provides a brief, yet suitable, discourse on music and manipulation and its implications for contemporary worship.

DISENTANGLING AFFECT AND MANIPULATION

One major problem surrounding the conversation of musical manipulation concerns the meaning of the term "manipulation." In English, we use the term in a few ways that typically have to do with control. For instance, we talk about a potter skillfully handling (manipulating) his or her clay or an analyst skillfully manipulating data for a presentation to highlight key trends and insights. Yet we also talk about manipulation as a form of *social* control. We might say a person manipulated someone into buying something he or she didn't want, or the government manipulated information to shape public opinion. The arguments surrounding music and manipulation assume a particular meaning of the term, but might draw inferences based on another definition. Someone might say, for instance, that the musicians are *manipulating* the note lengths of a musical passage to evoke expressiveness (e.g., playing in *tempo rubato*), and then say the musicians are therefore *manipulating* the listeners to feel a certain way. The first sense of manipulation concerns skillful handling of musical elements, and the second sense concerns social control through music. Thus, the term "manipulation" is subtly equivocated. The term gets more egregiously equivocated when ill-intent is assumed in the social control.

Psychologist Steven Brown shows that there are typically two ways to understand what is meant by the word "manipulation." The broad view of manipulation says that *all* communication is manipulation in that it leads to some sort of behavioral control. For instance, even a simple request such as "Could you please pass the salt?" is a form of manipulation as it seeks to control the behavior of another person. Thus, broadly speaking, manipulation means control. The narrow view of manipulation, on the other hand, says that manipulation is a specific form of communication that is used to intentionally influence the behavior of another person or group through deception. This narrow view typically refers to a disingenuous form of communication where "the sender's intentions are both selfish and concealed."[1] This view focuses on the *underlying intent* of the manipulation, which is to get the receiver to do something that will benefit the sender but may not be in the best interest of the receiver. The sender may wish to gain an unfair advantage over the recipient, strongly influence the recipient's outlook through deception, or force the recipient to do something they don't want to do. Thus, narrowly speaking, manipulation means *deceptive* control. The former definition sees manipulation as ethically neutral, whereas the latter sees manipulation as a vice.

Throughout this chapter, we will utilize the narrow sense of the term because this is what's implied when music is condemned as emotionally manipulative. For instance, when someone says worship music is used by the church[2] to manipulate people, they are assuming that the church has a hidden, ulterior motive. Instead of using the term "manipulation" in the broad sense, we'll use the term "persuasion." In this case, all communication is *persuasive* in that it seeks to influence or control human behavior. This point can be disputed, however, since some communication does not appear to have this need or ambition. Some speech, like the declarative statement "the sky is blue," seems to aim at "contact" without direction. Yet persuasion, according to Brown, is utilized when the sender seeks to modify the receiver's attitudes and/or behaviors.[3] In "The sky is blue," the sender is aiming to make the receiver believe something about the sky. Like manipulation, persuasion looks to influence a person's actions or beliefs, but unlike manipulation, persuasion is typically seen as "an honest, consensual, and interactive process in which the sender's intentions to influence are clear and open."[4] For instance, a salesman may show up at your door and say, "I would like to show you this product to see if you would consider buying it." Despite the salesman's obvious attempt at persuasion, he is not manipulative because he is upfront about his motivation. However, it would be manipulative if he pretended to be your friend who was trying to help you but then convinced you to buy something you didn't need or couldn't afford to gain a commission. We can say that music, rhetoric, and the arts are all, in general, persuasive, but only *intent* determines whether they are manipulative.

Another common confusion of terms when discussing music and emotions is when *affect* and manipulation are equivocated. Although these two terms are closely related, they are importantly different. Elsewhere, a colleague and I defined affect as "Being moved emotionally, which causes a change in someone or something."[5] Affect constitutes, essentially, the subjective and emotional components of experience. According to philosopher and psychologist William James, affect is an embodied force produced by perceptions and only transforms into "emotion" once it's codified into language.[6] As a result, not all affects become emotions, but all emotions are affects. The bodily manifestations and feelings that accompany a situation precede the particular emotion that's understood to be evoked. For instance, it has been observed that getting "gooseflesh," or "chills" is a common affective, bodily response to dynamic changes or crescendos in music.[7] One might respond, "the music manipulated me; I even got chills!" but this would only work for the broad sense of the term manipulation, that means mere behavioral control. Indeed, the music *did* affect the receiver, but his or her statement would not work for the narrow sense of manipulation, where the sender's intentions are selfish and concealed. What selfish intentions did the *music* have? We might say someone is using an affective medium like music in order to manipulate people, but that's not equivalent to seeing music as manipulative.

When a person uses music to manipulate others, it is *the person* who is manipulative, not the music. This is an important distinction to make because the statement "music is manipulative" is, as we've seen, often based on equivocations. As mentioned above, one might state that music is, by nature, manipulative (broadly as persuasion), and then condemn it for being manipulative (narrowly as selfish/concealed intent). One might also misconstrue art's ability to affect as being manipulative. The arts do not attempt to describe the world objectively without a filter. Nor do they attempt to argue through reason. The arts are fundamentally affecting—they engage human emotions and stir up particular reactions or feelings from perceivers. The arts convey a form of expression that is more immediate and evocative than traditional forms of communication. They evoke empathy and understanding, and help people connect on deeper levels. Artists skillfully utilize the formal elements of their art form to reveal the intricacies of the human experience. The arts are also human—they are the highest form of human expression. They are multifaceted and complex. They carry layered meanings and elicit myriad responses. They engage joy and sorrow, love and longing, exploring the shared vulnerabilities of the human condition. They make people receptive to deeper feelings, deeper thoughts, and deeper connections. They are, in a significant way, *about* affect.

Jean-Michel Basquiat famously stated, "Art is how we decorate space, music is how we decorate time."[8] Music is a temporal and auditory art form. It utilizes the formal elements of pitch, melody, harmony, rhythm, dynamics, timbre, and tempo to structure sound in time. These formal elements are combined in a way that evokes reactions and feelings. Just as good painters know what color schemes evoke certain moods, good musicians understand what sorts of emotions are typically evoked by various combinations of formal elements. Musicians use these combinations to urge listeners to pause amid the cacophony of life and zero in on something worth noticing.

Knowing music is affective, listeners *desire* to be moved. Listeners yearn to be transported, to be inspired, and to feel something. *Their* music speaks to them, touches them, and resonates with them. As listeners are moved by music, it becomes a part of their lives. Music is more than just an adornment to our lives; it is a way to express our emotions, to connect with others, and to find our own sense of self as expressed to the world. Because emotions are an essential part of our human constitution, we should not view music's ability to affect emotions as a negative thing. Reason and emotion were never meant to oppose each other but to collaborate as we move from perception to understanding. Emotions color our perceptions, and reason helps us determine what they mean.

Theologian Jeremy Begbie argues that music speaks to human emotion in a way that engages the whole person.[9] He sees three ways that people tend to describe a person's emotional state: (1) as an "interplay between conscious experience," which describes how people feel about an experience, (2) as "expressive bodily behavior," in which an emotion is physically expressed, or (3) as a "physiological activation," which is characterized by bodily fluctuations in an emotionally agitated person.[10] Begbie believes all three of these components are present in a listener's emotional connection to music. Thus, through emotion, the mind and body are more complexly connected than what a straightforward dualism might suggest. Our task is thus not to demonize music's ability to affect emotions but to determine how this influence can be rightly directed.

THE SPIRIT AND ARTISTIC INTENTION

We've determined above that while music affects, it does not necessarily manipulate. A person's intention determines if the music's affectability is used to manipulate or not. This means the ethical considerations that concern manipulation transcend the capacities of the art form. While art is affective in and of itself, the artist, or presenter of the art, is the one who utilizes the art with intention. Therefore, it is important to consider the potential for manipulation when engaging with music or any other art form, and to ensure that any intent to do so is carefully and ethically considered. A person at a regular concert assumes that music has the power to affect and does not really question if he is being manipulated by the music. Because a concert's purpose is entertainment, people open themselves up to being affected without worrying about underlying personal, social, or political agendas. They're there for a good time and expect to leave with nothing more than great memories. In other words, listeners appreciate the music for its own sake. Conversely, religious services utilize music in an encumbered way. In a worship service, listeners do not typically appreciate music for its own sake but as a means for expressing worship.

Christian worship music is performed in a context of religious persuasion—churches *want* participants to connect with God in worship and want people to grow in their devotion to God. Thus, religious music serves a distinct purpose that differs from the recreational purposes of secular music. These lines can, of course, be blurred as some "secular" songs function religiously with prophetic overtones (i.e., Kendrick Lamar's "Alright" or John Lennon's "Imagine"), and others overtly engage religious themes and modes of expression (i.e., U2's "I Still Haven't Found What I'm Looking For," Kanye West's "Jesus Walks," and Hozier's "Take Me to Church"). In other words, even things that are recreational can, at times, be "functionally" religious. Conversely, some church songs can be playful and not deeply religious (i.e., traditional Sunday school songs like "This Little Light of Mine" or "I've Got the Joy, Joy, Joy, Joy Down in My Heart"). Nevertheless, for the sake of simplicity, we'll think of church music as generally religious and secular music as generally recreational.

Philosopher James K. A. Smith says that worship music helps shape our Christian social imaginaries by being a "performative affirmation of our embodiment."[11] When we sing in worship, our whole body is activated. As Smith writes,

> Singing requires us to call on parts of the body that might otherwise be rather dormant—stomach muscles and vocal chords, lungs and tongues. And since singing seems to tap into our joints and muscles, song often pulls us into dance or raising our hands in praise.[12]

Singing thus enables a holistic worship expression, as our mind, body, and emotions revere God's worthiness in one accord. And because music involves our bodies in a special way, it has a "privileged channel to our imagination."[13] Because music is experienced in our bodies, it invokes in us a sense of time and place. It helps us recall how our experiences felt in the moment and contextualizes our memories. The theological belief of the church is that the Holy Spirit is already present, so the role of the worshiper is to turn his or her hearts and minds toward God, who's already there. Music is utilized as a tool to help the worshiper become sensitive to the presence of the Spirit—to open up and be receptive to an encounter with God.

In worship services, the music is not just about enjoying the experience, but about growing closer to God and deepening one's faith. Many of the suspicions surrounding Christian worship music have to do with receivers questioning the intentions of the leaders or institutions that present the music. Why are the receivers being persuaded with music? Is it only to connect with God, or is the church hiding another social or political motive? A listener's suspicion seems to have less to do with music's ability to affect than it does with a general distrust of the church's motives. These suspicions are, unfortunately, not without merit.

Recently, some prominent churches have experienced high-profile scandals where the church leaders in question were in some way involved with contemporary worship music. For instance, Hillsong Church, the home base of Hillsong Worship and Hillsong United, experienced a tumultuous period of scandal starting in 2019 when Marty Sampson, one of Hillsong Worship's main worship leaders, publicly denounced his faith.[14] Then, in 2020, Carl Lentz, the lead pastor of Hillsong Church in New York, was fired after being caught engaging in extramarital affairs.¹⁵ Then again in 2022, Hillsong Church founder Brian Houston resigned after being found engaging in inappropriate behavior with two women.¹⁶ These scandals and other allegations caused numerous reporters and documentarians to question Hillsong's power and organizational structures in general. Although most of these scandals were not directly associated with Hillsong's music, they still tainted public trust in Hillsong's usage of an affective medium like music to do anything that might result in social control.

While some may see Hillsong as abusing music's affect for ulterior social motives, there are also recent instances when contemporary worship has been used to persuade people toward political ends. Evangelical megachurches, for instance, are known to hold rallies for political candidates, and these rallies often begin with a worship set. But one major phenomenon exacerbated by the COVID-19 pandemic in 2020 was the advent of "worship protests." Worship protests combine music, prayer, and exhortation with public activism. Participants pray, sing, and discuss social or political issues at the same time. These protests often take place in public spaces, such as parks or in front of government buildings. These events typically include social or political messages about religious freedom, anti-wokeness, and other issues that align with conservative Christian values.¹⁷ The problem with worship protests is that they tie particular political positions to Christian worship. Is worship music being used manipulatively to get people to adopt a particular political view on certain issues? Worship protests can be damaging because they make musical worship into a political tool rather than a means to connect with God. People may also feel conflicted about their faith as they are pressured to conform to a certain political view in order to attend these worship gatherings. A sense of manipulation has permeated both the Hillsong scandals and the worship protests, causing many to lose trust in their intentions to present worship.

In 2023, *Christianity Today* ran an article titled "Worship Music in Emotionally Manipulative. Do You Trust the Leader Plucking the Strings?" by Kelsey Kramer McGinnis. In it, McGinnis does not condemn music's ability to affect but rather calls on worship leaders to be trustworthy when handling a highly affective art form like music. She writes, "Corporate worship invites us to open ourselves to spiritual and emotional guidance. That openness feels, and is, vulnerable. And as worship becomes a bigger production in churches and ministry events, a rising chorus has challenged whether our emotions are in safe hands."¹⁸ She rightly argues that worship leaders should respect the emotional vulnerability of their congregations and be trustworthy in the way they handle music, as it is a powerful tool in guiding people in their spiritual journeys.

McGinnis goes on to make two major points: (1) worshipers have agency and are able to decide rationally how much they open themselves up to emotional direction, and (2) the worship leader must display trust and authenticity when engaging in emotional shepherding.[19] While I'm in full agreement with the second point, the first point seems to bifurcate reason and emotion to the extent that the former takes precedence over the latter. If a worshiper enters a worship service, the clear expectation is to worship God. If, as noted above, manipulation entails a deceptive form of communication, then worship music should not, in general, be viewed as manipulative. As we'll see here, churches *purposefully* utilize music affectively at a service to encourage a person's receptivity to spiritual encounter. Because humans have agency, openness to God is essential for encountering God. A person's buffered demeanor jettisons experiential encounter the way wax sheds water.

A person's ability to rationally decide how much they'll open themselves up to emotional direction is a matter of control—one that is bracketed by a modern social imaginary that says a person *can* control how and in what way they'll be affected. Philosopher Charles Taylor sees the modern social imaginary as disenchanted and rationalistic. The medieval social imaginary saw no clear boundary between the mind and the world, whereas the modern social imaginary props up the "buffered self," who lives a life of self-determination. The buffered person is the rational individual who's protected from the whims of external forces.[20] The porous person is susceptible to the imaginary's external meaning because an enchanted worldview provides the rationale for any natural phenomenon.[21] Suzi Gablik has argued that art is a vehicle for *re-enchantment* in a modern, rationalized world. Every art form, including music, allows people to reconnect with the non-rational and mythical elements of life that were lost in modernity. The modern era replaced premodern Western theocentrism, which forced people to understand themselves, their purpose, and their telos through theistic constructs, with the secular, materialist, and mechanist constructs that emerged during the Enlightenment. Re-enchantment does not retreat back to premodern constructs but instead moves beyond the modern rule of disenchantment and toward a general openness to the mysteries of the world.[22]

If we view contemporary worship services as functioning under a frame of re-enchantment, then we can see why church practitioners and congregants generally come in with the expectation of being moved by external forces. As an affective medium, music has the ability to help people shift their mentalities from bufferedness to openness. It helps people adopt a posture of vulnerability to be open to what comes next. McGinnis' assumption that one can make a rational decision for how open he or she will be is like saying, "I will crack the door open and just let in a little light." Rather, one is *either* porous *or* buffered, either open or closed. The buffered self reflects a closed door, while the porous self reflects an open door.

As an affective medium, music helps set the stage for non-rational encounters. Non-rational encounters include emotional affect, but also spiritual and religious experiences. A popular YouTuber with the handle "Faith Free" made a video discussing how a church's music director utilizes tactics to manipulate people through music. He says the "feelings the church tries to sell us as an evidence for God" have a logical explanation. He says the skillful usage of formal musical elements in a worship service "starts to blur the lines between feelings and spirituality, between performance and manipulation. Our entire goal is to make people feel like they are connecting with God, to trigger that big emotional response and spiritual high. And we know exactly what works, we're professionals."[23] The emotional journeys people are supposed to go on are all planned out. The production seems larger than life, almost spiritual, and the group that's targeted by this is the emotionally vulnerable, like children and people who have gone through difficult times. They're being duped into the faith through emotional manipulation. The problem with this view is that it *assumes* there is no spiritual reality, and music's affect is utilized to make people believe something that's not true. This is viewed as manipulation because people are dishonestly made to believe something that's not the case. Christians, however, assume a completely different framework for encounter—one that assumes the existence of a porous spiritual reality.

Although abuses are possible, music is not generally utilized by the church in a manipulative way for at least three reasons: (1) people who enter a church setting know the church adheres to a theological framework of openness toward spiritual encounter; (2) people who enter a church know that every element of worship is designed to help people encounter God through worship; and (3) people who enter a church know that the majority of the people present already subscribe to the church's theological framework of spiritual openness. Thus, if a church is open and honest about its intentions to draw people into God's presence, and common sense tells us that excellent music is effective, no one is "duping" anyone into faith through emotional manipulation. One might retort that they are being misled by the experience itself, whatever their intention. Here again, we must ask, What are you being misled toward? Being *mis*led implies you were expecting to be led somewhere else. While the guide promised to bring you somewhere, they brought you elsewhere. If the church is forthright about its intentions and its usage of affective mediums, then the experiences they foster will not be misleading.

The assumption "Faith Free" is making is that when it is difficult to make a rational argument for belief in a faith, worship leaders rely on using emotion to convince others of that case. As another YouTuber asks, "If experiences of God's presence are real, they shouldn't require emotive ritual and music to occur. If the gospel is intellectually convincing, people shouldn't be emotionally primed before hearing it."[24] This assumption, however, is fundamentally dualistic and prioritizes the rational over the affective. It assumes that truth only comes about by way of intellect, and affect can be used to override rational belief. Rather, using an affective medium like music in worship is a recognition that humans are embodied, emotional, *and* rational beings. While reason is important, knowledge is holistic and not merely rational. Worshiping God *fully* entails worshiping God bodily and emotionally as well. It entails utilizing our greatest human expressions (the arts) in ways that glorify God and helps people draw into God's presence. Therefore, music lends itself ideally to expressing worship, as it allows for an embodied, emotional, and spiritual encounter.

CONCLUSION

Music in and of itself is not manipulative in the narrow sense, but, as an affective medium, it can be used to manipulate. We see this clearly when discussing the various intentions surrounding worship music. Both the trusting Christian and the skeptical atheist are making assumptions about intent when they enter a worship service. The Christian trusts the worship leader to faithfully lead him or her into God's presence, whereas the skeptical atheist questions whether the church leadership is using worship music to coerce its congregation toward an ulterior motive. How can we know if a group is truly attempting to use music to manipulate us into particular social or political actions? How can someone guard against an abuse of music's affect? The theological response to these questions of intent concerns *discernment.*

Discernment is a spiritual gift that involves relying on the Spirit for spiritual insight, testing teachings and experiences against Scripture, and cultivating a mindset that is consistent with biblical wisdom. According to Paul in 1 Cor. 2:14-16, the natural person cannot comprehend spiritual truths, but those who are in the Spirit can. Similarly, Paul encourages believers in 1 Thes. 5:21 to hold fast to what is right and to test everything. In other words, believers must use spiritual discernment and test their teachings and experiences against Scripture in order to determine what is true or false. Furthermore, Heb. 5:14 states that mature believers have their powers of discernment trained through constant practice to discern good from evil, implying that discernment is a skill that can be developed through spiritual maturity.

Because manipulation is not easy to spot, we must grow in our discernment to be better aware of the Spirit's activity. Hans Urs von Balthasar tells us that one way to test our experiences is to see if they renounce or hold fast to worldly ambitions. He writes, "God is essentially experienceable only in nonexperience. Or to translate it in more explicitly Christian terms: we can come to know God only by decisively renouncing what is ours, which is the very definition of faith, hope and love."²⁵ If your experience evinces a total dependence on God, then very likely you've experienced God.

While discernment helps us determine a person or group's intent, what should we do about the fact that music can be wielded in such a way that it manufactures responses in us? Art is, by design, affective, and music helps us fully engage our holistic, spiritual, and embodied selves. If the music in a worship service moves you, it could just be a masterful combination of formal elements that's evoking the bodily response of chills. Or it could be that music helped you open yourself up to encounter the Holy Spirit, and you felt it in your spirit and body. The assumptions we make really matter when we interpret our experiences. Maybe someone is engineering your experience by adjusting the thermostat, or maybe we feel fire when it's hot.

NOTES

1. Steven Brown, "Introduction: 'How Does Music Work?' Toward a Pragmatics of Musical Communication," in Steven Brown and Ulrik Volgsten, Eds., *Music and Manipulation: On the Social Uses and Social Control of Music* (New York: Berghahn Books, 2006), 22.
2. I should note that when I speak of the "church," I mean, in particular, the Evangelical and Pentecostal traditions that perform contemporary worship.
3. Brown, "Introduction," 21.
4. Brown, "Introduction," 21.
5. Steven Félix-Jäger and Yoon Shin, *Renewing Christian Worldview: A Holistic Approach for Spirit-filled Christians* (Grand Rapids: Baker Academic, 2023), 3.
6. William James, "What is an Emotion?" *Mind*, Vol. 9, No. 34 (1884), 190.
7. Scott Bannister and Tuomas Eerola, "Suppressing the Chills: Effects of Musical Manipulation on the Chills Response," *Frontiers in Psychology*, Vol. 9 (2018), 2.
8. Rachael Hope, "A Jean-Michel Basquiat Retrospective: Love Affair with Music and Art," Sound of Life (2022), https://www.soundoflife.com/blogs/people/jean-michel-basquiat-music-art (accessed 11/25/23).
9. Jeremy Begbie, "Faithful Feelings: Music and Emotion in Worship," in Jeremy Begbie and Stephen Guthrie, Eds., *Resonant Witness: Conversations Between Music and Theology* (Grand Rapids: Eerdmans, 2011), 324.
10. Begbie, "Faithful Feelings," 325.
11. James K.A. Smith, *Desiring the Kingdom: Worship, Worldview, and Cultural Formation* (Grand Rapids: Baker Academic, 2009), 170.
12. Smith, *Desiring the Kingdom*, 170.
13. Smith, *Desiring the Kingdom*, 171.
14. Lindsay Elizabeth, "'I'm Genuinely Losing My Faith': Hillsong Worship Leader Rejects Christian Beliefs," *CBN* (2019), https://www2.cbn.com/news/news/im-genuinely-losing-my-faith-hillsong-worship-leader-rejects-christian-beliefs (accessed 12/18/23).

15. Ruth Graham, "The Rise and Fall of Carl Lentz, the Celebrity Pastor of Hillsong Church," *The New York Times* (2020), https://www.nytimes.com/2020/12/05/us/carl-lentz-hillsong-pastor.html (accessed 12/18/23).

16. Anne Davies, "Hillsong's Brian Houston Resigns from Megachurch," *The Guardian* (2022), https://www.theguardian.com/world/2022/mar/23/hillsongs-brian-houston-resigns-from-megachurch (accessed 12/18/23).

17. For more on this, read Adam Perez, "'It's Your Breath in Our Lungs': Sean Feucht's Praise and Worship Music Protests and the Theological Problem of Pandemic Response in the U.S." *Religions*, Vol. 13, No. 47 (2022), 1–10.

18. Kelsey Kramer McGinnis, "Worship Music Is Emotionally Manipulative. Do You Trust the Leader Plucking the Strings?" *Christianity Today* (2023), https://www.christianitytoday.com/ct/2023/may-web-only/worship-music-emotionally-manipulative-leader-hillsong.html (accessed 12/2/23).

19. McGinnis, "Worship Music Is Emotionally Manipulative."

20. Charles Taylor, *A Secular Age* (Cambridge: Harvard University Press, 2007), 25–26.

21. Taylor, *A Secular Age*, 35.

22. Suzi Gablik, *The Re-Enchantment of Art* (New York: Thames and Hudson, 1991), 11.

23. "The Is How Church Music Manipulates You," Faith Free (2018), https://www.youtube.com/watch?v=XoaknMByfRs&t=0s (accessed 11/25/23).

24. "Church Services Are Designed to Influence You. Here's How." Genetically Modified Skeptic (2021), https://www.youtube.com/watch?v=7btz0ocXDeg&t=0s (accessed 11/25/23).

25. Hans Urs von Balthasar, *Spirit and Institution: Explorations in Theology IV*, trans. by Edward T. Oakes, S.J. (San Francisco: Ignatius Press, 1995), 348.

BIBLIOGRAPHY

Bannister, Scott, and Tuomas Eerola. "Suppressing the Chills: Effects of Musical Manipulation on the Chills Response." *Frontiers in Psychology*, Vol. 9 (2018): 1–16.

Begbie, Jeremy. "Faithful Feelings: Music and Emotion in Worship." In: Jeremy Begbie and Stephen Guthrie (eds.), *Resonant Witness: Conversations Between Music and Theology*. Grand Rapids: Eerdmans, 2011.

Brown, Steven. "Introduction: 'How Does Music Work?' Toward a Pragmatics of Musical Communication." In: Steven Brown and Ulrik Volgsten (eds.), *Music and Manipulation: On the Social Uses and Social Control of Music*. New York: Berghahn Books, 2006.

"Church Services Are Designed to Influence You. Here's How." Genetically Modified Skeptic (2021). https://www.youtube.com/watch?v=7btz0ocXDeg&t=0s (accessed 11/25/23).

Davies, Anne. "Hillsong's Brian Houston Resigns from Megachurch." *The Guardian* (2022). https://www.theguardian.com/world/2022/mar/23/hillsongs-brian-houston-resigns-from-megachurch (accessed 12/18/23).

Elizabeth, Lindsay. "'I'm Genuinely Losing My Faith': Hillsong Worship Leader Rejects Christian Beliefs." *CBN* (2019). https://www2.cbn.com/news/news/im-genuinely-losing-my-faith-hillsong-worship-leader-rejects-christian-beliefs (accessed 12/18/23).

Félix-Jäger, Steven and Yoon Shin. *Renewing Christian Worldview: A Holistic Approach for Spirit-filled Christians.* Grand Rapids: Baker Academic, 2023.

Gablik, Suzi. *The Re-Enchantment of Art.* New York: Thames and Hudson, 1991.

Graham, Ruth. "The Rise and Fall of Carl Lentz, the Celebrity Pastor of Hillsong Church." *The New York Times* (2020). https://www.nytimes.com/2020/12/05/us/carl-lentz-hillsong-pastor.html (accessed 12/18/23).

Hope, Rachael. "A Jean-Michel Basquiat Retrospective: Love Affair with Music and Art." Sound of Life (2022). https://www.soundoflife.com/blogs/people/jean-michel-basquiat-music-art (accessed 11/25/23).

James, William. "What is an Emotion?" *Mind* Vol. 9, No. 34 (1884): 199–205.

McGinnis, Kelsey Kramer. "Worship Music Is Emotionally Manipulative. Do You Trust the Leader Plucking the Strings?" *Christianity Today* (2023). https://www.christianitytoday.com/ct/2023/may-web-only/worship-music-emotionally-manipulative-leader-hillsong.html (accessed 12/2/23).

Perez, Adam. "'It's Your Breath in Our Lungs': Sean Feucht's Praise and Worship Music Protests and the Theological Problem of Pandemic Response in the U.S." *Religions*, Vol. 13, No. 47 (2022): 1–10.

Taylor, Charles. *A Secular Age.* Cambridge: Harvard University Press, 2007.

"The Is How Church Music Manipulates You," Faith Free (2018). https://www.youtube.com/watch?v=XoaknMByfRs&t=0s (accessed 11/25/23).

von Balthasar, Hans Urs. *Spirit and Institution: Explorations in Theology IV.* Trans. by Edward T. Oakes, S.J. San Francisco: Ignatius Press, 1995.

Chapter 4

"Everything Means Nothing to Me"

The Spirit of Wisdom within Qoheleth, Kierkegaard's Either/Or, and the Elliott Smith Songbook

Sophia A. Magallanes-Tsang

A musical duo called The Brilliance released an album on February 17, 2015, entitled *Brother*. Among the nine songs on the album, they have a song called "Does Your Heart Break?" The song asks the hearer if their heart breaks for a series of people who face troubling and even disturbing situations. The song begins by describing the cries of a hungry child. The singer asks if the audience's heart has broken upon hearing the child's cries or if their heart breaks now presumably in hearing the singer relate the scenario anew. He appears to answer his own question with the chorus of the song, which expresses the inability to feel it within his soul and articulates that he is unable to see the subject since the singer is alone. Then the singer asks if the blind can receive their sight. The singer then turns from addressing his hearers in order to address God directly. The singer asks God if the Lord can hear his people or if the blind may have their sight.

The next verse opens with a man crying out that he is being choked and that he cannot breathe. This song echoes a police brutality scenario that became known more widely after the George Floyd video went viral in May 2020. The singer returns to the chorus' repeated refrain that asks the audience if their hearts broke upon hearing his cry or if they break now. The half of the chorus that addresses the listeners remains the same and the other half that addresses God changes slightly. The singer asks God if he can hear his people when he sees them all alone. The chorus ends by echoing the last line of the first chorus as it asks if the blind may have their sight.

The third verse of the song clarifies that the singer is lamenting over the perceived apathy of God and his listeners. He sings that the world is burning as the listener stands by, just as God appears to be an unmoved spectator as his children die. This verse leads into a musical break that features another singer singing a descant found in Elliott Smith's song "Everything Means Nothing to Me." This descant is repeated four times, and then the musical interlude culminates in a crescendo of both electronic and orchestral resonance. After a brief break, the song resumes with a soft return to the first two first lines of the chorus, asking if the hearer's heart breaks. Those lines are repeated twice, which poses the question of whether or not the listener's heart breaks four times. The last line of the song ends with a question of solidarity: "When their hearts break, does your heart break?" This question appears to be addressing both God and the listener.

Upon hearing this song for the first time in the summer of 2020, I was deeply impacted in four ways: viscerally, spiritually, academically, and artistically. On a visceral level, my heart *did* break while listening to the song, especially because the second verse's subject and scenario had been witnessed by the whole world (as a captive audience) through the video of George Floyd crying out his last breaths from a policeman's chokehold. On a spiritual and academic level, this song embodied all that I study academically (which has enriched me spiritually) from the lament traditions of the Hebrew Bible and especially the pessimism of the books of Job and Qoheleth (Ecclesiastes). At an artistic level, I was ecstatic that The Brilliance, a well-known Christian band, was using a refrain from one of my favorite singer/songwriters of the turn of this century, Elliott Smith.

Elliott Smith (Steve Paul Smith) graduated as a double major in philosophy and political science from Hampshire College in Amherst, Massachusetts, in 1991. During his college years, not only did Smith become a student of Kierkegaard, but he also formed a band called Heatmiser with his classmate Neil Gust. Upon graduation, both Smith and Gust, along with two other members, began to perform back in Portland, Oregon, during Portland's '90s Music Renaissance. Since Smith was always reading one of Kierkegaard's works when he was not writing or performing music, his bandmates would introduce Smith among the other band members at their gigs with the statement, "We've got Søren Kierkegaard on guitar."[1]

After his first solo album, *Roman Candle* (1994), it became apparent that neither the melancholic and philosophical content of his songs nor Smith's deconstructed musical aesthetic were in keeping with that of Heatmiser's. Soon afterward, Smith started working on his self-titled second solo album, which was released a little over a year after his debut album on July 21, 1995. Smith's third solo album was entitled *Either/Or* (1997), after one of his favorite philosophical works by Kierkegaard. All three of these solo albums caught the attention of Gus Van Sant, an independent filmmaker. Six of Smith's songs ended up in Van Sant's film entitled *Good Will Hunting*. Smith's song "Miss Misery" was nominated for the Academy Award for Best Original Song in 1998. After this recognition, Smith remained true to his understated aesthetic as well as the philosophical content of his music. Smith produced two more albums (*XO* released in 1998, and *Figure 8* released in 2000) and composed several other songs which were released after his sudden and horrific death on October 21, 2003.

The Elliott Smith song that The Brilliance chose to incorporate for their song was a very interesting choice to me. It seemed obvious to me that the repeated descant from Smith's "Everything Means Nothing to Me" simply fits musically with the orchestration of "Does Your Heart Break?" But what was not as obvious was why they would choose this piece from among the wide array of songs in the Elliott Smith songbook. After all, what does the repeated refrain have to do with injustice and human beings' responses to it? Furthermore, how does the descant of "Everything means nothing to me" even relate to how we view God and the Holy Spirit? Does it mean that both humans and God are seemingly apathetic to human suffering, or is there something more that the Spirit of God has to say with the use of this lyric? Throughout this chapter, I wish to explore these questions further as we look to scripture, the philosophy of Søren Kierkegaard, and the artistry of Elliott Smith.

THE SPIRIT OF WISDOM IN SCRIPTURE

The Spirit's Association with Wisdom

The Spirit of God (רוּחַ אֱלֹהִים) within the whole of Scripture is often associated with wisdom. A part of this association recognizes God's Spirit not only as the one who inspires artistry but also as the one who reveals Godself through the abilities and skills of the artisans themselves (Exod. 35:30–36:1). The Spirit of God is also associated with the wisdom imparted from one skilled leader to another when Moses lays hands upon Joshua in the Book of Deuteronomy (Deut. 34:9). This association of wisdom with the Spirit of God even extends into the early church, as the Holy Spirit imparts Jesus' disciples when praying in Jerusalem on the day of Pentecost another skill set, that is, being polyglots in the language arts (Acts 2:4). Furthermore, the first deacons of the church at Jerusalem (Stephen being among them) are identified as having wisdom imbued by the Holy Spirit to serve the church and defend God's honor. The Spirit is the one who gives artisans, practitioners, and leaders their "know-how" in the application of their knowledge.

The Spirit's Association with Wisdom at Creation

The Spirit's association with wisdom should come as no surprise since the Spirit of God (רוּחַ אֱלֹהִים) is the one who establishes and incubates wisdom at the beginning of creation. The word wisdom חָכְמָה is not present in the Genesis accounts of creation, but the concept of wisdom is demonstrated in both Genesis 1 and 2. The Hebrew word for wisdom, חָכְמָה, at its most basic level refers to the application of knowledge. In the Genesis 1 account of the creation of the world, as God applies his knowledge at the beginning of creation, it is the Spirit of God who is incubating creation by hovering over the waters (וְרוּחַ אֱלֹהִים מְרַחֶפֶת עַל־פְּנֵי הַמָּיִם, Gen. 1:2). In the Genesis 2 account of creation, when God applies his knowledge to form his masterpiece, humanity (הָאָדָם), it is the Spirit of God who is actively participating when God breathes the "breath of life" (נִשְׁמַת חַיִּים) into humanity's nostrils, causing for humanity (הָאָדָם) to become a "living soul" (נֶפֶשׁ חַיָּה).

In a later tradition of the Lord's creation of the world, the creation account in Proverbs 8:22-31 expresses God's application of his knowledge through the personification of wisdom as God's co-worker and foreman. Wisdom הָכְמָה is named as the first of God's creation since it is by God's application of knowledge that the Lord sets up the foundations of the world (Prov. 8:22-31). Even before the depths that could be hovered upon by the Spirit were formed (Prov. 8:24), God named and designated wisdom as the master craftsman of God's work (Prov. 8:30-31). In this creation account, it almost appears as if Wisdom's inauguration coincides with creation itself. So, upon the application of God's knowledge, and in God's setting up of boundaries for God's creation, Wisdom is "born" (Prov. 8:24-29). As God applies God's knowledge in God's creation, the Spirit of God takes part in bringing order out of the chaotic primordial waters. The process of creation is wisdom itself. Throughout this process, it is the Spirit's wisdom that is embedded within creation, not only because creation is the product of the Spirit's creative activity but also because God's wisdom is on display within this process. The connection between the Spirit's wisdom embedded in creation and human creative processes, both ethical as well as within their artistry, is articulated in how the Spirit is understood within biblical wisdom traditions and literature.

The Spirit and Wisdom Literature

In two of the three canonical books linked to the Wisdom Literature of the Hebrew Bible (Job and Qoheleth/Ecclesiastes), the Spirit of God (רוּחַ אֱלֹהִים) is depicted mostly as *"the wind."* It is key to note that the biblical wisdom traditions are not a monolith, but they do share a great deal of overlap with each other in how they understand the world and the divine. One of the places where two of the three wisdom books overlap is in the way in which they link the Spirit of God to *the wind* as a force of nature. In the wisdom books, רוּחַ is used to convey the following concepts: (1) wind,[2] (2) the human person/spirit,[3] (3) breath,[4] (4) the Spirit of the Lord/God proper,[5] (5) as an emotional idiom, and[6] (6) futility (usually of speech).[7] In the book of Proverbs, the word is never overtly used to connote the Spirit of God nor breath, but rather is mostly used to convey an emotional idiom like grief or anger (Prov. 15:4, 13; 16:18, 19, 32; 17:22, 27; 18:14; 25:28; 29:11, 23) and the human spirit (Prov. 1:23; 11:13; 15:4; 16:2, 18, 19, 32; 17:22, 27; 18:14; 25:28; 29:23). Only once is the word used to speak of the concept of futility (Prov. 11:29). For the sake of brevity and clarity, we will focus on concepts 1, 3, and 6 in Job and Qoheleth/Ecclesiastes, with special attention to Qoheleth/Ecclesiastes.

The Spirit in Job

What is important to note is that in the book of Job, God reveals himself as a voice from a mighty whirlwind in his final confrontation and vindication of the title character, Job. Job is devastated by a mighty wind, which takes the lives of his children (Job 1:19). Eliphaz, Job's most outspoken critic from among his friends, indirectly insults Job by commenting that the children of the wicked person perish "by the breath (רוּחַ) of God" (Job 4:9). The wind is what God uses to confront Job at the end of the book. Job is unable to control the wind and in the same way he has to accept that God is like the wind, unable to be controlled or grasped fully.

At the end of Job's speeches, Elihu reveals himself as a young onlooker who has been among the company of Job and his companions throughout their poetic discourses (Job 32:1-22). In Job 32–37, six chapters are dedicated to Elihu's discourse on God in relation to Job's situation. He begins his discourse by drawing authority to speak from the Spirit of God (sometimes referred to as the "breath [רוּחַ] of the Almighty"; Job 32:8, 18; 33:4). Not only this, but Elihu also appeals to God's authority as the only one who can take his spirit from mortals back unto himself (Job 34:14). From this position of the Spirit's authority, he implicitly offers the possibility for Job to be vindicated by God in proposing a hypothetical theophany where God speaks to an innocent person directly. Elihu does not believe Job to be innocent, yet he presents a scenario of what divine vindication might look like if this were the case. The irony of Elihu's conclusion to his speech is that while he is articulating what Job's vindication would look like, God enters onto the scene exactly as Elihu describes, through a meteorological theophany (Job 37:1-21, especially "tempest" in v. 9 [וּמִמְּזָרִים] and "south wind" in v.17 [מִדָּרוֹם]; cf. "storm/whirlwind" in Job 38:24 [קָדִים]).

The whirlwind that God uses to "vindicate" Job through his final confrontation with him brings Job to a place of retreating to dust and ashes (Job 42:5-6). It is very important to understand that Job does not recant what he has spoken about God in his lengthy discourses, especially since God commends Job for speaking what was correct in direct contrast to what his friends had to say about God in their discourses (Job 42:7-8). What Job renounces is speaking of what was incongruent with his epistemological experience of God, that is, "speaking beyond his understanding" (Job 42:3,5). Also, his return to silence and mourning signals a relinquished entitlement to vindication. The Spirit of God has brought Job to a place where he must abandon the last possession that Job has, that is, his right to "be right." It is in the negation of his entitlement that Job comes to a place where everything he holds dear has truly become nothing to him.

The Spirit of Wisdom in Qoheleth/Ecclesiastes

With much learning and wisdom comes great sorrow. In the book of Qoheleth (Ecclesiastes) in particular, the grief of too much knowledge as well as the pain of wisdom is expressed through lament and existential exclamations. Qoheleth, the preacher persona of the book, has his fill of all human experience, both wise and foolish. At the end of this excessive sapiential banquet, he concludes that all is meaningless. Ultimately, the preacher articulates his angst and ennui with the repeated refrain הֲבֵל הֲבָלִים הַכֹּל הָבֶל, "meaningless, meaningless, all is meaningless" as he relates the wisdom of his experience of the world. It is this refrain that becomes the motto of the book.

Coupled with this articulation of life's meaninglessness, the preacher observes that trying to decipher the meaning of life is like the futility of trying to grasp the wind (רוּחַ). It is in the negation of everything that he comes to a newfound freedom to fear God. It is the preacher's observation of the wind (רוּחַ) that brings him to a deep reverence before his maker. The wind, like God's very Spirit, must be understood as beyond humanity's grasp. It is the preacher's observation of the wind (רוּחַ) as an uninterrupted force of nature that causes him to reflect upon the meaninglessness of the human experience with all of its joys and sorrows, especially in light of human mortality and also in comparison to the eternal.

The preacher's first observations concerning the wind (רוּחַ) are that, within his cosmology, it blows around the earth in an unending and uninterrupted circuit (Eccles. 1:6). The next time the preacher speaks of the wind is when he exclaims that all is meaningless and "chasing after the wind (רוּחַ)"

(Eccles. 1:14, 17). He repeats this sentiment periodically as he expresses his experiences of both wisdom/folly and his toil as well as wealth amassment (Eccles. 2:11, 17, 26). Qoheleth also uses the idiom "chasing after the wind" in expressing the futility of not enjoying the outcome of one's toil (Eccles. 4:4, 6, 16; 5:15 [16]). He uses the idiom to accentuate the futility of greed as well (Eccles. 6:9).

In Ecclesiastes 7:18, the preacher reveals to his audience/reader that they are to look to the eternal in order to avoid the extremes of being overly righteous or overly wicked. It is the one who fears God who avoids these extremes. In the next chapter, the preacher expresses that there is not one person who has power over the wind (רוּחַ) to restrain it, just as no one has power over the day of their death (Eccles. 8:8). In contrast to this, God is the one who has power over both wind/breath (רוּחַ) and the time of death (Eccles. 3:19, 21; 11:5; 12:7). It is within this context that the preacher bids his reader to remember their creator while they are still young (Eccles. 12:1-7) and the editor of the book concludes the book with an admonition to "Fear God and keep his commandments; for that is the whole duty of everyone" (Eccles. 12:13). It is the wind/Spirit (רוּחַ) of God that has brought Qoheleth to this newfound wisdom. Everything must become utterly meaningless, הֲבֵל הֲבָלִים // "a chasing after the wind (רוּחַ)" to the preacher in order for him to truly fear God.

The Spirit of Wisdom: Qoheleth's Negative Mode and Jesus

We can see that it is the Spirit of God who leads Jesus himself through Qoheleth's negative mode when the Spirit leads Jesus into the wilderness to confront the temptations of everything that the world has to offer (Mt. 4:1-11; Lk. 4:1-13). It is Christ himself who faces everything that the tempter presents to him and answers with a resounding "no." Everything that the world has to offer truly becomes nothing to Jesus. Jesus, by the leading of the Holy Spirit, demonstrates wisdom when he applies his knowledge of the Holy One in the desert confronting the tempter with a recitation of and obedience to God's commandments. It is in this application of knowledge that Jesus elevates obedience to God's commandments (that is, fear of God) and thus refuses and negates all earthly glory, honor, and riches. What remains is the word of God, which is exactly what Jesus uses to renounce everything that belongs to this existence. The Spirit of Wisdom, God's Holy Spirit, leads Jesus into an embodiment of what it means to truly fear the Lord. It is through the *via negativa*—the negative way—that Jesus can defeat the tempter in the wilderness. Jesus demonstrates what no human has ever been able to do before him that is, declare all is meaningless with an eternal hope.

THE SPIRIT IN KIERKEGAARD'S *EITHER/OR*

Qoheleth's negative mode of existence is comparable to Søren Kierkegaard's excursus on the aesthetic mode of human existence outlined in his debut publication, *Either/Or*. Using different writing personas, Kierkegaard sets out on a similar journey as Qohelteh's preacher. The aesthete persona (Persona A) of his two-volume work *Either/Or* embodies the sensuality of the Spirit, which brings him to a place where life is meaningless. The life of the aesthete is one of deepest sorrow and one of greatest beauty. It is in the embodiment of this dialectic that the poet finds purpose. It is not in choosing one thing or another but in accepting that everything is also nothing that a person has the freedom to live, create, and exist in the world.

The Negation of the Successive Dialectic

Within the first section of his writing as his artistic alter ego (Persona A), Kierkegaard expresses what it is to live an aesthetic lifestyle. Kierkegaard describes the poet as an "unhappy being whose heart is torn" and whose lips have become so disfigured by their secret sorrow that when "the sighs and the cries escape them, they sound like beautiful music."[8] Those who hear the cries of the poet relish his sufferings because they produce tormented cries that sound like the most "delicious" music to their ears.[9] Then Persona A exclaims that these hearers are absurd not only for their sadistic appetites for music but also for wasting their much-sought-after liberties on apathy, lethargy, and outright laziness.[10]

The aesthete (Persona A) then goes on to describe how both virtues and vices are essentially the same actions that swing from one extreme to another through Persona A's declaration that "the object of desire is first attainable through its opposite."[11] Persona A clarifies what he means by this statement by providing a litany of examples. Some of the examples he observes are that "the debauched often [are] the most moral" and "the doubtful often [are] the most religious."[12] This resembles Qoheleth's warning about being overly righteous as well as overly wicked in Eccles. 7:16, as well as Aristotle's expression that the golden mean (i.e., virtuous moral behavior) lies between the extreme of deficiency and excess. For Persona A, this phenomenon is the "chief imperfection of all things human."[13]

Persona A experiences deep despair as he observes the pendulum swing from what he later names as a "successive dialectic in either/or."[14] In observing the absurdity, apathy, and fickleness of his community, Persona A concludes that out of all his companions, "melancholy is the most faithful mistress" he has known.[15] The aesthete's melancholic existence is further expressed in the pages that follow with exclamations like "My view of life is utterly meaningless,"[16] "Life is so empty and meaningless,"[17] "my eyes are sated and weary of everything, and yet I hunger,"[18] and "My life is absolutely meaningless."[19]

Building upon his earlier description of how his apathetic community demonstrates what he calls the "chief imperfection of all things human," Persona A offers his solution to what he perceives to be a false dichotomy between opposites. The aesthete articulates that many people live as though they have to combine or mediate the opposites, but that is only a "misunderstanding . . . for the true eternity does not lie behind either/or, but before it."[20] The main contribution that Persona A makes in addressing the predicament presented in this dialectic is in his articulation of the problem. After this articulation, Persona A resolves the problem of the first dialectic through the negation of the dichotomy of "either/or."

Persona A makes a distinction between the "successive dialectic in either/or" and the "eternal dialectic" by stating that the latter is the negation of the former.[21] In other words, the solution to the successive dialectic is the negation of it. It is in this negation of the choice between "either/or" that makes an eternal dialectic possible. The aesthete does not describe the eternal dialectic any further than this. It comes after Kierkegaard presents his second persona in his section on an ethical life. What remains in the aesthete's section is his treatise on music and his practical solutions to "cure" boredom. Persona A begins speaking of the Spirit and Christianity in his preface on music before he goes into a rant about Mozart's *Don Giovanni* being the greatest opera of his time.

The Spirit and Music in Either/Or

One of the aesthete's greatest joys is music since, according to Persona A, "Music finds its way where the rays of the sun cannot penetrate."[22] Because Persona A categorizes music within the realm of the sensual, he sees fit to clarify that sensuality does not exclude the spiritual nor the religious[23] because it is Christianity that first posited sensualism. To Persona A, that which is sensual is first "posited through the act which excludes it, in that it posits the opposite principle."[24] He then clarifies that from the "standpoint of the Spirit," sensualism is spiritual since "Christianity is Spirit, and the Spirit is the positive principle which Christianity has brought into the world."[25] So, because Christianity has excluded it, sensualism now exists as a spiritual category through Christianity's negation of it.

After establishing sensualism as a spiritual category, Persona A speaks of music in an incarnational way.[26] The aesthete then uses the spiritual categories of Christianity to arrive at the concept of the "sensuous erotic genius,"[27] who "demands expression in all its immediacy," which "can only be expressed in music."[28] Music expresses immediacy that is,

> spiritually determined, and therefore, it is force, life, movement, constant unrest, perpetual succession; but this unrest, this succession, does not enrich it, it remains always the same, it does not unfold itself, but it storms uninterruptedly forward as if in a single breath.[29]

Therefore, spiritual immediacy itself is like a force of nature, like the wind that blows without interference.[30] This resembles the observation made by the preacher in Qoheleth/Ecclesiastes, where the wind is unable to be grasped but continues on its uninterrupted circuit throughout the world. Unlike the preacher, the aesthete offers music as an imperfect medium for spiritual immediacy.[31] Because by nature music expresses the Spirit's immediacy, music serves as the incarnational articulation of that immediacy. Persona A concludes that music must not be excluded but must be recognized in the "realm of the spirit."[32]

THE SPIRIT IN THE ELLIOTT SMITH SONGBOOK

Elliot Smith's musical catalog resonates with the existential and painful experience of both Qoheleth and Kierkegaard's aesthete persona in *Either/Or*. It is in the desperation and brokenness of Elliott Smith's ethos and lyrics that the Spirit of Wisdom has an opportunity to express Godself. Many would want to superficially link Smith to Kierkegaard just based on their shared experiences of depression and anxiety, but one does not have to listen very long to the Elliot Smith songbook to hear how Smith embodies the pathos and ethos of Persona A of *Either/Or*.

In her article entitled "Kierkegaard's Aesthetic Life View in Elliot Smith's Either/Or," Camille Richey makes a case for understanding Elliot Smith's *Either/Or* as being in keeping with the philosophy of Kierkegaard's Aesthete Persona. Richey observes,

> [W]hether Smith meant to deliberately engage Kierkegaard's version of the aesthete in this album [Either/Or] is questionable. Smith only mentions in interviews where the title came from and never elaborates on why he chose it. However, [w]hile reading *Either/Or*, Smith saw the aesthete in himself. If so, then he was doing exactly what Kierkegaard. wanted him to do: to struggle, to find his own meaning, to read himself into the works. Perhaps Smith not only saw himself in Author A or Johannes, but also in Kierkegaard, who was after all a literary, poetic writer—in truth, an aesthete.[33]

Richey is correct in her assessment of Smith's engagement with not only the philosophy of Kierkegaard's aesthete but also the philosophical approach of Kierkegaard himself. Whether it was his Community of Christ (RLDS) and Methodist upbringing as a child or his coursework as a philosophy major in college that led him to resonate with Kierkegaard's aesthete, what is clear is that Smith had reached a point in his life where he could no longer ignore the absurdity and meaninglessness of the world. Within both my and Kierkegaard's worldviews, this is only the work of the Spirit, who causes a person to negate everything the world has to offer. This is reflected in various songs but especially in the songs "The Ballad of Big Nothing," "Miss Misery," "Between the Bars," and "Everything Means Nothing to Me." Because "Everything Means Nothing to Me" is the song that captures the ethos of both the preacher of Qoheleth as well as Kierkegaard's aesthete persona, we shall focus on how the Spirit of wisdom reveals Godself in the music of Elliott Smith.

The Spirit in "Everything Means Nothing to Me"

The song "Everything Means Nothing to Me" consists of the contrast between delicate, whimsical piano playing and a gristly tenor voice that has been doubled in the studio because of its paper-thin quality. The voice sings very simple lyrics in the first verse, conveying that someone has decidedly made it their occupation to be a "statute in a fountain," standing at attention while looking backward into a pool of water. This appears to signal that the main figure of the song has decided to live a life "at attention," as possibly a military sort of person who waits to follow orders. Preoccupying his future with his job of waiting "at attention," he stands like a statue reflecting upon his past.

Because Smith's abusive stepfather was a military man whose perfectionism weighed heavily upon Smith as a child, I believe that here Smith alludes to how he tried to conform to his stepfather's expectations of him. This statue figure standing at attention is further depicted as wishing with a blue songbird on the statue's shoulder. The blue songbird sings the same song continuously. This song is revealed as the chorus, which is just one repeated refrain: "Everything means nothing to me." This appears to be a creature that echoes the melancholic aesthete, who negates everything that the world has to offer both to him and to the statue.

The second verse begins with the singer retelling another scenario. Here the singer says that he picked up the bluebird's song and ended up with his picture in the newspaper. This appears to refer to how Smith acquired fame by simply singing nature's song. The reflection in the "water" (or his image in the paper) demonstrates what he calls an "iron man still trying to salute."

He identifies that his portrait in the paper reveals that he is still the statue waiting for orders from people to be "everything he's supposed to be." Then the chorus begins again: "Everything means nothing to me."

This second verse is Smith reflecting on how both his past and present states are that of trying to conform to what others would have him be—first, his stepfather, and now, the music industry. The bluebird's cry is the cry of nature, creation itself, which reminds us that conformity to human expectations means absolutely nothing to nature and thus should mean absolutely nothing to the singer/songwriter. This cry of nature resembles the Spirit's cry that bids us to return to our creator in awe and wonder, thus compelling us to negate the expectations put upon us by anyone but God. The rest of the song is overrun by a crescendoing musical interlude and the repeated descent of "Everything means nothing to me" until the song's end.

CONCLUSION: THE SONG

So, why would Elliott Smith's song "Everything Means Nothing to Me" appear on The Brilliance's song "Does Your Heart Break?"? Perhaps The Brilliance noticed that the melody of the descant simply was compatible with the chord progression and tonality of their song. Or if my hunch is correct, Elliott Smith's ethos lends itself to the via negativa approach to spirituality that The Brilliance espouses in their aesthetic. This via negativa is readily made available to readers of the Bible, especially in the book of Ecclesiastes. It is further extrapolated philosophically in the works of Kierkegaard, especially in his work entitled *Either/Or*. It is then echoed in the groanings of Creation itself, which are articulated by the Spirit who intercedes for us (Rom. 8:22-27). A part of the Spirit's groans is the assertion and/or articulation that "Everything is meaningless" or that "Everything means nothing to me." And it is this negation of what the world has to offer that brings us to surrender to God's will.

Coming back to The Brilliance's song "Does Your Heart Break?" the descant of "Everything means nothing to me" is the Spirit asking us to align with the divine pathos for God's creation. This alignment is not possible unless the listener regards everything the world deems important as meaningless. When everything means nothing to the listener, they are now free to position themselves in obedient reverence before their creator. Positioned within the fear of God, we are forced to ask if our hearts break over what breaks the heart of God. As we do this, we are made aware that merely feeling what God feels is not enough; the Spirit's compassion must become embodied by the people of God. This creates an ethical imperative to act on behalf of those who need divine intervention. But instead of waiting for God's "heart to break," the listener must become aware that God's heart has already broken for humanity in the person of Jesus Christ. It is now the Body of Christ that must allow their hearts to break over the injustices of the world.

NOTES

1. William Todd Schultz, *Torment Saint: The Life of Elliott Smith*. New York: Bloomsbury, 2015, 200.
2. Prov. 11:29; 25:14, 23; 27:16; 30:4; Jb 1:19; 6:26; 8:2; 15:2, 30; 16:3; 21:18; 28:25; 30:15; 30:22; 37:21; 41:8 (16); [Job 37:9 וּמִמְּזָרִים; Job 37:17 מִדָּרוֹם; Job 38:24 קָדִים]; Ecc 1:6, 14, 17; 2:11, 17, 26; 4:4, 6, 16; 5:15 [16]; 6:9; 8:8.
3. Prov. 1:23; 11:13; 15:4; 16:2, 18, 19, 32; 17:22, 27; 18:14; 25:28; 29:23; Job 4:15; 6:4; 7:11; 10:12; 15:13; 17:1; 20:3; 32:8, 18; Eccles. 3:21; 7:8-9.
4. Job 4:9; 7:7; 9:18; 12:10; 19:17; 26:13; 27:3; Eccles 3:19; 11:5; 12:7.
5. Job 1:19; 4:9; 26:13; 27:3; 32:8; 33:4 [2x]; 34:14.
6. Prov. 15:4, 13; 16:18, 19, 32; 17:22, 27; 18:14; 25:28; 29:11, 23; Job 7:11; 21:4; Ecc 7:8-9; 10:4 [anger].
7. Prov. 11:29; Jb 8:2; 15:2; 21:18; 30:15; Eccles. 1:14, 17; 2:11, 17, 26; 4:4, 6, 16; 5:15 [16]; 6:9.
8. Søren Kierkegaard, *Kierkegaard's Writing, III, Part I: Either/Or*. Edited by Howard V. Hong and Edna H. Hong. Princeton University Press, 1987, p. 15.
9. Kierkegaard, *Either/Or*, 15.
10. Kierkegaard, *Either/Or*, 15.
11. Kierkegaard, *Either/Or*, 16.
12. Kierkegaard, *Either/Or*, 16.
13. Kierkegaard, *Either/Or*, 16.
14. Kierkegaard, *Either/Or*, 31.
15. Kierkegaard, *Either/Or*, 31.
16. Kierkegaard, *Either/Or*, 19.
17. Kierkegaard, *Either/Or*, 23.
18. Kierkegaard, *Either/Or*, 20.
19. Kierkegaard, *Either/Or*, 29.
20. Kierkegaard, *Either/Or*, 31.
21. Kierkegaard, *Either/Or*, 31.
22. Kierkegaard, *Either/Or*, 33.
23. Kierkegaard, *Either/Or*, 49.
24. Kierkegaard, *Either/Or*, 49.
25. Kierkegaard, *Either/Or*, 49.
26. Kierkegaard, *Either/Or*, 50–51.
27. Kierkegaard, *Either/Or*, 51.
28. Kierkegaard, *Either/Or*, 51.
29. Kierkegaard, *Either/Or*, 57.
30. Kierkegaard, *Either/Or*, 57.
31. Kierkegaard, *Either/Or*, 59.

32. Kierkegaard, *Either/Or*, 59.
33. Camille Richey, "Kierkegaard's Aesthetic Life View in Elliott Smith's Either/Or," *Criterion: A Journal of Literary Criticism.* Vol. 8, No. 2 (2015), 29.

BIBLIOGRAPHY

Camus, Alyson. *A Question Mark: An Investigation into the Mysterious Death of Elliott Smith.* Los Angeles: Genius Book Publishing, 2021.
Dansby, Andrew. "Smith Comes Up Roses." *Rolling Stone.* 1 Oct. 2007. Web. 22 Mar. 2014.
Gungor, David. 2024. Interview by Sophia A. Magallanes-Tsang. Zoom. March 7, 2024.
Kierkegaard, Søren. *Kierkegaard's Writing, III, Part I: Either/Or.* Edited by Howard V. Hong and Edna H. Hong. Princeton: Princeton University Press, 1987.
Nugent, Benjamin. *Elliott Smith and the Big Nothing.* Cambridge: Da Capo, 2005.
Alastair Hannay. *Kierkegaard: A Biography.* Cambridge: Cambridge University Press, 2001.
Richey, Camille. "Kierkegaard's Aesthetic Life View in Elliott Smith's Either/Or." *Criterion: A Journal of Literary Criticism.* Vol. 8, No. 2 (2015): 19–30.
Schultz, William Todd. *Torment Saint: The Life of Elliott Smith.* New York: Bloomsbury, 2015.

Part II

MUSIC AS CULTURAL EXPRESSION

Chapter 5

The Spirit-Haunted Lyrics of Jason Isbell

Amber Benson

Jason Isbell is an American singer-songwriter who publishes music both as a solo artist and as the frontman for the band the 400 Unit. Described by former Drive-By Truckers bandmate Patterson Hood as "maybe the most threatening triple threat I've ever met,"[1] Isbell has received critical acclaim as a perceptive songwriter, a powerful singer, and a proficient guitar player. A stalwart of the Americana genre, he has received four GRAMMY awards for four nominations in the Americana and American Roots categories and has won nine awards from the Americana Music Honors & Awards, voted on by the Americana Music Association, for both songwriting and recorded performances, including 2014 Artist of the Year.[2]

If, as Flannery O'Connor said, the South is "Christ-haunted,"[3] then Americana music might be said to be "Spirit-haunted." The genre of Americana, or roots music, draws on the varied musical heritage of distinctly American forms, including blues, country, jazz, bluegrass, folk, and gospel—all styles heavily influenced by Pentecostal worship. While many Americana artists can trace the provenance of their influences to church music, singer-songwriter Jason Isbell's lyrics reflect a Pentecostal sensibility rooted in its practice in the rural American South. This chapter will explore the evolution of theological concepts in Isbell's discography, with an emphasis on pneumatological themes.

RAISED IN THE CHURCH, WASHED IN THE BLOOD

Michael Jason Isbell was born on February 1, 1979, in Greenhill, Alabama, an unincorporated community in Lauderdale County, just two miles from the Tennessee state line and not far from Muscle Shoals, the famous Alabama community that spawned FAME Studios and Muscle Shoals Sound Studio, where iconic gospel soul performances such as "I'll Take You There" by the Staple Singers were recorded. *Rolling Stone* editor David Fricke has described that recording as "the epitome of the Muscle Shoals sound."[4]

Isbell is the only child of Angela Hill Barnett and Michael Isbell, who were teenagers when Jason was born; they later divorced. While his parents were at work, Isbell spent much of his childhood at his grandparent's farm. Although his parents were not musicians, many members of Isbell's extended family played instruments. He credits his paternal grandfather, Carthel Isbell, a preacher in the Holiness Pentecostal movement, and other family members with teaching him how to play the guitar and various other instruments. Isbell attended both Pentecostal and Church of Christ church services as a young man.[5]

Isbell has acknowledged the influence of his Pentecostal upbringing on his music—not only stylistically but also thematically. He has described the Pentecostal worship he experienced as "rock and roll music in church."[6] The influence of Pentecostal worship on the genesis of rock and roll is well-documented, with icons such as Jerry Lee Lewis, James Brown, and even the king himself, Elvis Presley, crediting their Spirit-filled upbringing for their unique contributions to the genre.[7] The worship in the church Isbell's grandfather pastored featured full bands, including drums, bass, and electric guitars. Isbell concedes that this style of gospel music, combined with knowledge of older country music, shapes the structure of his melodies. But he also notes that he was influenced by the redemptive presence he experienced in the church as well. As Isbell states:

> I don't know if it was unique, but the church had a quality of sort of redemption that I think that a lot of churches didn't necessarily have. There were a lot of people in my grandfather's church who had either been to prison or had been drug addicts or alcoholics in the past. And I think that happens a lot with your fire-and-brimstone Holiness churches in the South and in rural areas; you get a lot of people who had done some really bad things before and had cleaned up their act and come to Jesus, so to speak. And I think my narrative follows that now, probably more closely than I realize sometimes.[8]

Isbell has also acknowledged his training in the Bible as an input into his craft. In an interview with NPR after the release of the *Weathervanes* album, Isbell shared how, frightened by the threat of eternal damnation as a child, he studied Bible passages to ensure his salvation. While he admits this may not be "the most psychologically healthy thing, you can very easily trace an unintended formalist reading of each of the songs" back to the Bible.[9]

There is some direct evidence of Jason Isbell's Pentecostal heritage within the lyrical content of his songwriting. In the song "Something to Love" from the album *Something More Than Free* (2015), Isbell dispenses fatherly advice to an unnamed daughter. Unusually, the song begins with the chorus refrain urging the young child to find "something to love," a creative act that would inspire her through the vicissitudes of life. With this scaffolding set, Isbell builds an image of his own childhood in a "tiny Southern town." The next lines paint a familiar picture of the rural South a family front-porch band including "old men with old guitars smoking Winston Lights." In the next stanza, we see a clear influence of church music in the life of the songwriter.

Old women harmonizing with the wind
Singing softly to the savior like a friend[10]

The "old women harmonizing with the wind" conjures images of the Protestant tradition of congregational harmony singing. Harmonies influenced by shape-note singing would have likely been prevalent in both the Church of Christ and Pentecostal traditions he was exposed to as a child. The lyric "singing softly to the savior like a friend" connotes a very realized Christology present among his family members. Jesus was an intimate companion— not an abstract concept. It was among men and women of deep faith that Isbell learned the craft of playing and performing music. It is no wonder that these themes persist in his catalog.

One of the next lines of the stanza said, "I'm still singing like that great speckled bird,"[11] and this is perhaps the most telling sign of Isbell's Pentecostal upbringing in his songwriting. Based on a reference from Jeremiah 1:29, "The Great Speckled Bird" is a Southern hymn written by Guy Smith and first recorded by Roy Acuff in 1936.[12] Written to the tune of a traditional folk melody (probably most recognized as the melody of the song "It Wasn't God Who Made Honky Tonk Angels" by Kitty Wells), the song was a response to the Fundamentalist-Modernist Controversy within the Presbyterian Church but became a staple of country music artists and has been recorded by the likes of Johnny Cash, George Jones, and Lucinda Williams.[13] This sort of "deep cut" demonstrates the depth of Isbell's saturation in Southern gospel culture.

The song "Children of Children" from the same album also offers some autobiographical information about Isbell's family. The song, which addresses his parents' relationship and the fact that they themselves were just teenagers when they had Isbell, offers a glimpse into the family. The first verse finds the narrator looking through family photographs:

Pictures of the farm before us
Old men in a gospel chorus[14]

The "old men in a gospel chorus" likely refer to Isbell's paternal grandfather and his brothers, who also played instruments and sang church music.

At twenty-one, Jason Isbell was signed to a publishing deal by FAME Studios, and he remained with the studio for fifteen years, through the release of his solo album *Southeastern*.[15] His Pentecostal background, combined with his connection to the Muscle Shoals music scene, would have exposed Isbell to an amalgamation of influences that sit at the unique intersection of white and black gospel music, both of which heavily influenced American roots music. White and black gospel share a common heritage in Pentecostal worship, likely due to the interracial nature of the movement's origins. Craig Mosher has defined the following distinctives of Pentecostal worship: strongly rhythmic music, use of a wide variety of instruments, highly emotional singing, the interpolation of testimony within singing, improvisation, and vocal techniques like melisma and call-and-response elements. These can be seen across American roots music genres, including country, bluegrass, folk, blues, jazz, and especially the gospel-tinged soul music that characterizes the Muscle Shoals sound.[16]

Although Isbell does not identify as a Christian or claim association with any denomination, his background provides him with a deep reservoir of theological concepts to draw from. It is within this context that we examine the lyrical content of Jason Isbell's catalog of songs.

SELECTED DISCOGRAPHY FOR ANALYSIS

This analysis will focus on Jason Isbell's studio album discography, both as a solo artist and with his backing band, the 400 Unit. It excludes his songwriting credits with the Drive-By Truckers, live recordings, and other songs written by Jason Isbell for projects such as movie soundtracks or special collaborations. Jason Isbell is unique among modern songwriters in that he is typically credited as the sole songwriter with no co-writers. By focusing

Table 5.1 Selected Studio Recordings of Jason Isbell

Album Title	Release Date	Label
Sirens of the Ditch	July 10, 2007	New West
Jason Isbell and the 400 Unit (with the 400 Unit)	February 17, 2009	Lightning Rod
Here We Rest (with the 400 Unit)	April 12, 2011	Lightning Rod
Southeastern	June 11, 2013	Southeastern
Something More Than Free	July 17, 2015	Southeastern
The Nashville Sound (with the 400 Unit)	June 16, 2016	Southeastern
Reunions (with the 400 Unit)	May 8, 2020	Southeastern
Weathervanes (with the 400 Unit)	June 9, 2023	Southeastern

Source: Created by the author.

on his studio albums, where he is given sole songwriting credit, we can use an insistency-based analysis as a quantitative research method. Insistency analysis "supports content analysis by considering lyrical repetition (motifs) over time as significant of artistic intent" within a given corpus of lyrics.[17]

Using these criteria, Jason Isbell's studio discography includes three solo albums and five albums released as Jason Isbell and the 400 Unit. One studio album, *Georgia Blue* (2021), was excluded from this analysis because it consists of cover versions of songs written by Georgia artists and not original songwriting by Isbell. (See table 5.1.)

QUANTITATIVE METHOD OF LYRICAL ANALYSIS

Using a modified version of Paul Linden's two-stage methodology for insistency-based analysis, a corpus of Jason Isbell's lyrics was created from the selected discography. This total number of songs in this corpus is eighty-five, which excludes three instrumental tracks with no lyrical content. The lyrics from each song were downloaded and then verified by reading along to the studio albums and correcting for spelling. Nonsense words or vocalizations were omitted. Extremely repetitive phrases caused by vamping at the end of songs were cut down by half of their original amount. The total word count for the study is 22,831. The full corpus of lyrics was entered into a word frequency software program (AntConc).

Once the corpus was loaded, AntConc functions were used to identify a list of theologically relevant keyword clusters appearing in the corpus. Those keywords were then viewed in context to assess how many times they appear, how many songs they appear in, and across how many "eras" of Isbell's songwriting they appear in, supporting the following research questions:

RQ1: What are the theologically relevant lyrics used by Jason Isbell across his entire work?
RQ2: What theological, and specifically pneumatological, themes are revealed by these frequent words?
RQ3: Can an evolution of theological expression be ascertained when assessed across the studio discography (diachronically) and within a given era (synchronically)?

THEOLOGICALLY RELEVANT KEYWORD CLUSTERS FREQUENCY ANALYSIS

A review of the frequency of keywords in the corpus revealed the following theologically relevant keyword clusters. Keyword clusters include derivations of the keyword, including plurals, possessives, and verb variations (see table 5.2).

Many theologically relevant themes in Isbell's catalog are ambiguous in their intent, as these same broad themes such as love, life, and death can be used in contexts of interpersonal relationships, non-theological expression, or as figurative language, that is, "hotter than hell." However, it is

Table 5.2 Frequency of Theologically Relevant Keyword Clusters in the Corpus of Jason Isbell's Songwriting

Keyword(s) Cluster (Includes Derivations)	Frequency in Corpus	Number of Songs in Which the Keyword Appears	% of Songs in Corpus
Love	73	29	34.1
Life	69	34	40.0
Death	48	24	28.2
Hope	20	10	11.8
God*	20	10	11.8
Saved	14	7	8.2
Devil*	11	3	3.5
Hell	10	8	9.4
Truth	9	6	7.1
Pray*	9	9	10.6
Sunday*	8	5	5.9
Forgive	8	4	4.7
Church*	7	5	5.9
Lord*	6	3	3.5
Sin*	6	5	5.9
Faith*	5	5	5.9
Savior*	4	2	2.4
Bless*	4	2	2.4
Jesus*	3	3	3.5
Heaven*	2	2	2.4
Bible*	2	2	2.4
Christian*	1	1	1.2
Evil	1	1	1.2
Gospel*	1	1	1.2
Holy Ghost*	1	1	1.2
Profane*	1	1	1.2
Redemption*	1	1	1.2
Sacred*	1	1	1.2
Scripture*	1	1	1.2
Sermon*	1	1	1.2
Total Number of Theologically Relevant Keyword Clusters= 29	343	75	88.2
*Keyword Clusters Excluding Broad Themes	92	42	49.4

Source: Created by the author.

relevant to note that these larger existential themes permeate Isbell's catalog, with a full 88 percent of songs in the corpus containing lyrics related to these theologically relevant keyword clusters. Even when not expressing explicitly theological sentiments, Isbell works with a songwriting toolbox that is pregnant with the language of theology. When the broad themes are excluded, leaving only the more explicit keyword clusters associated with the Christian experience, these keyword clusters still appear in nearly half of the songs in Isbell's discography. This includes direct references to all three Persons of the Trinity, the Bible, church, and related concepts such as sin and redemption.

THEOLOGICAL THEMES IN THE CORPUS

Key themes that are evident in the quantitative insistency analysis can be qualitatively approached through a more traditional textual analysis of the lyrics.

Presence of the Godhead

Isbell's catalog contains direct references to all three Persons of the Godhead: Father, Jesus, and the Holy Spirit. Almost always referenced obliquely, these keywords appear to be used more colloquially than theologically; however, there are a few uses that make strong theological statements.

The song "Soldiers Get Strange" from the *Jason Isbell and the 400 Unit* (2009) album deals with the challenges faced by deployed soldiers when they are reintroduced into the civilian world. The song tells the story of a soldier who is struggling to connect with a woman he loves now that he has returned home. Struggling to find his footing, he hears words of comfort from the woman, who reminds him that everything is "watched by the eyes of God."[18]

These lines recognize an omnipresent deity that is capable of steadying the soldier with constancy and eternal vigilance. In the song "Last of My Kind," the narrator claims that "Mama says God won't give you too much to bear."[19] This God is present throughout the corpus of Isbell songs, a God that is thanked in gratitude, called upon to bless "the broken ships that bring us back,"[20] and prayed to even when it is not clear the narrator believes those actions might be efficacious. For example, Isbell's teenage parents in "Children of Children," "Pray to God that God was bluffing,"[21] when they found out they are expecting a child.

In "24 Frames," Isbell reflects upon the changes in behavior required to maintain sobriety in what might be the most overtly theological lyrics in his corpus.

You thought God was an architect, now you know
He's something like a pipe bomb waiting to blow[22]

    The lyrics here demonstrate an evolving understanding of the relationship between God and humanity, shifting from the puppet-master God of determinism and foxhole prayers to a more dynamic presence orchestrating lessons in humility.

    Jesus is mentioned three times in the corpus by name, and once as "the Savior" when referencing the elder women of his family in "Something to Love."[23] In "Down in a Hole," from Isbell's first solo album, *Sirens of the Ditch* (2007), a prosperity gospel hypocrite is thanking Jesus for his wealth and power:

Had a real big wife, a real big grin
He gave thanks to Jesus for the shape that he was in[24]

    Another reference, from "The Life You Chose" from *Something More Than Free* (2015), evokes the name Jesus in a similar, if more gracious, manner. In this song, the narrator has a conversation with a woman he knew when they were younger. Trying to assess whether she has demonstrated agency over the choices that led to her current life circumstances, he asks her, "Where's the Jesus that you swore you'd find? After running the last line?"[25] This use of theological language to confront hypocrisy will be further explored, as it is a recurring motif in Isbell's songwriting.

    There's only one direct reference to the Holy Spirit in Isbell's catalog. In the song "Only Children," he reflects on the time spent with a childhood friend upon the occasion of that friend's death. The first chorus refrain ponders the possibilities of divine inspiration:

The Holy Ghost could get inside you
You'd do whatever you put your mind to[26]

The use of "Holy Ghost" versus "Holy Spirit" is indicative of Southern Pentecostal nomenclature for the third Person of the Trinity and adds a sense of place to the lyrics. Coupled with the next line, the narrator demonstrates an understanding of the Holy Spirit as a form of empowerment and inspiration, enabling humans to access the full capabilities of their creative capacities.

Conviction of Sin and Condemnation

Another persistent theme in Isbell's writing is that of an awareness of sin as a paradigm over against perceived righteousness. The characters in Isbell songs struggle with conviction of sin even while rejecting condemnation. On *Weathervanes* (2023), the song "White Beretta" addresses this directly. The song centers on an abortion procured by a young woman but is told from the perspective of the man who impregnated her. The chorus recognizes that the singer was raised in church and, purportedly, received salvation as a child. Still, his current decisions are leaving him feeling disconnected and unsettled.

If His love is unconditional
Why do I feel so miserable?[27]

In this chorus, the male narrator's acknowledgment that they were "raised in the church" and "washed in the blood" is ambiguous. Is the implication that they, like Adam and Eve in the garden, are aware of their sin and now feel exposed? Or rather, are they rejecting the condemnation because they know that the love of God is unconditional? "Why do I feel so miserable?" describes the paradox between the Spirit-led, liberating conviction and the shame of condemnation. The alternate lyrics in the second refrain of this chorus further illuminate the narrators existential struggle with the idea.

I thank God you weren't brought up like me
With all that shame and uncertainty[28]

The narrator is envious of the young woman's worldview, that doesn't associate sin with this action. Curiously, the song ends with the man thanking the young woman "for her grace" by making a decision that freed them both to pursue their dreams unencumbered by unexpected parenthood. The narrator finds grace, not in God, but in the fact that she felt no condemnation and thus, was able to move forward without guilt, ultimately liberating him.

"White Beretta" sees Isbell addressing a topic close to his family: reproductive rights. His wife, Amanda Shires, has long championed access to abortion and shared her personal experience of an ectopic pregnancy in 2020 in an op-ed in *Rolling Stone* magazine.[29] In 2022, in the wake of the Supreme Court decision that overturned *Roe v. Wade*, Isbell spoke to *GQ* magazine about the topic.

> I think if people would just tell the truth, that would help a whole lot. Because a whole lot of us men have benefited from women having the right to choose. And if you don't know that you've benefited from that, the reasons could either be that a woman was too kind to tell you or that she was afraid to tell you. This is the privilege of ignorance. If by some chance we could reveal all the men who have benefited from abortion, it would become very clear and obvious just what a woman's right to choose does for society in general.[30]

"White Beretta," which was released in 2023, appears to be Isbell making good on this statement.

Churches, the Bible, and Hypocrisy

Churches populate the landscape of Isbell's songwriting. In "Cumberland Gap," the narrator complains about the limited options the pass affords its residents by saying, "there's nothing here but churches, bars, and grocery stores."[31] In the working-class anthem "Something More Than Free," Isbell's blue-collar worker states that "On Sunday morning I'm too tired to go to church / but I thank God for the work."[32] In the chorus of "White Beretta," the young couple was "raised in the church."[33] In Isbell's lyrical universe, church attendance is an assumed marker of righteous living. Or at least the appearance of it.

Churches are often deployed as symbols of hypocrisy in Isbell's lyrics, a white-washed tomb that hides deeper sins. In "Songs That She Sings in the Shower," the narrator laments his poor choices that led to the loss of his female companion, who, as the title suggested, used to sing in the shower. As he comes to terms with the fact that she isn't going to return despite his efforts to sober up, he sings, "And the church bells are ringing for those who are easy to please."[34] There is a sense that organized religion is a crutch, or a panacea for the simple-minded. This theme appears again in the song "Relatively Easy," where Isbell sings, "Is your brother on a church kick? Just a different kind of dope sick."[35] Here, church attendance is analogous to drug addiction, something that fills a void. So, even though churches are omnipresent in Isbell's writing, they are places of performative righteousness rather than sincere devotion.

References to the Bible and scripture are similarly ambient and ambiguous. In "Hudson Commodore," an instant sense of place is established when he states the female protagonist was "in her 20s in the Bible Belt."[36] In "What've I Done to Help?" the narrator reflects on a previous marriage and subsequent divorce where he "lied on a Bible just to feel a little free."[37] Isbell sets the scene in "Dress Blues" by mentioning "scripture on grocery store signs,"[38] a common sight in the rural South. Here we see how Isbell uses the trappings of Christianity as set pieces rather than sacred objects in his catalog.

EVOLUTION OF THEOLOGICAL EXPRESSION

Within the eight studio albums included in this analysis, one can distinguish three "eras" within Isbell's career. The first three albums, *Sirens of the Ditch* (2007), *Jason Isbell and the 400 Unit* (2009), and *Here We Rest* (2011), were written at a time when Isbell was in active addiction to drugs and alcohol. Theological references in this era are often oblique, including biblical allusions with a focus on sin, hypocrisy, and condemnation. After an intervention by fellow musicians in 2012, Isbell achieved long-term sobriety.[39] At this same time, Isbell launched his own independent record label, Southeastern, which afforded him complete creative control over his recordings. The following two solo albums, *Southeastern* (2013), *Something More Than Free* (2015), and *The Nashville Sound* (2017), which was recorded with his band, the 400 Unit, reflect this process. These two solo albums are considered by critics to be seminal works of Jason Isbell, and *The Nashville Sound* was considered a breakout album for the full band. Here, the theological themes are more pronounced and focused on redemption and hope. The final era, including *Reunions* (2020) and *Weathervanes* (2023), is less autobiographical in nature, seeing Isbell settling into his role as a Gothic storyteller, and the theological themes here lean more toward the prophetic with an emphasis on social justice.

Quantitative analysis of the corpus demonstrates that theological terms and themes have been present in all three "eras" of Isbell's songwriting, peaking in his post-sobriety era. However, it should be noted that the most recent era is theologically rich as well. A qualitative analysis will demonstrate a shift in the type of theological expression across eras. (See table 5.3.)

Era A

In the first era, theological language consists of passing biblical allusions such as "Don't roll that stone away"[40] or references in the service of indictments on hypocrisy. In the song "However Long," we see a harbinger of the prophetic voice that will shape the more recent era, but this song is an exception in this phase of his songwriting. The song is commenting on a "man with a military mind":

Table 5.3 Frequency and Percentage of Theologically Relevant Keywords within Jason Isbell's Songwriting Corpus across Three "Eras"

	Number of Songs Containing Theologically Relevant Keyword	Total Number of Songs in Era	Percentage of Era Catalog Containing Theologically Relevant Keywords	Percentage of Total Catalog
Era A	23	30	76.6	27.1
Era B	30	32	93.8	35.3
Era C	21	23	91.3	24.7

Source: Created by the author.

Try to recollect the sermon on the mount
Blessed are the poor when they're all swinging from the gallows[41]

This distortion of the Beatitudes demonstrates Isbell's familiarity and facility with scriptural references.

Era B

The release of *Southeastern* marks the beginning of a three-recording cycle consisting of *Southeastern*, *Something More Than Free*, and *The Nashville Sound*, which includes much more autobiographical content and, in this era, the theological themes center on confession, forgiveness, redemption, and hope. "If It Takes a Lifetime," from *Something More Than Free*, describes a distinctly Wesleyan view of sanctification:

And I thought that I was running to but I was running from
Oh, our day will come if it takes a lifetime[42]

When asked what the narrative arc of his career might be, Isbell has said, "For me, it is the work of understanding yourself and improving yourself. If I did that today, it was a good day. And if I didn't, I'll try again tomorrow."[43] This grace-filled notion of self-reflection and movement toward maturity pervades this era of Isbell's songwriting.

Era C

In the most recent era, consisting of *Reunions* and *Weathervanes*, Isbell's prophetic voice has emerged. Building on the political sensibilities of "Hope the High Road" and "White Man's World" on *The Nashville Sound* and *Reunions*, the songwriter's first studio recording since the MeToo movement, Black Lives Matter, and the COVID-19 pandemic, solidified Isbell as a protest songwriter. "What've I Done to Help" served as an examen on the songwriter's own sense of privilege in a world of stark inequality.

Sent our thoughts and prayers to loved ones on the ground
And as the days went by we just stopped looking down, down, down[44]

The chorus refrain, "What've I Done to Help?" further illustrates the songwriter's sense of obligation to the "loved ones on the ground." This expression of neighborly love is continued in other songs that act as commentaries on social injustice. In "Cast Iron Skillet," Isbell focuses on the entrenched despair and casual racism in a small town:

Jamie found a boyfriend with smiling eyes and dark skin
And her daddy never spoke another word to her again[45]

Isbell spoke to *Time Magazine* about how addressing issues of social justice is an exercise in truth and authenticity for him. "I believe that people should be allowed to be who they want, to love who they want. I think there is a big systemic racial issue in our country. I think a lot of people are pushed to the margins intentionally. I think the system is set up that way," he says. "And if those are the things I believe and I don't say them out loud then I'm being dishonest with myself, and that's the last thing I want to be."[46]

In "Save the World," Isbell addresses the issue of gun violence in the wake of a school shooting. In the song, Isbell himself is the narrator as he struggles with feelings of helplessness in protecting his own daughter, after hearing a "balloon popping in the grocery store."[47]

Although not overtly theological in its expression, this era of Isbell's writing rings with the hallmarks of Spirit-filled prophecy: addressing what is and declaring a just and equitable future reflective of the kingdom of God.

CONCLUSION

While not categorized or self-identified as a Christian artist, Jason Isbell uses theological concepts as a prism, refracting the human condition into perspectives that are both "sacred and profane."[48] Theologically salient terms are found throughout his catalog, reflecting an insistent use of these keywords both diachronically and synchronically. His rural Alabama upbringing is demonstrated not only in his musical influences but lyrically as well, providing a rich sense of place and depth of character development to his songs. From a pneumatological perspective, while not explicit, the Spirit does indeed haunt Isbell's songwriting. Themes of conviction of sin, redemption, sanctification, and prophecy are as omnipresent in his writing as the Spirit.

NOTES

1. Matt Hendrickson, "Jason Isbell Picks a Legacy," *Garden & Gun* (2023), https://gardenandgun.com/feature/jason-isbell-picks-a-legacy/.

2. "Winners and Honorees, 2014," American Music Association, https://americanamusic.org/awards/winners (accessed 3/5/24).

3. Flannery O'Connor, *Mystery and Manners: Occasional Prose* (New York: Farrar, Straus and Giroux, 1970).

4. Peter Meltzer, *So You Think You Know Rock and Roll?: An In-Depth Q&A Tour of the Revolutionary Decade 1965–1975* (New York: Skyhorse Publishing, 2017), 287.

5. "Jason Isbell," *The Encyclopedia of Alabama*, https://encyclopediaofalabama.org/article/jason-isbell/ (accessed 12/31/23).
6. Bill Kopp, "Jason Isbell on Muscle Shoals, Politics, Religion and Sobriety," *Musoscribe* (2018), https://blog.musoscribe.com/index.php/2018/12/06/jason-isbell-on-muscle-shoals-politics-religion-and-sobriety/.
7. Craig Mosher, "Ecstatic Sounds: The Influence of Pentecostalism on Rock and Roll," *Popular Music and Society,* Vol. 31, No. 1 (2008), 96.
8. Kopp, "Jason Isbell on Muscle Shoals, Politics, Religion and Sobriety."
9. Jefferson Cowie, "The Rebuilt Heart of Jason Isbell," *NPR Music* (2023), https://www.npr.org/2023/06/21/1183194069/jason-isbell-weathervanes-profile.
10. "Something to Love," words and music by Jason Isbell © 2017 Southeastern Records.
11. "Shape Note Singing," *The Library of Congress Digital Collections: The Library of Congress Celebrates the Songs of America*, https://www.loc.gov/collections/songs-of-america/articles-and-essays/musical-styles/ritual-and-worship/shape-note-singing/ (accessed 12/31/23).
12. "The Great Speckled Bird," hymnstudiesblog, https://hymnstudiesblog.wordpress.com/2021/02/20/the-great-speckled-bird/ (accessed 5/13/24).
13. "The Great Speckled Bird."
14. "Children of Children," words and music by Jason Isbell © 2015 Southeastern Records.
15. "Jason Isbell," *The Encyclopedia of Alabama*, https://encyclopediaofalabama.org/article/jason-isbell/ (accessed 12/31/23).
16. Mosher, "Ecstatic Sounds," 96.
17. Paul Linden, "Insistency: A New Methodology for Lyrical Analysis," *The Journal of the Music and Entertainment Industry Educators Association,* Vol. 15, No. 1 (2016), 127.
18. "Soldiers Get Strange," words and music by Jason Isbell © 2009 Lightning Rod Records.
19. "Last of My Kind," words and music by Jason Isbell © 2017 Southeastern Records.
20. "New South Wales," words and music by Jason Isbell © 2013 Southeastern Records.
21. "Children of Children," words and music by Jason Isbell © 2015 Southeastern Records.
22. "24 Frames," words and music by Jason Isbell © 2015 Southeastern Records.
23. "Something to Love," words and music by Jason Isbell © 2017 Southeastern Records.
24. "Down In a Hole," words and music by Jason Isbell © 2007 New West Records.
25. "The Life You Chose," words and music by Jason Isbell © 2015 Southeastern Records.
26. "Only Children," words and music by Jason Isbell © 2020 Southeastern Records.
27. "White Beretta," words and music by Jason Isbell © 2023 Southeastern Records.

28. "White Beretta."

29. Amanda Shires, "Amanda Shires on Why Abortion Rights Matter," *Rolling Stone* (2020), https://www.rollingstone.com/music/music-country/amanda-shires-abortion-rights-op-ed-1082647/.

30. Jason Isbell, "We Believe Access to Abortion is a Basic Human Right," *GQ* (2022), https://www.gq.com/story/the-roe-project?utm_source=twitter&utm_brand=gq&mbid=social_twitter&utm_medium=social&utm_social-type=owned.

31. "Cumberland Gap," words and music by Jason Isbell © 2017 Southeastern Records.

32. "Something More Than Free," words and music by Jason Isbell © 2015 Southeastern Records.

33. "White Beretta."

34. "Songs That She Sang In the Shower," words and music by Jason Isbell © 2013 Southeastern Records.

35. "Relatively Easy," words and music by Jason Isbell © 2013 Southeastern Records.

36. "Hudson Commodore," words and music by Jason Isbell © 2015 Southeastern Records.

37. "What've I Done To Help," words and music by Jason Isbell © 2020 Southeastern Records.

38. "Dress Blues," words and music by Jason Isbell © 2007 Southeastern Records.

39. Dwight Garner, "Jason Isbell, Unloaded," *The New York Times* (2013), https://www.nytimes.com/2013/06/02/magazine/jason-isbell-unloaded.html

40. "The Blue," words and music by Jason Isbell © 2009 Lightning Rod Records.

41. "However Long," words and music by Jason Isbell © 2009 Lightning Rod Records.

42. "If It Takes a Lifetime," words and music by Jason Isbell © 2015 Southeastern Records.

43. Cowie, "The Rebuilt Heart of Jason Isbell."

44. "What've I Done to Help."

45. "Cast Iron Skillet," words and music by Jason Isbell © 2023 Southeastern Records.

46. Silas House, "*Jason Isbell Is Finding His Purpose*," Time (2023), https://time.com/6285952/jason-isbell-interview/.

47. "Save the World," words and music by Jason Isbell © 2023 Southeastern Records.

48. "Children of Children."

BIBLIOGRAPHY

Cowie, Jefferson. "The Rebuilt Heart of Jason Isbell." *NPR Music* (2023). https://www.npr.org/2023/06/21/1183194069/jason-isbell-weathervanes-profile.

Garner, Dwight. "Jason Isbell, Unloaded." *The New York Times* (2013). https://www.nytimes.com/2013/06/02/magazine/jason-isbell-unloaded.html.

Hendrickson, Matt. "Jason Isbell Picks a Legacy." *Garden & Gun* (2023). https://gardenandgun.com/feature/jason-isbell-picks-a-legacy/.

House, Silas. "Jason Isbell is Finding His Purpose." *Time Magazine* (2023). https://time.com/6285952/jason-isbell-interview/.

Isbell, Jason. "24 Frames." *Something More Than Free*, Southeastern Records, 2015.

———. "Cast Iron Skillet." *Weathervanes*, Southeastern Records, 2023.

———. "Children of Children." *Something More Than Free*, Southeastern Records, 2015.

———. "Cumberland Gap." *The Nashville Sound,* Southeastern Records, 2017.

———. "Dress Blues." *Sirens of the Ditch,* New West Records, 2007.

———. "Down In a Hole." *Sirens of the Ditch,* New West Records, 2007.

———. "However Long." *Jason Isbell and the 400 Unit*, Lightning Rod Records, 2009.

———. "Hudson Commodore." *Something More Than Free*, Southeastern Records, 2015.

———. "If It Takes a Lifetime." *Something More Than Free*, Southeastern Records, 2015.

———. "Last of My Kind." *The Nashville Sound,* Southeastern Records, 2017.

———. "New South Wales." *Southeastern*, Southeastern Records, 2013.

———. "Only Children." *Reunions*, Southeastern Records, 2020.

———. "Relatively Easy." *Southeastern*, Southeastern Records, 2013.

———. "Save the World." *Weathervanes*, Southeastern Records, 2023.

———. "Soldiers Get Strange." *Jason Isbell and the 400 Unit*, Lightning Rod Records, 2009.

———. "Something More Than Free." *Something More Than Free*, Southeastern Records, 2015.

———. "Something to Love." *The Nashville Sound*, Southeastern Records, 2017.

———. "Songs That She Sang In The Shower." *Southeastern*, Southeastern Records, 2013.

———. "The Blue." *Jason Isbell and the 400 Unit*, Lightning Rod Records, 2009.

———. "The Life Your Chose." *Something More Than Free*, Southeastern Records, 2015.

———. "We Believe Access to Abortion is a Basic Human Right." *GQ* (2022). https://www.gq.com/story/the-roe-project?utm_source=twitter&utm_brand=gq&mbid=social_twitter&utm_medium=social&utm_social-type=owned.

———. "What've I Done To Help." *Reunions*, Southeastern Records, 2020.

———. "White Beretta." *Weathervanes*, Southeastern Records, 2023.

"Jason Isbell." *The Encyclopedia of Alabama.* https://encyclopediaofalabama.org/article/jason-isbell/ (Accessed 12/31/23).

Kopp, Bill. "Jason Isbell on Muscle Shoals, Politics, Religion and Sobriety." *Musoscribe* (2018). https://blog.musoscribe.com/index.php/2018/12/06/jason-isbell-on-muscle-shoals-politics-religion-and-sobriety/.

Linden, Paul. "Insistency: A New Methodology for Lyrical Analysis." *The Journal of the Music and Entertainment Industry Educators Association.* Vol. 15, No. 1 (2016): 125–150.

Meltzer, Peter. *So You Think You Know Rock and Roll?: An In-Depth Q&A Tour of the Revolutionary Decade 1965–1975.* New York: Skyhorse Publishing, 2017.

Mosher, Craig. "Ecstatic Sounds: The Influence of Pentecostalism on Rock and Roll." *Popular Music and Society.* Vol. 31, No. 1 (2008): 95–112.

O'Connor, Flannery. *Mystery and Manners: Occasional Prose.* New York: Farrar, Straus and Giroux, 1970.

"Shape Note Singing." *The Library of Congress Digital Collections: The Library of Congress Celebrates the Songs of America.* https://www.loc.gov/collections/songs-of-america/articles-and-essays/musical-styles/ritual-and-worship/shape-note-singing/ (Accessed 12/31/23).

Shires, Amanda. "Amanda Shires on Why Abortion Rights Matter." *Rolling Stone* (2020). https://www.rollingstone.com/music/music-country/amanda-shires-abortion-rights-op-ed-1082647/.

"The Great Speckled Bird." Hymnstudiesblog. https://hymnstudiesblog.wordpress.com/2021/02/20/the-great-speckled-bird/ (Accessed 5/13/24).

"Winners and Honorees, 2014." American Music Association. https://americanamusic.org/awards/winners (Accessed 3/5/24).

Chapter 6

The Spirit in Neoclassical, Wordless Music

Marc Byrd and Aaron Gabriel Ross

THE BOUNDLESS ALLUSIVENESS OF MUSIC

It is not uncommon to understand music as a polyvalent art form, one that can be seen from the perspective of its creator or from the perspective of the listener. This includes how the listener chooses to engage with the music, be that by casual listening in a car, on public transportation to block out the world around one's self, or the intentional creation of space and time by the avid listener. Music, perhaps differing from other forms of art, is an art that technology has formed as non-sedentary. Music is the art of movement, physically changing spaces, and asking to be engaged within various contexts, not only by the listener but through the surroundings it is manifest within.

As an art form engaged in countless contexts, music, in all of its various forms, genres, and means of participating with that music, whether playing the music or listening, inherently resists simplistic codification. Speaking more broadly of art, Jeremy Begbie argues,

> I have suggested that most if not all the activities we habitually place under the umbrella of "the arts" are marked by a boundless or inexhaustible allusiveness. We suggested also that just to the extent that the arts operate in this way, they can attest to the boundlessness of the world's meaning, and, pressing that a stage further, to the infinitely generative character and activity of the Creator. Music seems especially relevant here, just because it does not depend for its power on directing our attention to particular ideas, objects, and events in the world. Indeed, music theorists have notoriously struggled to account for the fact that music is "meaningful" it is not perceived as a random, senseless conglomeration of sounds, and seems to be able to present or show forth realities beyond itself and that it clearly does not "mean" in the manner of descriptive, representative language.[1]

If Begbie is correct, music actively counters being concretely interpreted. Neither the creator who gives their creation to the world, nor the listener who engages with that music, owns a singular interpretation. The interpretive frameworks of each individual are not only active within listening to music but are both necessary and encouraged in order for meaning to be made manifest within the listener.[2] The reality that music resists being overly defined and static in its interpretation does not mean that music cannot be interpreted and therefore has no meaning for individuals.[3] In fact, the openness of the interpretation of music provides a greater expanse for humanity to participate within the world the music is creating.

It should come as no surprise, then, that music, in all of its genres, types, instrumentation, ways and means of recording, and ways to listen to it, is an expanse and open space for the work of the Spirit within humankind. Music, like the Spirit, cannot be dictated in how it moves throughout the world and engages with humanity. Within this line of reasoning, it would be ironic, then, for this chapter and its writers to attempt to codify the Spirit's work within music, attempting to dictate what the Spirit may or may not do in and through the creators and engagers of music. Rather, this chapter sets out to explore the awareness of and delight in the Spirit's work through music, which is underrealized in Christian theology, and to provide ways for Christian theology to explore, with an open hand, how to theologize within the vast potential of the Spirit's work through music.

We'll engage this topic through our Pentecostal sensibilities.[4] The uniqueness of reflecting on this topic through Pentecostal thought is such that "Pentecostals can serve academic theology by suggesting creative ways in which the gap between charismatic experience and academic theology might be bridged."[5] This exploration is not carried out under obedience to the rules of academic theology, but as a means by which to understand the work of the Spirit in places that may surprise both the reader and the one who encounters the Spirit through music. Further, given the near endless genres of music, and in an attempt to be able to speak with some specificity to the work of the Spirit within music, this chapter will engage with one specific genre: neoclassical, wordless music.[6] As such, this chapter is not meant to be a framework to think about the Spirit's work in *all* music but to provide an outline of a theology of the Spirit's work that may also be useful to examine other genres of music. This constructive theology is, as Amos Yong argued, a "pneumatology of quest," which "allows only a provisional certitude at every turn."[7] Within such a quest, this chapter is meant to spark the engagement of the theological and metaphysical hypothesis of the Spirit's work within humanity through neoclassical, wordless music. We encourage readers of this chapter to actively listen to a curated playlist of neoclassical, wordless music while reading the chapter. These playlists can be found on Apple Music here:

https://tinyurl.com/AppleMusicWordless and Spotify here: https://tinyurl.com/SpotifyWordless.

GROANS TOO DEEP FOR WORDS[8]

Neoclassical, wordless music is just that—wordless.[9] Within such a genre, many composers seek to engage their listeners not through words and the interpretation of those words to create meaning, but primarily through beauty.[10] Neoclassical music usually begins with the ambient soundscape, not as a feature, but more like a space or horizon that surrounds the composition, which is mainly translated and performed using traditional classical instrumentation. It usually consists of piano, a string section, and sometimes a choir. The choral elements are sometimes intentionally recorded and mixed in a way that blurs the distinction between the human voice and the music. Rather than a linear, sequential vocal narrative meant to stand out in front of the sculpted soundscape, the choir becomes just another instrument that blends and merges into the horizon of the soundscape. When approached this way, the finished work can, for the most part, remain wordless.

Unlike the soundtrack for consumerism, such as Muzak[11] or the major key uplift of most new age music, listeners of wordless, neoclassical music (also known as "classical crossover"), have conveyed their experience of this music as a type of audio space for contemplative reflection. The music, when deeply felt, can provoke an awareness of freshness within the familiar or a realization of the gratuity of life, a sense of awe over one's own existence, and the strangeness of being alive. Unlike music that is strictly ambient, this music, like most music, is meant to be experienced and appreciated through the practice of deep listening. Paradoxically, it can also be effective as a type of wallpaper music when the music seems to settle into a non-intrusive atmosphere. It is in this mode of listening when our attention can be interrupted, when the music strikes something within, and we are surprised by the gentle wounding of beauty. Even the most indurated defenses can crumble under the unbending beauty and weight of this music.[12] Can these experiences be sacred or used as a theological source? Would it be theologically proper to classify these experiences as the forming of humanity in divine ways, or simply human and emotional responses to the music with no theological significance?

Experience as a theological source has been debated for some time, and does not need to be rehashed here. However, it is important to determine as a starting point what can be said about the experience in relation to music and what place it may take in our theologizing. In reviewing the state of music and theology, Jonathan Arnold asks a pointed question as a summation of the debate between Jeremy Begbie's ideas and those of David Brown and Gavin Hopps: "Is a 'sacred' encounter one that is defined purely by what is subjectively experienced, or defined apart from that subjective experience, or perhaps both? Can one have a 'transcendent' and 'natural' experience that is sacred but not realize it?"[13] This question is fair as it attempts to situate Begbie's Trinitarian and transcendent approach to music and theology that finds its rootedness through Christian Scripture, and Brown's arguments toward a natural theology within the "post-biblical tradition."[14] The debate on the role of music within Christian theology has at times suffered in either the requirement of a transformational experience through music to be translated against a logocentrism bound by the biblical text or the argument that such experiences need to have no anchoring point in Christian theology. What we surmise and hope to show, however, is that what has been missing in the dialogue of the experience of music is the theological considerations of pneumatological rootedness, a mooring of the Spirit's and humanity's participation that is not static but rises and falls with the tides of human experience.

It is necessary to find a framework by which experiences of music are neither a prime theological source, nor devoid of any theological significance. Stephen Parker has offered that Paul Tillich may provide a pneumatological approach that may overcome some of the unique issues in discussing experience as a theological source. Parker explains that for Tillich, "experience is a 'medium' but not a 'source' of theology."[15] While Parker argues that at times Tillich's desire to mediate between the positions of Friedrich Schleiermacher (experience as a source of theology) and the neo-orthodox position in which "experience has no role in theology," he astutely notes that, "Tillich is not always consistent in his explanation of the relationship of revelation to knowledge. This inconsistency leads in turn to confusion over the relationship of religious experience to revelation and to knowledge."[16] Parker argues that while inconsistent, what can be understood from Tillich, "suggests two criteria for evaluating purported instances of revelatory experiences and for distinguishing true from false occurrences: (1) true revelation conjoins ecstasy and reason, and (2) true revelation does not confuse finite media with their infinite ground."[17] Parker's conclusion on Tillich leads to two implications for the work of the Spirit in wordless music.

First, in the conjoining of ecstasy and reason, the experience of the Spirit within wordless music leads those who have had an experience with the Spirit to ask, "What does this mean?"[18] As such, experiences must lead the person to a place of desire to understand what the experience has done within them. This understanding is not an understanding of certitude of a concept of truth (e.g., this experience confirms God's existence), but an interpretation of the experience that leads one to the greater wonder and mystery that is beyond one's self. Such experiences, as those who experienced the Spirit on the day of Pentecost, upon the reflection of the meaning of the experience, must continue to move beyond one's self by asking, "What shall we do?"[19] In this way, "No individual receives revelation for himself. He receives it for his group, and implicitly for all groups, for mankind as a whole."[20] Experiences of the Spirit in wordless music, precisely because they are experiences of the Spirit, move us beyond ourselves, pushing for further engagement in the building of the kingdom of God as the telos of creation.

Second, in the experience of the Spirit through the medium of wordless music, we must not "confuse finite media with their infinite ground" or alternatively put, one must not confuse the medium of wordless music and the experience found in the moment of participation with it as that which is infinite, or with God's self. Wordless music as a medium cannot be elevated to the divine; nothing created can. Therefore, it does not and cannot in and of itself divinize or sanctify the hearer. In practicality, to conflate participation in wordless music as a participation with the divine would be "idolizing" the music. Thus, Parker quotes Tillich in that "Idolatry is the perversion of a genuine revelation; it is the elevation of the medium of revelation to the dignity of revelation itself . . . The claim of anything finite to be final in its own right is demonic."[21] Following this line of thought, we would have to conclude that the experience of the Spirit in wordless music as such is not a foundational source of theology, nor should the medium of the experience of the Spirit in wordless music be elevated to the place of the divine. It is, as Tillich argues, a medium by which one experiences the divine which moves one beyond one's self. Still, given the creativity of the Spirit, such a medium can become, and be, itself and even more than itself, so that hearers are taken up by the experience into the transcendent and communion with Christ.

Pentecostals are not strangers to the idea of the work of the theophanic revealation of the Spirit in unexpected ways. The aurality of music, from when it is first heard in full anticipation to the point of memorization through repeated listening, opens one to something beyond one's self. Makoto Fujimura puts it well:

> The power of art is to convey powerful personal experiences in distilled language and memorialize them in a cogent manner . . . precisely because God has poured his grace in all of creation, and every artist, consciously or not, taps into the 'groaning' of the Spirit.[22]

As the listener has no control over the melody or construction of the piece, one must open oneself to the music itself in order to participate in it. Neoclassical, wordless music provides a space in beauty for the groanings too deep for words, a space in which the ability for one to express oneself through language to God through prayer.

The groaning of the Spirit that can be found in the experience of wordless music moves one to engage with their faith in unexpected ways. The Spirit who points to Christ does not need verbal language in order to express something about Christ, to teach and to move one toward the love of Christ and imitation of him. Wordless music, as it is wordless, provides a necessary counterbalance to music that attempts to expressly tell one what to believe or to know. Lyrically, worship music attempts to speak directly and cataphatically about or to God, attempting to express aspects of the Christian life as well as the life of God. As such, it acts as a teaching tool for the church.[23] In wordless music, however, the Spirit moves within the listener in both cataphatic and apophatic engagement—at times teaching the individual who Christ is, but more uniquely moving the listener to explore the boundaries of who Christ is *not*, particularly in relation to what the listener has been led to believe and taught to presume. It uniquely affords the deconstructing and reconstructing work of the Spirit in ways that move beyond verbal language and resist indoctrination—defying the idea that God can be captured by language.

Further, wordless music provides a counter-cultural expression. It does not tell one what one wants to hear, whether that is the self-reflection of pop music or the desire for rebellion and resistance within the cries of punk or hardcore music. The space created by neo-classic wordless music provides the mirror by which one must hear and know is made open within the person, not at the direction of spoken or sung language, but by the work of the Spirit, revealing to the person in a moment of vulnerability, drawing one into the life of Christ. In this way, wordless music is a "significant form," and "its significance is that of a symbol, a highly articulated sensuous object, which, by virtue of its dynamic structure, can express the forms of vital experience which language is peculiarly unfit to convey. Feeling, life, motion and emotion constitute its import."[24] These unexpected expressions push back against the requirements of cultural mores and act in subversive ways.

Wordless music finds a commonality with the subversive soundscape of early Pentecostalism. As David Daniels argues, the "riot of sound" coming from early Pentecostals "undermined the dominant sound of Protestantism." Further,

> While Pentecostal soundways traveled along a circular continuum, most Protestant soundways travel along a linear continuum. . . . Most U.S. Protestants stopped along the continuum at speech and music, declining even to travel further to where ambient sounds could be utilized within worship.[25]

The interpretation of wordless music within congregational settings cannot be controlled, precisely as the work of the Spirit within the person as they engage with such music cannot be controlled. The lyrics crafted in music, whether they're specifically Christian or otherwise, provide a sense of controlling the meaning, even if that control is not complete. Lyrics that speak to God's grace argue a point—a point that the composer of the song wants to provide to those who sing-along with the music, especially in the use of repetition within lyrics. Wordless music is a risk to those who encounter it, as what springs from that music cannot be controlled. Wordless music removes control and power from leaders in congregational settings, offering an experience whose interpretation and meaning cannot be dictated by a musician, pastor, or leader. The Spirit makes wordless music more than just the music itself.

What is necessary to focus on is the way in which the Spirit works within humanity, opening humanity up to the language of the divine, through which we must ask, "how is it that each of us hears them in our native language?" (Acts 2:8). The language of beauty found in wordless music can be likened to glossolalia, a language being interpreted by the Spirit for the breaking down and building up of the individual or community, such as found on the Day of Pentecost.

> The dramatic descent of the Spirit on the Day of Pentecost was a kind of theophany, accompanied by the sound of a mighty wind and tongues of fire . . . Pentecostal spirituality has tended to highlight this theophanic theme in Scripture, developing a church life characterized by a fervent expectation for the signs and wonders of God's Spirit.[26]

Music can at times be the glossolalic theophany of Christ through the Spirit, precisely because the Spirit has been poured out on all flesh. Pentecost acts as the sign of the age of the Spirit, wherein the Spirit engages with humanity in ways that are bound to surprise humanity. Music as the glossolalic sounds of the Spirit act at times as the groans too deep for words, as music, particularly wordless music, fulfills a space within the human experience of aurality.[27] Where language and words fail, the Spirit takes up surprising avenues and mediums by which humanity can express the deep and mysterious realities of life.

The aurality of wordless music creates a space in which the "deep calls to deep,"[28] a space where words are no longer necessary for the human experience to be embraced and groanings too deep for words are made manifest. Wordless music provides a space for the Spirit to prepare humanity to be cultivated into the life of Christ, at times being torn asunder and at others being created anew. The Spirit hovers over the primeval depths of human life, and as such, humanity is opened up to the Spirit, primed again to have the chaos of life subdued by the Spirit's presence. Wordless music functions as a medium for many to be opened up to the hovering of the Spirit, by which the Spirit calls out to the depths of human experience and life.

The Spirit's engagement with humanity through aurality is what Frank Macchia calls a "dynamic pneumatic experience."[29] The concern for theology and theologians is not rooted in Christ's analogy of the Spirit and those born of the Spirit to the wind, which "moves freely wherever it wishes."[30] Rather, the

> lack of theological attention to tongues and other forms of dynamic pneumatic experience . . . is because theology has accented the *logica* of faith and has thus been ill-equipped to respond to the kind of dynamic pneumatic experience that borders on the non-rational. Theology has served only to shun and stifle the creative manifestations of the Spirit, which continue to be a "bug-bear" for theologians.[31]

The work of the Spirit through the aurality of music is a struggle for those who would attempt to define exactly the framework by which the Spirit must work, rather than being open to the dynamism found in the Spirit's theophanic engagement with humanity. Thus, as we have attempted to express, what is being offered is not a theology born of pure logic in how the Spirit will work within people through the extravagance and aurality of music, but rather what the Spirit does and may do in humanity through the experience of wordless music.[32]

As a dynamic pneumatic experience, the engagement with Spirit through wordless music, though not limited solely to wordless music, speaks directly to the context of human life and experience, offering shadows of divine revelation that pull humanity toward the revelation of Jesus Christ made known through Scripture. There's no need to dismiss the Spirit's influence in the lavishness of music over concerns it might overshadow Christ's revelation in Scripture. Similarly, we shouldn't insist that the Spirit's work is confined to Scripture, which would restrict the Triune God to the text rather than aligning Scripture with God's broader work. What must be recognized is that the Spirit will always be drawing humanity to itself and therefore to the Triune Godhead made known through Jesus Christ. The route of these revelations may not appear to be a directly scripturally rooted path, but one that will ultimately end in the revelation of Christ made known within Scripture as the work of the Spirit is ultimately and always pointing to Christ, a path bound in beauty.

PARTICIPATING IN THE DECENTERING OF IMMEASURABLE BEAUTY

Hans Urs von Balthasar offers that

> beauty is the word that shall be our first. Beauty is the last thing which the thinking intellect dares to approach, since only it dances as an uncontained splendor

around the double constellation of the true and the good and their inseparable relation to one another.[33]

> Music serves as a potent reminder of just these features and limitations of language, the relative inadequacy and inevitable 'openness' of all speaking and writing, an openness that obviously becomes crucially important when we dare to speak of, or to, the living God.[34]

Music, as a means of opening one up to the work of God through the Spirit, is inevitably necessary since verbal language can only provide a limited means by which to describe the divine. Beauty, in fact, frees humanity from the notion that, within language, we can define and therefore capture some of the ineffable. Balthasar further argues the outcome of a religion which no longer "believes" in beauty when he claimed that "We can be sure that whoever sneers at [beauty] as if she were the ornament of a bourgeois past—whether he admits it or not—can no longer pray and soon will no longer be able to love."[35] Beauty, in an act of "mysterious vengeance," breaks one down from the notion of capturing that which can never be contained through the overreach of certitude while opening one up to the realization that what is or can be known is ultimately only known in part. Wordless music asks those who participate with it to engage from a place of uncertainty, for as much as one can deconstruct the music, its melody, instrumentation, composure, and so on. One cannot be certain of the meaning the music offers, as its meaning in the life of the listener is bound to the listener. Yet, in the mystery of the beauty of wordless music, it not only breaks down certainty but in wordless music, "Beauty is the inconceivable made so intimate that it illuminates our hearts."[36] Perhaps this is why Pope John Paul II, in his "Letter to Artists," called for the creation of "epiphanies of beauty" as necessary as a means of renewal for humanity.[37]

Wordless music opens up humanity to the possibility that the desire for certainty is contrary to the art itself. Wordless music demands that the listener be a part of the interpretative process. There are no lyrics for listeners to attempt to master, but rather listeners are moved to consider their own experiences and context. It is here, within this pushback against certainty, that humanity can participate in the work of the Spirit, as the Spirit draws the listener not to certainty but rather to constant re-engagement and reinterpretation, not only of the music but of one's own life. It is in this interpretative loop where humanity, in participation with the Spirit, is drawn to the likeness of Christ, even when the person may not recognize this process as an act of the *imitatio christi*.

Further, the work of the Spirit resists simple codification, as the Spirit often works with humble anonymity. One must recognize that not only must we appreciate the mysterious ways in which the Spirit works, but also that, at times, in its work, the Spirit is not attempting to draw attention to itself and explicitly reveal the outcome of its participation with the person. There is a tendency to attribute the Spirit's work only to moments that lead to a direct cataphatic moment in which the person recognizes their need of Christ and finds ways to express how their experience with the Spirit is moving them closer to Christ. Just because it cannot be easily explained with christocentric language, that does not mean it's not a work of the Spirit—in fact, the Spirit does work within the person in subtle yet profound ways. The Spirit, at times, takes upon itself humble anonymity in leading one to their telos in ways that may not be explainable nor attributable to the Spirit. The Spirit's work is a work of leading all of creation to its telos, and this work is at times slow, a work that cannot be attributed, nor is it necessary to, as the Spirit does not draw attention to itself, but rather points to the work of Christ within the world.[38] The theophanic work of the Spirit in wordless music is the work of wounding and healing, cataphatically and apophatically, breaking down and lifting up so that the hearer may be brought closer to an epiphany that is deeper and higher than human awareness, even if the person may not cognitively know how the Spirit is preparing and working within them. This is the vulnerable power of the Spirit: at once wounding and healing, breaking down and building up, moving creation and therefore humanity to its ultimate telos while not demanding to be known by name. Humanity exists within cycles of breaking down and building up. Music, just as art, has a vital role in this process. By bringing people to the brink of what they can understand, know, or speak of, music reminds humanity there is something beyond itself. The Spirit is at work within these cycles, breaking humanity open to what it has forgotten, what it refuses to see, or even what it fears to consider.

When we are present with it, wordless music can become a vehicle for transformation. The minimal chord structure, deceptive simplicity, and patterned repetition of this music share a similarity with the repetition of liturgical participation, exposing the deepest places of self-enclosure and wounds too real to face. As simple as a lump in the throat or an ache in the chest, a memory of things done and left undone. And like the ritual of liturgy, the more open our hearts and minds are when we approach this music, the more likely we are to be moved and broken open by it, perhaps even gifted with a moment of clarity and insight. It should remain somewhat astonishing that these experiences are the direct result of listening to music; the phenomenon of organized soundwaves and vibrations entering from the outside while simultaneously interpenetrating and seemingly coming from the interior space of the listener. We have suggested here that this is another way the Spirit moves within, to bring the darkness we live with into the light, so that, as translated through the music, the darkness is illuminated by the one who reveals to us in the dark what needs to be shared in the light.

CONCLUSION

We do not deny our romanticized view and understanding of the work of the Spirit within music, nor do we claim that this is the common outcome of a person's engagement with wordless music. To claim that either the Spirit must act or must not act within the person through wordless music is theologically problematic as it attempts to argue for what the Spirit can or cannot do. What can be said is that the Spirit is at work within all humanity, and neoclassical wordless music profoundly moves humanity to a place to engage with the Spirit. Rather than make claims to what the Spirit can or cannot do, we are recognizing how neoclassical music is a powerful medium by which humanity and the Spirit participate together. What has been offered is an exploration of the way in which the Spirit may work, and in fact has worked in the lives of the authors.

This exploration has risen from our firsthand accounts. I, Marc, have found this exploration to be uniquely true in the many messages I've received from people who have engaged with the music I've produced as one-half of the band, Hammock. It is common for listeners to reach out and express how, as they listened to our music, there were times of being overwhelmed, moments of despair and hope, fear and peace, that led them to reconnect with estranged family members, come to repentance (whether to God or to another individual), or a desire to know something beyond themselves. They are at times spiritual responses and at times human responses, but as this exploration argues, within the anonymous humility of the Spirit, whether the individual is aware or not, the work of the Spirit within their engagement of the music ultimately points to the person of Christ and the hope of the world in the kingdom of God as it is and as it will be.

This exploration only exists precisely because of the work of the Spirit in neoclassical wordless music. Some years ago, I, Aaron, listened to the music Marc produced, and in a moment of what felt like being moved by the Spirit, I decided to send Marc's band a message, simply to thank them for the music they made and how it had affected me (this was before Marc and I knew each other). It was from that message that Marc and I would continue to connect, grow in a friendship, and, among many other things, began our discussion on the work of the Spirit in wordless music.

As we have attempted to express, wordless music, through the work of the Spirit, can translate the wordless depths of ourselves when we are "defenseless and terribly naked."[39] This is who the Spirit is for us, that in those times when "we need the music more," the Spirit will generously comfort and companion us. Often, this is done without us noticing. Bidden or unbidden, the Spirit, in humble anonymity, hides within the music of things, moving within the ache of our deepest longings and living and breathing within the wordless depths of our lives. When we let go and allow ourselves to be attuned, maybe one day it will be revealed that the Spirit was and always has been moving us into an ever-deeper harmony with the one who sings us like a love song into existence. Not only the fullness of ALL but also the ache of emptiness in those who grope after the divine through the pursuit of beauty—the Word within the wordless.

NOTES

1. Jeremy Begbie, *Redeeming Transcendence in the Arts: Bearing Witness to the Triune God* (Grand Rapid: Eerdmans, 2018), 169.

2. Daniel Barenboim, Edward W. Said, and Ara Guzelimian, *Parallels and Paradoxes: Explorations in Music and Society*, 1 (New York: Vintage Books, 2004); Begbie, *Redeeming Transcendence in the Arts*, 170. As Begbie notes, "The conductor and pianist Daniel Barenboim caught something of this in a tribute to his friend Edward Said: "Edward saw in music not just a combination of sounds but he understood the fact that every musical masterpiece is, as it were, a conception of the world. And the difficulty lies in the fact that this conception of the world cannot be described in words—because were it possible to describe it in words, the music would be unnecessary. But he recognized that the fact that it is indescribable doesn't mean it has no meaning."

3. David Brown and Gavin Hopps, *The Extravagance of Music* (New York: Palgrave Macmillan, 2018), 5–6. It must be noted that there is a larger debate regarding the metaphysical framing of music that cannot be engaged here. Browns and Hopps, for instance, have engaged in scholarly arguments with Begbie, both in the metaphysical framing of music and in the idea of transcendence and extravagance of music. The means of the debate and disagreements have been argued elsewhere, summated succinctly by Jonathan Arnold. Jonathan Arnold, "New Directions in Music and Theology," *Theology,* vol. 126, no. 1 (2023): 36–44. This debate is not just amongst theologians, but musicologist and philosophers alike. This chapter will engage with various interlocutors within this debate, not in a means of favoring one means of engaging with the philosophy of music over another, but rather to find where these writers may or may not within the pneumatological framework being explored here. As such, the authors are not asking whether or not music can be understood as

transcendent, extravagant, or other means that musicologist speak of music, but rather understand the Spirit's work within humanity through music and what that may mean for both music and humanity. As such, the authors are seeking to not engage within the "either-or-ism" of the debate, as, according to Browns and Hopps,

> What tends to get lost in the 'either-or-ism' of recent debates about music's aesthetic autonomy and deconstructions of its apparently transcendent self-sufficiency is the possibility that music's distance from quotidian reality—which is, of course, a thoroughly worldly construction—may itself have a mimetic dimension. One may thus acknowledge the constructedness of musical forms and their embeddedness within 'the densely compacted, concretely situated worlds of those who compose, perform and listen' while simultaneously recognizing their ability to augment our vision of the real and to offer us intimations of transcendence (6).

4. In order to undertake this task, the writers of this chapter have engaged with the method of constructive theology, a fitting methodology as constructive theology is both interdisciplinary as well as resists the urge to create theologies that are "timeless" or unchanging. Jason A. Wyman, *Constructing Constructive Theology: An Introductory Sketch* (Minneapolis: Fortress Press, 2017), 174. Wyman, upon reviewing the state of constructive theology, including the work done by the "Workgroup on Constructive Theology" founded at Vanderbilt University in 1975, provide four common features of constructive theology: (1) Persistently open-ended. (2) Based in the insight that Christian theology is constructed, that is, imaginatively and creatively produced human thoughts about God and God's work. (3) Almost always doctrinally based. (4) Suspicious of systems or confession-based theology. Reviewing Wyman's work provides a more in-depth overview of the work of constructive theology, particularly in how it is differentiated to systematic or dogmatic theology.

5. Frank D Macchia, "Sighs Too Deep for Words: Toward a Theology of Glossolalia," *Journal of Pentecostal Theology,* vol. 1, no. 1 (1992): 47–73, 50.

6. We encourage readers of this chapter to actively listen to this playlist of neoclassical, wordless music while reading the chapter. These playlists can be found on Apple Music here: https://tinyurl.com/AppleMusicWordless and Spotify here: https://tinyurl.com/SpotifyWordless

7. Amos Yong, *Discerning the Spirit(s)* (Sheffield: Sheffield Academic Press, 2000), 314.

8. Rom. 8:26.

9. For the purpose of clarity and brevity, when we speak of wordless music, we are using this as a shorthand to the specific genre of neoclassical, wordless music.

10. In describing the late Jóhann Jóhannsson's influential album *Orphée*, it was noted that the album "was inspired by a range of readings of the Orpheus myth and draws on a varied sonic palette, both acoustic and electronic, to explore the boundaries between darkness and light. It contemplates impermanence, memory and the elusive nature of beauty, ultimately celebrating art and its power of renewal." The music of legendary producers such as Max Richter (https://www.yourclassical.org/story/2021/09/01/eclectic) and Jón "Jónsi" Birgisson (https://chimesnewspaper.com/21177/archives/features/victory-rose-sigur-ros-creates-beauty-music/) are often

described with the language of beauty, attempting to capture something beyond just the mechanics of the music. Beauty is a familiar term within neoclassical wordless music, a term and idea that is used to capture the ineffable within music and what is produced in the listener of such music.

11. "Muzak" is a specific brand of music, the label of which has been used since the first half of the twentieth century. It is the background music that is commonly played in retail stores, such as shopping centers and grocers.

12. I, Marc, have seen the truth of this based on the myriad emails and messages I have received. Further, while not the focus of this paper, it is important thatwe also mention the genre of music known as post rock. This music can have the atmosphere of ambience as well as traditional classical instrumentation, but for the most part, it is instrumental music made with traditional rock instrumentation: drums, bass, guitars, and sometimes synthesizers. It is known for dramatic and emotional musical peaks and valleys, with the peaks building toward a melodramatic wall of sound.

13. Jonathan Arnold, "New Directions in Music and Theology," *Theology,* vol. 126, no. 1 (2023): 36–44, 38.

14. Begbie, *Redeeming Transcendence in the Arts*; Jeremy Begbie, *Music, Modernity, and God: Essays in Listening* (Oxford: Oxford University Press, 2013); David Brown and Gavin Hopps, *The Extravagance of Music.*

15. Stephen E. Parker, "Led by the Spirit: Toward a Practical Theology of Pentecostal Discernment and Decision Making," *Journal of Pentecostal Theology,* vol. 7 (1996).

16. Parker, "Led by the Spirit."

17. Parker, "Led by the Spirit," 155.

18. Acts 2:12.

19. Acts 2:37.

20. Paul Tillich, *Systematic Theology. 1: Reason and Revelation, Being and God* (Chicago: University of Chicago Press, 1951), 127–128.

21. Parker, *Led by the Spirit*, 156; Paul Tillich, *Systematic Theology. 1*, 133–134.

22. Makoto Fujimura, *Refractions: A Journey of Faith, Art, and Culture* (Colorado Springs: NavPress, 2009), 39.

23. Whether what is taught is theologically healthy or unhealthy in these songs is a subject for a longer treatise.

24. Susanne Katherina Langer, *Feeling and Form: A Theory of Art Developed from Philosophy in a New Key* (New York: Scribner, 1953), 32.

25. David Douglas Daniels III, "'Gotta Moan Sometime': A Sonic Exploration of Earwitnesses to Early Pentecostal Sound in North America," *Pneuma,* vol. 30, no. 1 (2008): 5–32, 12.

26. Frank D. Macchia, "Tongues as a Sign: Towards a Sacramental Understanding of Pentecostal Experience," *Pneuma,* vol. 15, no. 1 (1993): 61–76, 73.

27. Steven Félix-Jäger, *Spirit of the Arts: Towards a Pneumatological Aesthetics of Renewal* (New York: Palgrave Macmillan, 2017), 94. Félix-Jäger properly argues, "Pentecostals and charismatics come from a tradition that values the spoken word as a primary means of theological reflection, pastoral care, witnessing, and preaching." Both Daniels and Félix-Jäger are correct, while Pentecostals use spoken language in

order to discuss and disseminate their theologies, they also engaged in non-verbal means of engaging with the Divine, such as the "moanings" in the Spirit, that would only afterward be interpreted and given meaning through language.

28. Psalm 42.7.
29. Frank D Macchia, "Sighs Too Deep for Words: Toward a Theology of Glossolalia," *Journal of Pentecostal Theology,* vol. 1, no. 1 (1992): 47–73, 49.
30. John 3:8.
31. Frank D Macchia, "Sighs Too Deep for Words," 47–73, 50
32. One further note must be made here. The Spirit is not bound by intent of authors, music producers, artists, or musicians. As such, within wordless music there is no sense of "sacred" or "secular," a divide which is arbitrary at best. However, when one attempts to define these terms in relation to music, whether that is based on the language used within the song, the intention of the creators of the song, or other such arguments, we must be careful not to limit the work of the Spirit within the person's engagement with music. A claim that the Spirit may only work in an through the person when that person engages with music with "Christian" lyrics, or rather lyrics that use the common, shared language of Christian communities, is a claim of the limited ability of the Spirit, that somehow the Spirit is constrained by what the composer of a song intends within the music. Just as the Spirit cannot be controlled by the worship artist who seeks to engage worships through clever melodies and moving lyrics, the Spirit cannot be relegated to spaces that have Christian lyrics or intention.
33. Hans Urs von Balthasar, *The Glory of the Lord: A Theological Aesthetics,* 2nd ed (San Francisco: Ignatius Press, 2009), 18.
34. Begbie, *Redeeming Transcendence in the Arts,* 171.
35. Balthasar, *The Glory of the Lord,* 18.
36. John O'Donohue, *Beauty: The Invisible Embrace,* (New York: HarperPerennial, 2005), 211.
37. John Paul II, "Letter to Artists, (April 4, 1999): John Paul II," *Letter to Artists, (April 4, 1999)* | *John Paul II,* https://www.vatican.va/content/john-paul-ii/en/letters/1999/documents/hf_jp-ii_let_23041999_artists.html. (accessed 1/14/2024).
38. John 16:13-15.
39. Ted Hughes, *Collected Poems,* ed. Paul Keegan, (London: Faber and Faber, 2005), 742.

BIBLIOGRAPHY

Arnold, Jonathan. "New Directions in Music and Theology." *Theology,* vol. 126, no. 1 (2023): 36–44.

Balthasar, Hans Urs von, Joseph Fessio, and John Kenneth Riches. These translators? Check out a Turabian style guide to see how to write that. This citation needs to be redone. *The Glory of the Lord: A Theological Aesthetics.* 2nd ed. San Francisco, New York: Ignatius Press ; Crossroad Publications, 2009.

Barenboim, Daniel, Edward W. Said, and Ara Guzelimian. *Parallels and Paradoxes: Explorations in Music and Society.* New York: Vintage Books, 2004.

Begbie, Jeremy. *Music, Modernity, and God: Essays in Listening*. Oxford: Oxford University Press, 2013.

———. *Redeeming Transcendence in the Arts: Bearing Witness to the Triune God*. Grand Rapids: Eerdmans, 2018.

Brown, David, and Gavin Hopps. *The Extravagance of Music*. New York: Palgrave Macmillan, 2018.

David Douglas Daniels, III. "'Gotta Moan Sometime': A Sonic Exploration of Earwitnesses to Early Pentecostal Sound in North America." *Pneuma*, vol. 30, no. 1 (2008): 5–32.

Félix-Jäger, Steven. *Spirit of the Arts: Towards a Pneumatological Aesthetics of Renewal*. New York: Palgrave Macmillan, 2017.

Fujimura, Makoto. *Refractions: A Journey of Faith, Art, and Culture*. Colorado Springs: NavPress, 2009.

Hughes, Ted. *Collected Poems*. Ed. by Paul Keegan. London: Faber and Faber, 2005.

Langer, Susanne Katherina. *Feeling and Form: A Theory of Art Developed from Philosophy in a New Key*. New York: Scribner, 1953.

O'Donohue, John. *Beauty: The Invisible Embrace*. New York: HarperPerennial, 2005.

Parker, Stephen E. *Led by the Spirit: Toward a Practical Theology of Pentecostal Discernment and Decision Making*. Journal of Pentecostal Theology 7. Sheffield, England: Sheffield Academic Press, 1996.

Tillich, Paul. *Systematic Theology. 1: Reason and Revelation, Being and God*. Chicago: University of Chicago Press, 1951.

Wyman, Jason A. *Constructing Constructive Theology: An Introductory Sketch*. Minneapolis: Fortress Press, 2017.

Yong, Amos. *Discerning the Spirit(s)*. Sheffield: Sheffield Academic Press, 2000.

Chapter 7

Spiritual Longing in the Music of Jimi Hendrix

Blaine Charette

It would not be inaccurate to describe Jimi Hendrix (1942–1970) as a misunderstood artist. In the over fifty years since his death, his reputation as a guitar virtuoso and "a musician's musician" is firmly established and yet in the popular imagination, he continues to be regarded as an icon of the excesses of the late 1960s. Misconceptions regarding his legacy are largely due to the considerable difference between Hendrix, the private person, best described as a sensitive introvert burdened by feelings of loneliness and alienation, and his public persona, largely cultivated by the man himself, of blistering self-confidence and sexually charged performance. There are several avenues one could explore when considering the significance of Hendrix, and it is fair to say that his contribution to the cultural and social context of his time has yet to be fully examined. For example, when *The Jimi Hendrix Experience* was formed in late 1966, it was certainly a radical, almost militant, step for a black man to front a band with white musicians.[1] Moreover, his social impact on America in the midst of the Vietnam conflict was significant.[2] The purpose of this chapter is to move beyond the public image of Hendrix in order to explore various spiritual elements present in his music that are more reflective of his private interior life as an artist. Specifically, those elements will be examined that relate to the theme of spiritual longing, a theme that distinctly infuses the lyrics and musical texture of his songs.

Hendrix, due to his popular image, is not generally regarded as an artist of particular spiritual interest or depth. For most people, his music is reflective of his milieu and thus sprinkled with drug references and sexual innuendo, in keeping with the blues-influenced rock with which he is most closely identified.[3] If a spiritual element is acknowledged in his music, it is largely seen as dark or mysterious, as in "Voodoo Child (Slight Return)."[4] Many would be surprised that "Purple Haze," often considered Hendrix's signature song, was initially entitled "Purple Haze, Jesus Saves."[5] Moreover, a song like "Foxy Lady," arguably his most sexually charged song, was regarded by Hendrix as something of an anomaly to the extent that it was a happy song. As he reflected in a 1967 interview, "Foxy Lady" is about the only happy song he had written. In his words, "I can't write no happy songs . . . Don't feel very happy when I start writing."[6] It is this melancholic feature of Hendrix's songwriting that gives his music its distinctive quality. He does not often directly address matters of spiritual import, but there is nonetheless a note of longing and a search for connection that infuses his music. As a writer, Hendrix was not too interested in religion or theology, but he is spiritual in the sense of expressing an awareness that there must be something other and more than the mere material or natural. It is perhaps ironic that the most overtly theological lyric he ever wrote was composed the day before he died and discovered after his death. Interlaced throughout the song, entitled "The Story of Life," are phrases that indicate Hendrix's deep desire for assurance and comfort. He writes, for instance, "Oh, the story of Jesus is the story of you and me. No use in feeling lonely, I am searching to be free."[7] The song, which, of course, was never recorded, does, in many ways, represent a fitting conclusion to Hendrix's songwriting. It addresses the loneliness so often expressed in his lyrics, speaks of his search to find a freedom that was so often fleeting, and ponders the easy yet difficult way of living in an integrated manner that might result in love and authentic freedom.

The songs discussed in this chapter are among those for which Hendrix is best known.[8] It is primarily in his most representative songs that the themes and topics explored here are most evident. Although there are many recordings of Hendrix released after his death, attention is directed to the songs that appear on the albums released during his lifetime. However, since at the time of his death he had made significant progress in recording songs for a projected fourth studio album, *First Rays of the New Rising Sun*, many of those songs are also examined.[9] Those songs, written and recorded in the final months of his life, are important in that they suggest possible future directions in his writing and music. It is difficult to envisage the kind of music Hendrix would have continued to produce, but his early death must certainly be regarded as one of the great tragedies in music history. Moreover, it is evident from these final compositions that a longing for greater spiritual connection remained a constant theme in his music.

LONGING WITHIN A THEOLOGICAL FRAMEWORK

A biblical text that provides a framework for such artistic longing is Paul's profound statement in Rom. 8:19: "the longing (aÓpokaradoki÷a) of creation awaits the revelation of the sons of God." It is significant that Paul makes "longing" the subject of the sentence.[10] What he wishes to affirm is that a feeling of longing defines and characterizes the present fallen age. As he goes on to observe in verses 20–23, this sense of longing persists because creation has been subjected to "futility" (mataio/thß). As such, it longs to be set free from "the bondage of decay" and is presently "groaning" as with labor pains. Paul's diagnosis of the present age is that it is marked by futility and thus seemingly lacks meaning and purpose. He is almost certainly alluding to the judgment pronounced upon humans in Gen. 3:17-19. Due to disobedience, human work becomes drudgery and "thorns and thistles" frustrate and diminish human accomplishment. Although humans subsist, in the end they return to the dust from which they came. It is this condition that is the cause of so much longing and discontent in the present. This sense that "things are not as they should be" resonates deeply, particularly within an artistic disposition. In certain cases, futility provokes the artist to raise a fist against the universe or, in despair, to rail against God himself. But it also inspires a yearning for something better, awakening a sense of hopefulness that there is indeed purpose and meaning at the heart of reality. In such cases, the artist may grasp onto a hope in what is not yet seen or catch a vision of the glory which, for Paul, will be ultimately revealed.

Throughout his writings, C. S. Lewis formulated what can best be described as a theology of longing. As a writer of significant artistic sensibility, Lewis recognized the tug of the beautiful, which he notes may come through a variety of natural and artistic channels that give one a glimpse of something more and better. In his essay "On Three Ways of Writing for Children," Lewis, a very accomplished children's author in his own right, explores this topic of longing. He observes that for the reader,

> fairy land arouses a longing for he knows not what. It stirs and troubles him . . . with the dim sense of something beyond his reach, and far from dulling or emptying the actual world gives it a new dimension of depth.[11]

He often used the German word *Sehnsucht* to describe this romantic longing, which at times he translated by the English word "Joy." In his essay "Christianity and Culture," he describes *Sehnsucht* as "spilled religion," emphasizing that the spilled drops may be full of blessing to the unconverted person who licks them up and begins to search for the cup from which they were spilled.[12] In perhaps his most famous essay, "The Weight of Glory," Lewis speaks of "our life-long nostalgia, our longing to be reunited with something in the universe from which we now feel cut off, to be on the inside of some door which we have always seen from the outside." This feeling is not "a neurotic fancy" for Lewis, but "the truest index of our real situation."[13] In a similar way, Lewis writes in *Mere Christianity*, "If I find in myself a desire which no experience in this world can satisfy, the most probable explanation is that I was made for another world."[14] Through these and other statements, Lewis effectively provides a personalized commentary on Rom. 8:18-23. He gives voice to that longing which is awakened by the echoes and intimations of God felt in the present, despite the obscuring pervasive futility, and which looks to ultimate satisfaction in some other place or, better, some other Person. By returning so regularly to this topic, Lewis is able to clearly articulate what is commonplace in the human condition and what generates so much artistic expression in the present age. Lewis expresses this longing from the position of a person of faith, yet his description would find resonance with anyone who acutely feels an alienating restlessness in the present and, for that reason, aches for something or someone other.

In one of his final compositions, recorded during the last three months of his life, Hendrix gives voice to such feelings of *Sehnsucht*.[15] The song "Drifting" is an exquisite piece, featuring layers of guitars and other effects that lend it a haunting melancholy. Lyrically one of his briefest songs, Hendrix describes an existence of "drifting on a sea of forgotten teardrops" and later of "drifting on a sea of old heartbreaks," suggesting a life of sadness and hurt adrift without purpose or direction. And yet there is a hopefulness in the responding lines, which now place him "on a lifeboat sailing for your love," indeed "sailing home." In a few short lines, he expresses, on the one hand, the despair and meaninglessness of life, and, on the other, a sense of purpose, evident in the shift from drifting to sailing, and the hope of reaching love and home. It is not clear whose love stands at the end of this passage and what or whom he identifies as home. Yet the song captures well the sense of longing. This lyric is very evocative of another quotation from Lewis. In his novel *Till We Have Faces* the character Psyche declares: "Do you think it all meant nothing, all the longing? The longing for home? For indeed, it now feels not like going, but like going back . . . I am going to my lover."[16] It is significant that near the end of his life, Hendrix expressed this longing for true love and for an actual home. Especially since so much of his lyrics were about alienation and loneliness.

"LONELINESS IS SUCH A DRAG"

One of Jimi Hendrix's earliest recordings, "Manic Depression," from his first album, *Are You Experienced* (1967), has given rise to much speculation about whether he suffered from bipolar disorder. The song has been described as "a sound poem in psychosis, an angry cry of despair and rage at a world full of misery and pain."[17] Yet, the artist also clearly affirms in the song that it is in music he finds solace: "Feeling, sweet feeling, drops from my fingers." Despite the ups and downs of life, there is "Music, sweet music," but if he were to "turn myself off," that would mean to "go on down. All the way down." On the same album appears an even bleaker song, "I Don't Live Today." The opening question, "Will I live tomorrow?" is answered with a tentative response, "I just can't say," but this is then followed by a definitive declaration, "But I know for sure, I don't live today." It is somewhat unsettling that even as Hendrix enjoys initial success, he writes of existential emptiness. These lyrics might give the impression that the mood of Hendrix's music is one of unyielding sadness, but this is not the case. Despite his assertion that he could not write happy songs, he was always capable of composing and recording songs about love and his desire for social harmony. Even so, disconnection and isolation were always major elements of his music.

It would be true to say that as his songwriting evolved, Hendrix addressed the theme of loneliness with ever greater frequency. A song that establishes the mood of his third studio album, *Electric Ladyland* (1968), is "Burning of the Midnight Lamp." Regarded by Hendrix as one of his favorite songs, it is intensely introspective and steeped in gloom. The song was composed at a time when Hendrix was frustrated with his management and a punishing touring schedule, and he was also annoyed that he could not achieve the sounds he imagined with the recording techniques and technology available. The song is essentially about the heartbreak and abandonment felt at the end of a relationship: "the smiling portrait of you is still hanging on my frowning wall," the unbearable stillness and emptiness provoked by the absence, "There's nothing left here to leave me, but the velvet moon," and the enveloping experience of loneliness, "I continue to burn the midnight lamp, alone."[18] The most poignant and provocative declaration of the song is, "All my loneliness, I have felt today. It's a little more than enough to make a man throw himself away." is punctuated by the wailful, "Lonely, lonely, lonely. Loneliness is such a drag."[19] This highly personal and emotionally weighted song stands testament to the artist's isolation and alienation from persons and places that would connect him to purpose and fulfillment in life.

It is especially in the songs he was preparing for his fourth studio album, *First Rays of the New Rising Sun*, that the theme of loneliness becomes even more pronounced. Most of these songs were written and recorded in the final months of his life. A sampling of lyrics is sufficient to give a sense of Hendrix's state of mind at the time. There is the ineffectual quest for love: "Searching for his heaven above, but he's dying to be loved, dying to be loved!" ("Ezy Ryder"), the perception of isolation: "I used to live in a room full of mirrors, all I could see was me." ("Room Full of Mirrors"), which finds its complement in the troubled solitude of "My Friend": "I feel so dizzy I take a quick look in the mirror to make sure my friend's here with me too."

the chorus of which sighs, "And sometimes it's not so easy, especially when your only friend, talks, sees, looks and feels like you; you do just the same as him." Finally, the fateful assertion of "Straight Ahead": "I was so alone, all by myself, I just couldn't make it." Several other songs also reveal that, near the end of his life, Hendrix often voiced feelings of isolation and detachment. This is not to suggest that Hendrix was suicidal during this period in his life. The lyrics do reveal, however, his weariness and distraction.[20] He was unable to find the solace he was seeking.

SONGS OF INNOCENCE AND EXPERIENCE

In the compilation of illustrated poems by William Blake, *Songs of Innocence and Experience*, innocence and experience are set in a form of dialogue. Innocence, associated with the world of the child, is characterized by purity and represents a state of freedom and simplicity over against the harsher realities of life. Yet innocence can easily become toppled and corrupted by the intrusive adult world of experience.[21] Typical of Romanticism, the condition of the child represents a more natural and positive state of human existence prior to the spoiling and distorting influence of experience. One finds a similar contrast between innocence and experience in the artistry of Hendrix. His popular image, as noted earlier, was defined by pushing the limits on alternative experience. It is no accident that he burst on the scene fronting a band called *The Jimi Hendrix Experience* and that his first album was titled *Are You Experienced.*[22] At the same time, there is an innocence that pervades his lyrics, which is more reflective of his reserved and diffident personality. There are indications that during times of pressure, Hendrix's imagination moved toward a more childlike world as a source of comfort, seeking to find in such notions a refuge from the unpleasant realities of celebrity and the music business.

There was a childlike quality to Hendrix. When asked on one occasion where his songs came from, his response was, "I spend a lot of time daydreaming, they come from there." In a comment given to *Life* magazine in 1969, he reflected, "A musician, if he is a messenger, is like a child who hasn't been handled too many times by man, hasn't had too many fingerprints across his brain." In the final interview he gave, Hendrix observed, "Most of my writing was a clash between fantasy and reality and I felt you had to use fantasy to illuminate some aspect of reality. Even the Bible does that. You have to give people something to dream on."[23] The songs of Hendrix often register an objection to those experiences that generate a sense of disenchantment with the world and can be seen as a musical and lyrical expansion toward re-enchantment. In "May This Be Love," from *Are You Experienced*, the cause of the love he feels is a personified waterfall: "My worries seem so very small, with my waterfall." In the opening of "The Wind Cries Mary," he marks the change from a more tranquil time in a romantic relationship to the tumult of breakup as an end of innocence: "After all the jacks are in their boxes, and the clowns have all gone to bed, you can hear happiness staggering on down the street." In "One Rainy Wish," from his second album *Axis: Bold as Love* (1967), he writes of a dream he had distinguished by colors: "gold and rose . . . misty blue and lilac too, never to grow old." In "Castles Made of Sand," from the same album, he describes the story of a young crippled girl who decides to end her life but is healed as she jumps up to exclaim, "Look, a golden winged ship is passing my way"; the lyric continues, "And it really didn't have to stop, it just kept on going." The feminine figure of "Little Wing," also from *Axis: Bold as Love*, which will be discussed further in the next section, is described as "walking through the clouds, with a circus mind that's running wild." All she ever thinks about is "Butterflies and zebras and moonbeams and fairy tales." A final example is from "Burning of the Midnight Lamp" in which he observes, anticipating a possibly happier future, "And soon enough time will tell about the circus and the wishing well." It is helpful to view Hendrix as standing in the Romantic tradition, experiencing the disenchantment of the modern age and protesting against it through a longing for the simplicity and innocence of childhood and thus the greater significance and resourcefulness of enchantment.

THE ANGELIC FEMININE AS A SACRAMENTAL PRESENCE

A common feature of many of Hendrix's most beautiful songs is that of a mystical feminine figure. She is presented as a powerful, wise, and caring presence, able to guide and rescue him. This woman stands in deliberate contrast to the more predacious femme fatales in songs like "Foxy Lady" ("You know you're a cute little heartbreaker") and "Dolly Dagger" ("She drinks her blood from a jagged edge") who are reflective of the typical women Hendrix, as a rock star, would have encountered. This angelic ideal originates, to some extent, in the loss Hendrix experienced as a boy when his mother died, yet in interviews and conversations, he spoke of various sources of inspiration.[24] What is certain is that the "angel" represents the purity and innocence cherished by Hendrix and thus one who offers him comfort and freedom when the complications of life are too pressing. She comes from outside and beyond but is able to break into the present to uplift and inspire.

There are three songs, in particular, that highlight this angelic figure. She makes her first well-defined appearance in "Little Wing," arguably one of Hendrix's most enchanting compositions and certainly one of his most popular and widely covered songs.[25] Her otherworldly essence is noted in that she is "walking through the clouds" and "riding with the wind." It is the effect of her presence that elevates the song: "When I'm sad, she comes to me, with a thousand smiles she gives to me free." It is through the innocent generosity of her smiles that freedom is found. Additionally, her love is unreserved: "It's alright," she says, "It's alright, take anything you want from me, Anything." In two later compositions, both from *First Rays of the New Rising Sun*, the portrait of the angelic feminine is further developed. The song "Angel," a majestic poetic ballad, opens with the declaration, "Angel came down from heaven yesterday. She stayed with me just long enough to rescue me." Why he needs saving is not stated, but she rescues him by telling a story about "the sweet love between the moon and the deep blue sea" which points again to the longing for a childlike innocence. She promises to return the next day, and true to her word, "this morning came on to me; silver wings silhouette against a child's sunrise." At her arrival, she announces, "Today is the day for you to rise." The song concludes with his hopeful avowal: "forever I will be by your side." In the slower and wistful "Hey Baby (New Rising Sun)," a song that well illustrates the new musical direction in which Hendrix was moving when he died, the female figure is not identified as an angel but does come from the beyond, specifically "from the land of a new rising sun." Her mission is to spread peace of mind and love to people everywhere. Hendrix asks if he might come along with her, "can I step into your world a while?" a request which she grants. This angelic redemptive figure aligned with the image of a new rising sun indicates hopefulness in the midst of despair and disillusionment. The "angel" assumes an almost sacramental quality, re-enchanting the present and filling it with the promise of a new day.

Whatever might be the source of inspiration for this angelic figure, she is much more than a muse. She certainly inspires some of Hendrix's most subtle and elegant compositions, yet she is also the object of his longing. It is in her presence and by her strength that he hopes to find purpose and redemption. It is noteworthy that in Rom. 8, the Spirit of God not only inspires the longing intrinsic to fallen creation but is also the power that pulls creation toward the glory that defines its redemption. The angelic presence in Hendrix's songs introduces an important element that balances the loneliness and despair that infuse his music. Moreover, in theological terms, the angelic feminine can be seen as a representation of the Spirit, which Hendrix, as an artist, intuitively sensed as both a stimulus to longing and also the One who satisfies such longing. The longing felt by Hendrix was unquestionably a spiritual longing, which formed within him the need for someone from above and beyond who could bring salvation.

CONCLUSION

Like *Qohelet* of the biblical book of Ecclesiastes, Hendrix, as a man and artist, experienced everything under the sun and found it all to be vanity or futility. Although this provoked feelings of alienation and despondency, it never devolved into sullen cynicism. Rather, the discontent he felt awakened a hopefulness for something or someone beyond himself that was both enchanting and redemptive. In his case, disenchantment was a productive condition, as he found ways through his music to re-enchant the world. It is significant that in the final months of his life, he directed his artistic attentions to the first rays of a new rising sun, which, in his final poem, he associates with the idea of resurrection. It is as though he knew he was nearing the end of a journey which was bringing him closer to the object of his longing. One might hope that in the end he did find the love and home to which he was sailing and will perhaps be raised to participate in that ultimate dawn.

NOTES

1. Like other African American musicians before him, Hendrix moved to Europe to find initial success. The emergence of *The Jimi Hendrix Experience* in London made a startling impression, with the flamboyant Hendrix flanked by two waifish white British musicians, Mitch Mitchell (drums) and Noel Redding (bass). As one might expect, his appearance gave rise to implicit racist comments since he was quickly dubbed by the British press, "the Wild Man of Borneo"; see Jas Obrecht, *Stone Free: Jimi Hendrix in London, September 1966-June 1967* (Chapel Hill: University of North Carolina Press, 2018), pp. 91–92, for a discussion of this appellation and its place within the history of racist projections onto black entertainers. Although steeped in the various traditions of American black music, Hendrix's identification with the style of rock music emerging from Britain in the late 60s as well as his popularity among white audiences meant that he was not fully understood or accepted by an extensive black audience.

2. Hendrix's interpretive performance of "The Star Spangled Banner" near the end of the 1969 generation-defining Woodstock concert, at which Hendrix was the top-billed performer, is widely regarded as one of the definitive protest statements of the Vietnam era. It is also important to note the impact of his music on soldiers serving in Vietnam, on which see Michael J. Kramer, *The Republic of Rock: Music and Citizenship in the Sixties Counterculture* (New York: Oxford University Press, 2013), pp. 144–151.

3. This association with drugs and the blatant sexuality that often distinguished Hendrix's early performances, most notably his American "debut" at the Monterey Pop Festival in June 1967, meant that most Christians, including Pentecostals, regarded Hendrix and his style of music as objectionable and even harmful to Christian young people. The electric guitar, since its invention, has had phallic

connotations. Hendrix certainly exploited this early in his career and thus precluded his general acceptance within conventional American, not to mention Christian, culture.

4. The companion piece, "Voodoo Chile" (both tracks appearing on the 1968 double album *Electric Ladyland*) contains the ominous lyric, "The night I was born, I swear the moon turned a fire red." It is perhaps not surprising that in Africa certain tribes use Hendrix' music in their Voodoo rituals since the beat and ambiance of his music resemble their own rhythmic style; Michael Drewett, "Chapter 4: Censorship, religion, and popular music" in C. Partridge and M. Moberg, eds. *The Bloomsbury Handbook of Religion and Popular Music*. London: Bloomsbury, 2023. p. 46.

5. That longer title was ultimately cut out along with most of the lyrics, much to the disappointment of Hendrix, who felt that much of what he wanted to say was removed from the song; Charles R. Cross, *Room Full of Mirrors: A Biography of Jimi Hendrix* (New York: Hyperion, 2005), p. 176.

6. From an interview originally published in *Beat Instrumental*; reprinted in Steven Roby, ed., *Hendrix on Hendrix: Interview and Encounters with Jimi Hendrix* (Chicago: Chicago Review Press, 2017), pp. 11–12.

7. Photographs of the handwritten lyrics to the song can be found in *Jimi Hendrix: The Ultimate Lyric Book* (Milwaukee: Backbeat Books, 2012), pp. 286–87.

8. Two of his most popular recordings, "Hey Joe" (1966) and "All Along the Watchtower" (1968), are not discussed since they are cover versions of songs written by others.

9. A compilation album, *First Rays of the New Rising Sun* was finally issued in 1997. Many of the songs included there had appeared on earlier posthumous albums, principally *The Cry of Love* (1971) and *Rainbow Bridge* (1971). With respect to the title of this projected album, it is striking that in the poem "The Story of Life" Hendrix reflects on the death and ongoing life of Jesus by noting that the angels of heaven made "Easter Sunday the name of the Rising Sun."

10. It is not uncommon for modern translations to make "creation" the subject of the sentence, as in the NRSV: "the creation waits with eager longing for the revealing of the children of God." Yet, more accurate and preferable are earlier translations (e.g., KJV, ASV) that make longing the subject of the sentence.

11. C. S. Lewis, "On Three Ways of Writing for Children" in Walter Hooper ed., *On Stories and Other Essays on Literature* (New York: Harcourt Brace Jovanovich, 1982), p. 38.

12. C. S. Lewis, "Christianity and Culture", in Walter Hooper, ed., *Christian Reflections* (Grand Rapids: Eerdmans, 1980), p. 23, n. 1.

13. C. S. Lewis, "The Weight of Glory", in Walter Hooper, ed., *The Weight of Glory and Other Addresses* (New York: Macmillan, 1980), pp. 15–16.

14. C. S. Lewis. *Mere Christianity* (Glasgow: Collins, 1980), p. 118.

15. In the summer of 1970, Hendrix opened his own recording studio, Electric Lady Studios, in Greenwich Village, NYC. He spent only about ten weeks recording there before his death in September 1970.

16. C. S. Lewis, *Till We Have Faces* (New York: HarperCollins, 1984), p. 87.

17. Harry Shapiro and Caesar Glebbeek, *Jimi Hendrix: Electric Gypsy* (London: Heinemann, 1990), p. 170.

18. The song, in many ways, echoes an earlier composition, "The Wind Cries Mary," from *Are You Experienced*. Both are beautiful songs, distinguished musically by a delicate and disorienting fragility, and both concern the breakup of a relationship. "The Wind Cries Mary" contains some of the best poetry found in Hendrix's work: "A broom is drearily sweeping up the broken pieces of yesterday's life." and "The traffic lights, they turn blue tomorrow, and shine their emptiness down on my bed."

19. The journalist Meatball Fulton, who interviewed Jimi Hendrix at the time of the release of "Burning of the Midnight Lamp" later reflected, "I had the impression that he had few friends if any that could see him as a person, not as a pop star or a thing." *Hendrix on Hendrix*, p. 77.

20. Complaints of exhaustion are a common element in many interviews Hendrix gave in the final months of his life. Typical of his schedule, the day after the official opening of Electric Lady Studios, he left for a European tour, from which he never returned. Yet given that he now had a studio of his own, a new musical direction, and collaborative projects lined up with other musicians, it is clear that he had much to live for. It is best to see his death as an unfortunate accident, albeit one largely brought on by the negligence of those who were to look after his interests.

21. For an helpful discussion of the poems, see Leo Damrosch, *Eternity's Sunrise: The Imaginative World of William Blake* (New Haven: Yale University Press, 2015), pp. 50–95.

22. An interesting feature of the album title is the absence of a question mark, making the title more of an assertion than a query.

23. The previous three quotations, respectively, are from *Hendrix on Hendrix*, pp. 29, 328, 320.

24. The fullest account of the feminine ideal that haunts Hendrix's lyrics is in Charles Shaar Murray, *Crosstown Traffic: Jimi Hendrix and Post-war Pop* (London: Faber and Faber, 1989), pp. 75–77. Shapiro and Glebbeek, *Jimi Hendrix: Electric Gypsy*, p. 314, claim that Hendrix was possibly making an oblique reference to the feminine side of his own psyche.

25. Most notably by Derek and the Dominos, released on *Layla and Other Assorted Love Songs* (1970) and Stevie Ray Vaughan, released on *The Sky is Crying* (1991). The former, recorded nine days before Hendrix's death, was initially intended as a tribute by Eric Clapton and Duane Allman, yet curiously evokes the pathos and dignity of a lament.

BIBLIOGRAPHY

Cross, Charles R. *Room Full of Mirrors: A Biography of Jimi Hendrix*. New York: Hyperion, 2005.

Damrosch, Leo. *Eternity's Sunrise: The Imaginative World of William Blake*. New Haven: Yale University Press, 2015.

Drewitt, Michael, "Chapter 4: Censorship, Religion, and Popular Music." In: C. Partridge and M. Moberg (eds.), *The Bloomsbury Handbook of Religion and Popular Music*. London: Bloomsbury, 2023, pp. 45–55.

Hendrix, Jimi. *Jimi Hendrix: The Ultimate Lyric Book*. Milwaukee: Backbeat Books, 2012.

Kramer, Michael J. *The Republic of Rock: Music and Citizenship in the Sixties Counterculture*. New York: Oxford University Press, 2013.

Lewis, C. S. "Christianity and Culture." In: Walter Hooper (ed.), *Christian Reflections*. Grand Rapids: Eerdmans, 1980, pp. 12–36.

———. *Mere Christianity*. Glasgow: Collins, 1980.

———. "On Three Ways of Writing for Children." In: Walter Hooper (ed.), *On Stories and Other Essays on Literature*. New York: Harcourt Brace Jovanovich, 1982, pp. 31–43.

———. *Till We Have Faces*. New York: HarperCollins, 1984.

———. "The Weight of Glory." In: Walter Hooper (ed.), *The Weight of Glory and Other Addresses*. New York: Macmillan, 1980, pp. 3–19.

Murray, Charles Shaar. *Crosstown Traffic: Jimi Hendrix and Post-war Pop*. London: Faber and Faber, 1989.

Obrecht, Jas. *Stone Free: Jimi Hendrix in London, September 1966-June 1967*. Chapel Hill: University of North Carolina Press, 2018.

Roby, Steven ed., *Hendrix on Hendrix: Interview and Encounters with Jimi Hendrix*. Chicago: Chicago Review Press, 2017.

Shapiro, Harry and Caesar Glebbeek, *Jimi Hendrix: Electric Gypsy*. London: Heinemann, 1990.

Chapter 8

"The Answer, My Friend"

A Pneumatological Reading of Bob Dylan's "Blowin' in the Wind"

Jeffrey S. Lamp

Perhaps no song in Bob Dylan's oeuvre is more well-known and anthemic than his 1963 release, "Blowin' in the Wind." My first encounter with the song happened in the second grade in a small South Dakota elementary school chorus in 1967, when it seemed every such elementary school chorus felt compelled to perform the song. It has been covered by more than 300 artists, making it one of his most covered songs. Dylan himself has performed it live 1,585 times.[1] As is his wont, Dylan borrowed the music for the song from an old abolitionist Negro spiritual, "No More Auction Block."[2] The story goes that when African American singer Sam Cooke heard it, it moved him to write his own civil rights anthem, "A Change Is Gonna Come" (1964). "Blowin' in the Wind" was performed at Martin Luther King, Jr.'s March on Washington in 1963. It has also been identified as the anthem not only of the Civil Rights Movement, but also of the "peace movement" of the 1960s.[3] This song, among others, led to Dylan's anointing as the pre-eminent "protest" singer of the day, and even the "voice of a generation," labels vehemently rejected by Dylan. To call "Blowin' in the Wind" an epochal entry in Dylan's catalog is the acme of understatement, especially considering that the song occurred so early in his career.

Interpretations of the song are myriad, though on the surface, the structure and the message of the song seem quite evident, even simplistic. The present essay will add to this tradition, examining the imagery of "wind" in the song "Blowin' in the Wind" in conversation with passages drawn from both Testaments of the Christian Bible. Noting that the Hebrew *ruah* and Greek *pneuma* are both translatable into English either as "s/Spirit" or "wind," the essay will read the song through an interplay of the meanings of *ruah/pneuma* to suggest that the song may be read pneumatologically to indicate that the answer to the questions posed in the song is found in and through the Spirit.

To structure our discussion, I have chosen to look at the performance of the song at two junctures in Dylan's career. The first occurs in the summer of 1963, with two live performances separated in time by about a month. In many ways, these are iconic moments for the song, showing how it earned its reputation as an anthem of many social movements of the 1960s. The first performance took place in the finale of the Newport Folk Festival in Newport, RI, on July 26, 1963, in which Dylan performed the song with many others who performed at the festival. The second occurred on the day of Martin Luther King, Jr.'s, "I Have a Dream" speech during the March on Washington on August 28. Interestingly, the song was not performed by Dylan, but rather by Peter, Paul, and Mary, who had a huge hit with the song at the time. The second juncture we will examine took place during Dylan's so-called "born again period," typically dated 1979–1981. One particular performance will occupy our attention here: his performance in Lakeland, FL, on November 21, 1981.

We will begin by describing the contexts of these two junctures in order to ascertain how the song was esteemed during each period. The essential distinction between the two periods is that in 1963, the song functioned as an anthem for social action and change, while in the "born again" period, the song is subtly framed within a gospel context. Each of these periods invites distinct pneumatological readings of the song.

NEWPORT AND WASHINGTON—SUMMER 1963

By the time of the Newport Folk Festival in Newport, RI, Dylan had established himself firmly within the Greenwich Village folk scene. Having arrived in New York City in 1961, Dylan presented himself in the persona of an heir of Woody Guthrie, even crafting his appearance, wardrobe, and vocal presentation in the likeness of Guthrie.[4] He recorded his first album in 1962, the eponymous *Bob Dylan*, consisting of covers of traditional folk and gospel songs with only two original compositions, one of which was titled "Song for Woody." The album initially sold only about 5,000 copies. His second album, *The Freewheelin' Bob Dylan*, established Dylan as a songwriter, containing many songs that would position him as a leading voice in the social movements of the day, including "Blowin' in the Wind." The album was released on May 27, 1963, a mere two months before the Newport Folk Festival. At the direction of Albert Grossman, manager of both Dylan and Peter, Paul, and Mary, the trio released their version of the song as a single in June of that year, becoming one of the group's biggest hits. Dylan himself wrote and first performed the song in April 1962.

At this time, Dylan's career was closely associated with that of singer Joan Baez, one of the most influential performers in folk circles and a passionate social activist. Dylan's star was rising, in large measure due to his many vocal collaborations with Baez at her concerts and festivals. He would later become romantically entwined with Baez. Moreover, at this time, Dylan was romantically involved with Suze Rotolo, who is widely credited for getting Dylan involved with social causes.[5] Though Dylan patterned his persona at this time after Guthrie, in many ways, Dylan's social consciousness was informed by the women in his life.

Dylan's set list for the evening performance on Friday, July 26, included five of his most poignant "finger-pointing" songs, a designation often attributed to Dylan's compositions early in his career, also known as "protest" songs. Of course, the songs fit well with the folk aura of the festival, especially its focus on socially pertinent music.[6] For the finale of the evening concert, Dylan was joined on stage by several other performers, notably Pete Seeger, a well-known folk singer, Baez, Peter, Paul, and Mary, The Freedom Singers, and many others, to perform "Blowin' in the Wind" and the anthem of the Civil Rights Movement, "We Shall Overcome."[7] This performance helped cement Dylan's reputation as the "voice of his generation," a designation he would soon resoundingly reject to the consternation of his folk following.

About a month after the Newport festival, on August 28, 1963, Rev. Martin Luther King, Jr., led the massive March on Washington for Jobs and Freedom, gathering near the Lincoln Memorial. While Dylan, at this point a mere twenty-two years old, performed a set of four songs,[8] it was Peter, Paul, and Mary who performed "Blowin' in the Wind." To be sure, at the time it was Peter, Paul, and Mary's single that would have been the most widely known version of the song. As it was performed, it became a sing-along among the more than 250,000 attendees of the march, uniting the massive crowd in asking the poignant questions posed in the song. In light of this performance giving way to Rev. King's "I Have a Dream" speech, the song became identified with the Civil Rights Movement.

In this context, what pneumatological reading of the song emerges? While an exhaustive biblical pneumatology is far beyond the scope of this discussion, one theme of such a pneumatology evident at this juncture in Dylan's career and the performance of the song is the prophetic role of the Spirit. At this point, we must again restate that Dylan, even at this early stage of his career, adamantly rejected claims that he was a prophet in any sense. Indeed, in the song "Long Time Gone," an unreleased song first performed live on November 8, 1962, Dylan sang, "But I know I ain't no prophet/an' I ain't no prophet's son," echoing Amos' protest in Amos 7:14.[9] Though Dylan may not have accepted the mantle "prophet," it is evident that many among his audience esteemed him as such.

Jenny Leeden, in her study of Dylan, *Prophecy in the Christian Era*, looks at Dylan's career during the period 1962–1966, focusing specifically on how "Blowin' in the Wind" functioned to establish Dylan as the major prophetic voice of what she labels the "peace movement," a convergence of social protests against racism, militarism, and authoritarianism.[10] In fact, Leeden dates the beginning of the "peace movement" to the song's first live performance, April 16, 1962,[11] interestingly again, not by Dylan himself. The story goes that Dylan arrived at Gerde's Folk City, a club in Greenwich Village, with the lyrics to the song and his guitar, auditioning it for Gil Turner, who was serving as master of ceremonies at the club that night. When Turner heard the song, he asked Dylan if he could perform it. Dylan agreed and was a member of the audience for its first live performance.[12] Leeden argues that from that moment, more than a year before the song received widespread radio play in Peter, Paul, and Mary's version, the song was widely circulating as an effective confrontational device and instructional vehicle on ethical issues important to people in the "peace movement."[13]

Leeden acknowledges that Dylan would rebuff any suggestion that he was a prophet or voice for any cause. Nevertheless, she sees commonalities in Dylan's function within the "peace movement," intentional or not, with the biblical prophets. Drawing on Martin Buber's characterization of Israel's prophets, Leeden sees a kinship in function between Dylan and the prophets:

> [The prophets] never announced a God upon whom their hearers' striving for security reckoned. They always aimed to shatter all security and to proclaim in the opened abyss of the final insecurity the unwished for God who demands that His human creatures become real, and that they become human.[14]

If Dylan functioned as a prophet for the "peace movement," then "Blowin' in the Wind" was his first oracle. And in the vein of the prophets, Dylan's questions in the song function as an enigma with two primary possibilities of meaning: the judgment of God at the end of the age or revolution in the present.[15] "'Blowin' in the Wind' drew people together; it put words of protest into the mouths of millions of people, and it created a spectacle that was revolutionary."[16] Dylan was calling society to account for the sins of racism, militarism, and authoritarianism in an idiom at home in the folk music culture of the day. "Blowin' in the Wind" energized a generation to take on the social ills of the times.

But "Blowin' in the Wind" was not alone in this regard in Dylan's catalog in the early years of his career. As Leeden notes, Dylan wrote several songs in the period 1962–1966 that drew upon meteorological phenomena to describe the judgment of God against social injustices. Following "Blowin' in the Wind" in 1962 were "A Hard Rain's A-Gonna Fall" (1962), "When the Ship

Comes In" (1963), "The Times They Are A-Changin'" (1963), "Chimes of Freedom" (1964), "Gates of Eden" (1964), "It's All Over Now, Baby Blue" (1964), "Desolation Row" (1965), and "Visions of Johanna" (1965).[17] It has been widely acknowledged that Dylan drew from the Bible for his lyrics from the beginning of his career, and prior to his focus on writing his own songs, he was immersed in the old folk and gospel songs of earlier times, many of which drew extensively on biblical imagery. Though this period of his career took place many years before his conversion to Christianity in 1978, Dylan was conversant with the Bible and drew from it in his own compositions. The question remains for us, how might the Bible be seen to contribute to a pneumatological reading of "Blowin' in the Wind"?

Conceding that Dylan probably did not have in his mind the concern to present a pneumatological prophecy in the song, we might still see how the song achieved this effect. Second Peter 1:21 reminds us that "no prophecy ever came by human will, but men and women moved by the Holy Spirit spoke from God."[18] While Dylan would deny speaking for God at this point in his career, as noted above, he spoke in concert with the prophets of old. In the Hebrew Bible, what Christians call the Old Testament, the prophets addressed the social shortcomings of the Israelites. And in several of the Old Testament prophets, particularly Ezekiel,[19] the Spirit of God is said to have come upon the prophets as they spoke their oracles against the people. Indeed, in the so-called "Nazareth Manifesto" of Jesus in Luke 4:16-21, Jesus reads from Isa. 61:1-2:

The Spirit of the Lord is upon me,
    because he has anointed me
        to bring good news to the poor.
He has sent me to proclaim release to the captives
    and recovery of sight to the blind,
        to let the oppressed go free,
to proclaim the year of the Lord's favor.

In the Hebrew of the Isaiah passage, the Spirit of the Lord God (*ruah adonai yahweh*) comes upon the prophet to proclaim relief for those who suffer, including especially those outcasts who were suffering the social ills that provoked the judgment of God against the oppressors. Jesus' ministry is cast in terms of breaking the bonds of social oppression. The thematic concerns of both Jesus and Isaiah are reflected in the lyrics of "Blowin' in the Wind."

Dylan begins the song by asking, "How many roads must a man walk down/before you call him a man?" This elicits comparisons to Isaiah's and Jesus' mission to let the oppressed go free. In the context of the March on Washington, where protests against the denial of basic human dignity found expression, Dylan's opening question resonated loudly as it was sung by many in attendance. In the second verse, the question is reiterated with precision: "Yes, 'n' how many years can some people exist/before they're allowed to be free?" The question is asked and sung with prophetic fervor.

Jesus' ministry saw several miracles that restored sight to the blind (e.g., John 9). These miracles not only enabled recipients to see in physical terms, but also enabled them and subsequent readers to see the kingdom of God encroaching into a broken reality. Dylan's stinging indictment in the second verse, "Yes 'n' how many times can a man turn his head/pretending he just doesn't see?" is a call for society to open its eyes to the injustices around them. The question is restated poignantly in the third verse: "How many times must a man look up/before he can see the sky?" The imagery of looking up may be seen as a call to look heavenward for a proper response to injustice. The biblical prophets and Jesus, heir and Lord of the biblical prophets, urge people to seek out God's revelation and to respond obediently to God's law, to respond justly to the social injustices prevalent among ancient Israelites, and by extension, to the social injustices of the 1960s.

Indeed, the final reference in the Isaianic prophecy quoted by Jesus is to the "acceptable year of the Lord," which virtually all biblical scholars agree refers to the Year of Jubilee in Lev. 25. This legislation called for the release of slaves, the forgiveness of debts, and the return of lands to their original owners. It is, in short, the abrogation of all forms of oppression that bring suffering. Dylan's question, "Yes, 'n' how many ears must one man have/before he can hear people cry?" draws attention to the general condition of social suffering, the conditions addressed by the Jubilee legislation.

If the March on Washington provides a setting that draws attention to those questions in the song that address matters of oppression, the performance at Newport a month earlier, given in the context of a folk music festival, seems to focus on other elements of the song. Rather than focusing on elements of social injustice in the United States (though these issues were clearly in view), the context seemed more directed at anti-war sentiments. In the first verse, references are made to a "white dove sail[ing]" and "cannonballs fly[ing]/before they're forever banned." The third verse asks, "Yes, 'n' how many deaths will it take till he knows/that too many people have died?" Concerns related to the anti-war component of the "peace movement" prevail in this context. The prophetic Spirit here calls attention to the intention to work for peace in the spirit of Jesus' statement in the Beatitudes that asserts, "Blessed are the peacemakers" (Matt. 5:9).

This juncture in Dylan's career avails itself to a pneumatological reading in terms of the prophetic Spirit. As St. Peter asserts, prophets in the Old Testament spoke at the moving of the Spirit (2 Pet. 1:21). Old Testament prophets spoke largely in terms of social injustice. Jesus spoke in continuity with the prophets as fulfilling the oracle of Isaiah 61. In the early 1960s, Dylan, the folk singer and songwriter, articulated concerns of the prophets in "Blowin' in the Wind." If Dylan asserts that the answer to his queries is found "blowin' in the wind," a pneumatological reading understands this to be the Spirit who moved the prophets to speak. This Spirit calls for society to address the entrenched injustices prevalent at the time. The interplay found in the Hebrew and Greek words *ruah* and *pneuma*, respectively, may be appropriated to show that the wind Dylan identifies as holding the answers to these injustices is located in the Spirit who moved the prophets to speak out. The next section of our discussion will address another aspect of this Spirit, the Spirit of new creation, more prevalent in the "born-again" juncture of Dylan's career and performance of the song.

THE "BORN-AGAIN" PERIOD: 1979–1981

Bob Dylan's career has been a series of personal and artistic reinventions. The first such reinvention took place at the Newport Folk Festival in 1965, a mere two years after his triumph at Newport discussed above, when he famously "went electric," alienating many of his traditional folk fans. There would be many other reinventions in his over sixty-year career, but perhaps none was more shocking and seemingly inexplicable than his conversion to Christianity in 1978, resulting in a "Gospel only" tour and a series of three studio albums in which Dylan seemed to take on the guise of a fire-and-brimstone preacher.

Dylan's conversion to Christianity occurred in 1978. As he recounts the moment, he had returned to his hotel room after a performance in Tucson, AZ, feeling ill. As he lay on the bed, he held a silver cross that a fan had tossed on stage a few nights earlier. It was then that Dylan saw Jesus in his room, and as he recalls it, "Jesus put his hand on me. It was a physical thing. I felt it. I felt it all over me. I felt my whole body tremble. The glory of the Lord knocked me down and picked me up."[20] Dylan's early Christian nurture took place in the Vineyard Fellowship, a church started in Los Angeles in 1974 by Kenn Gulliksen, a pastor on staff at Chuck Smith's Calvary Chapel. In early 1979, Dylan's girlfriend at the time, Mary Alice Artes, arranged a meeting between Dylan and two pastors on staff at the Vineyard church, Larry Myers and Paul Emond.[21] Dylan even felt compelled to enroll in Vineyard's three-month-long School of Discipleship following his conversion.[22] The newly converted Dylan imbibed the fervent charismatic ethos of Vineyard, providing him with fresh theological (particularly eschatological) content to integrate into his established practice of drawing on Scripture for his lyrics.[23]

Dylan's conversion also reshaped his artistic and performance output. In 1979, he released his first of three gospel-themed albums, *Slow Train*

Coming. In a way, it was a return to his "finger-pointing" era, offering biblical commentary on social and political issues (e.g., "Slow Train"). But there was also a new focus in the lyrics, namely, the wrath of God to be poured out when Jesus returns (e.g., "When He Returns"). The album was acknowledged as a well-produced record, and it won a Grammy award, though the subject matter left many confused and even angry.

After *Slow Train Coming*'s release, Dylan embarked on what is called The Gospel Tour, which ran in three legs from November 1, 1979, through May 21, 1980. Opening with fourteen shows in sixteen days at San Francisco's Warfield Theater, audiences were treated to shows that featured only Christian-themed music, consisting of songs from *Slow Train Coming*, songs written during the tour in preparation for his next album, *Saved*, and some covers of popular Christian songs (e.g., "Rise Again" by Dallas Holm). Missing were the standards that established him as the "voice of his generation" or as the "poet laureate of rock 'n roll." Again, audience responses ranged from outrage from those who felt betrayed by this latest change of persona to hand-raising and shouts of "Hallelujah" and "Amen" among those who rejoiced at Dylan's conversion.

Following The Gospel Tour, Dylan returned to the studio to record *Saved*, critically less well-received than *Slow Train Coming*, but a record saturated with the sounds of black gospel music and overall a much more emotional response to his conversion than the more polished previous disc. That fall, Dylan embarked on another tour, called "A Musical Retrospective Tour." It too began with an extended residency at the Warfield Theater beginning November 9, 1980, this time with twelve shows. After a hiatus to record the third album of the so-called "gospel trilogy," *Shot of Love*, Dylan spent the summer of 1981 with a short stint of shows in the United States followed by a European tour. The year concluded with a tour of the United States and Canada in October and November of 1981.

The concerts in 1980 and 1981, however, deviated from those of The Gospel Tour in a significant way. No longer would Dylan play only gospel-themed music. While the set lists continued to be mostly populated by songs from the albums of the "born again period," some older favorites began to reappear, among them "Blowin' in the Wind."

While bootleg audio and video recordings of many of these shows appear in various internet forums and in the thirteenth entry in Dylan's official Bootleg Series titled *Trouble No More* (2017), the final performance of the tour, November 21, 1981, in Lakeland, FL, is emblematic of Dylan's performance of the song at this juncture in his career.[24] Gone is the stark folk arrangement of the performances from the summer of 1963. Even though Dylan began introducing early songs back into his concerts, the arrangements were distinctly gospel in feel. Dylan begins the song at the piano, toward the back of the stage, with traditional black gospel fervor, midway through the performance, getting up and moving to the front center of the stage and playing the guitar. The black gospel sound is furthered by a group of African-American female backing singers, known as the Queens of Rhythm, as well as an organ. Many in the audience are seen raising their hands with their eyes closed, more typical of a revival service than a rock concert.

Indeed, in this arrangement, the song communicates in a way that differs drastically from the performances we noted from 1963. Context is the key. Whereas the Newport Folk Festival and March on Washington were grounded in scenes of protest, exhibiting the tone of the prophetic Spirit challenging the unrighteousness of society, the "born again" ethos of 1981 provides the song with a less directly challenging effect, offering something else in terms of an answer.

The episode of Nicodemus coming to Jesus in John 3:1-21 is the key text in this context. Nicodemus, a Jewish leader (v. 1), comes to Jesus at night to avoid being seen by others, to speak to Jesus. After Nicodemus' seemingly flattering statement that Jesus is indeed one who comes from God (v. 2), Jesus takes the discussion in another direction. In v. 3, Jesus in a non sequitur states, "Very truly, I tell you, no one can see the kingdom of God without being born from above." English translations differ on how to translate the term *anothen*, translated "above" in the NRSV. It may indicate a sense of "a source that is above," as indicated here, or "from a point of time marking the beginning," granting the sense of "again."[25] Nicodemus misunderstands Jesus' words, querying how one who is old can be born after growing old (v. 4). "Can one enter a second time into the mother's womb and be born?" he asks. Jesus' extended response is crucial to a pneumatological reading of the song.

Jesus informs Nicodemus that no one enters the kingdom of God without being born of water and Spirit. Bypassing the question of the referent of "water" here, Jesus indicates that one can only enter into the kingdom of God by the agency of the Spirit. Verse six affirms the key principle: "What is born of flesh is flesh, and what is born of the Spirit is spirit." His assertion that one must be born from above should not surprise Nicodemus, as Jesus states (v. 7). Here Jesus says, "The wind blows where it chooses, and you hear the sound of it, but you do not know where it comes from or where it goes" (v. 9). Jesus' punchline follows: "So it is with everyone who is born of the Spirit."

The word translated as "wind" here is the word *pneuma*, which may be translated as either "wind" or "s/Spirit." Jesus plays on the dual referent of the term to illustrate to Nicodemus that, in the way that human beings may experience the effects of wind without knowing either its source or destination, so too is the work of the Spirit among those who have been born from above. The key contrast is between a human perception of what is happening and a spiritual perception that is granted to those who are born from above.[26] To the one who is "born from above/again" the Spirit gives insight into the nature of things. Indeed, the Spirit will bring to mind for Jesus' followers all those things Jesus said (14:26; 15:26; 16:12-13). This would ostensibly include Jesus' words in Nazareth quoting Isa. 61:1-2. On the one hand, this would essentially repeat the sense of Jesus' words from that oracle in the sense they might be understood in the lyrics of "Blowin' in the Wind," as we discussed earlier. But in John, there is another sense communicated. The performance of the song in the summer of 1963 might represent a more "fleshly" sense, a focus, though in line with the Spirit, that is essentially a call to address the questions of the song through social action and human effort apart from, though consonant with, the Spirit. Jesus' words in John 3 indicate that something else is needed to address the questions raised in the song. While the "peace movement" of the 1960s did indeed arguably contribute to some successes in terms of civil rights and anti-war activism, the fact is that they were not unqualified successes. Work remains to be done. The "born again" context of "Blowin' in the Wind" suggests that answers to the questions raised in the song are only discernible in the Spirit, the *ruah/pneuma* that blows in the world and among human beings. Human efforts, though commendable, are limited in effect, and only in the Spirit is potential resolution found. Dylan's contribution in 1963, though pneumatological, was at least analogically, of limited effect, needing that component that would be articulated later in his career, the work of the Spirit. It takes the work of God to effect the transformation suggested in the question of "Blowin' in the Wind." The *ruah* that hovered over primordial creation to bring order (Gen. 1:2), the wind that blew through the valley of dry bones in Ezekiel 37, that blew through those in the upper room in Acts 2, that raised to new life a society that had effectively died, that empowered a new community to bring new life to the world, is the Holy Spirit that Dylan came to know personally with his conversion, the wind that brings with it the divine power to change the world. This is a world that would ultimately, in Dylan's estimation, not come through human political and social effort, important though they are, but through the transformative move of the Spirit that blows life into all things. It is an eschatological vision, though one worth emulating in the present.

CONCLUSION

On September 27, 1997, Bob Dylan performed a concert at the World Eucharistic Conference in Bologna, Italy, before an estimated 300,000 attendees. The most prominent person in this throng was Pope John Paul II, at whose invitation Dylan performed. Interestingly, future Pope Benedict

XVI attempted to keep Dylan from performing, deeming Dylan to be the wrong kind of "prophet" for such an occasion.[27] John Paul II prevailed and Dylan indeed performed. Dylan opened with two songs, his early "protest" song "A Hard Rain's A-Gonna Fall" and "Knocking on Heaven's Door." In a homily that followed the performance, the Pontiff said, "You say the answer is blowing in the wind, my friend. So it is: but it is not the wind that blows things away it is the breath and life of the Holy Spirit, the voice that calls and says, 'Come!'"[28] This sentiment sums up "Blowin' in the Wind" in the two junctures in Dylan's career examined here. The prophetic Spirit exemplified in the summer of 1963, the wind that is the Spirit who calls human beings to account in revolutionary terms that foresee the judgment of God that is to come if repentance is not forthcoming, is a wind that blows away corrupt structures. But the renewing Spirit of the "born again" period that comes through Jesus is a wind that is a breath of new life, a divine power that transforms corrupt systems and structures. Perhaps the way to characterize these junctures is in terms of a problem-solution relationship. While a prophetic assessment of the situation is indeed a Spirit-inspired assessment, the solution is only found in the work of the Spirit itself. Blowin' in the wind? Yes, indeed, if we understand that wind to be the Spirit.

NOTES

1. Bob Dylan, "Blowin' in the Wind," Warner Bros., Inc., 1962, https://www.bobdylan.com/songs/blowin-wind/. The first time was April 16, 1962, and the most recent was July 14, 2019.

2. Though there was a disproved conspiracy theory that Dylan stole the song from a New Jersey high school student.

3. Jenny Leeden, *Prophecy in the Christian Era* (St. Louis, MO: Peaceberry Press of Webster Groves, 1995).

4. Timothy Hampton, *Bob Dylan's Poetics: How the Songs Work* (New York: Zone Books, 2019), 45–81.

5. Suze Rotolo, *A Freewheelin' Time: A Memoir of Greenwich Village in the Sixties* (New York: Crown Publishing Group, 2008).

6. The songs were "Talkin' World War III Blues," "With God on Our Side," "Only a Pawn in Their Game," "Talkin' John Birch Paranoid Blues," and "A Hard Rain's A-Gonna Fall."

7. For a video of the performance, see Bob Dylan, "Blowin' in the Wind—From Newport Folk Festival 1963," YouTube, 4:04, November 6, 2013, https://www.youtube.com/watch?v=jleLj9Pj1Gw.

8. Dylan performed "Only a Pawn in Their Game," a song about the murder of black civil rights activist Medgar Evers, in which Dylan powerfully focuses attention on those whose rhetoric and policies drove the assassin Byron de la Beckwith to kill Evers. He also sang his songs, "When the Ship Comes In," and "With God on Our

Side," and a traditional spiritual "Keep Your Eyes on the Prize," a song that became a staple during the Civil Rights Movement.

9. The song was eventually released on *The Bootleg Series, Vol 9: The Witmark Demos: 1962–1964* in 2010.

10. Leeden, *Prophecy in the Christian Era*, 6. See also, Stephen Brandon, Isaac Maupin, and Mark Goodman, "Bob Dylan: The Prophet of Social Change in the 1960s," *Media Watch* 8:3 (2017): 366–77.

11. Leeden, *Prophecy in the Christian Era*, 1.

12. This is the account of David Blue recounted in Robbie Woliver, *Bringing It All Back Home: Twenty-five Years of American Music at Folk City* (New York: Pantheon, 1986), 83–84.

13. Leeden, *Prophecy in the Christian Era*, 1. Leeden (3) notes that Joan Baez and Pete Seeger played the song live often in the year before its radio popularity, and the words and music appeared in an issue of *Broadside* magazine (May 1962), a periodical dedicated to disseminating folk music to fans and activists.

14. Martin Buber, *Eclipse of God*, trans. Maurice Friedman (New York: Harper, 1954), 97.

15. Leeden, *Prophecy in the Christian Era*, 6.

16. Leeden, *Prophecy in the Christian Era*, 101.

17. Leeden, *Prophecy in the Christian Era*, 11. For a discussion of these songs, see 11–25.

18. Unless otherwise noted, all biblical quotations are from the New Revised Standard Version.

19. Leonard P. Maré, "Ezekiel, Prophet of the Spirit: חור in the Book of Ezekiel," *Old Testament Essays* 31:3 (2018): 553–70.

20. Dylan interviewed by Karen Hughes, May 21, 1980, in *Bob Dylan: The Essential Interviews*, ed. Jonathan Cott (New York: Wenner Books, 2006), 276.

21. Clinton Heylin, *Trouble in Mind: Bob Dylan's Gospel Years—What Really Happened* (New York: Lesser Gods, 2017), 23–25; Scott M. Marshall, *Bob Dylan: A Spiritual Life* (Washington, DC: WND Books, 2017), 34–35.

22. Dylan interviewed by Robert Hilburn, November 23, 1980, in *Bob Dylan: The Essential Interviews*, 298.

23. Jeffrey S. Lamp, "The Hal Lindsey Effect: Bob Dylan's Christian Eschatology," *Dylan Review* 3:1 (Summer 2021): 87–111. https://thedylanreview.org/2021/07/25/the-hal-lindsey-effect-bob-dylans-christian-eschatology/.

24. This performance of "Blowin' in the Wind" is part of a display at the Bob Dylan Center, Tulsa, OK.

25. Walter Bauer, *A Greek—English Lexicon of the New Testament and Other Early Christian Literature*, rev. and ed. Frederick William Danker, 3rd ed. (Chicago: University of Chicago Press, 2001), 92.

26. George R. Beasley-Murray, *John*, Word Biblical Commentary (Dallas: Word, 1999), 49.

27. Sean Curnyn, "The Pope and the Pop Star," *First Things*, May 10, 2007, https://www.firstthings.com/web-exclusives/2007/05/the-pope-and-the-pop-star.

28. Allison Rapp, "25 Years Ago: Bob Dylan Plays for the Pope," *Ultimate Classic Rock*, September 27, 2022, https://ultimateclassicrock.com/bob-dylan-pope-performance/.

BIBLIOGRAPHY

Bauer, Walter. *A Greek—English Lexicon of the New Testament and Other Early Christian Literature*. Revised and edited by Frederick William Danker, 3rd edition. Chicago: University of Chicago Press, 2001.

Beasley-Murray, George R. *John*. Word Biblical Commentary. Dallas: Word, 1999.

Brandon, Stephen, Isaac Maupin, and Mark Goodman. "Bob Dylan: The Prophet of Social Change in the 1960s." *Media Watch* 8.3 (2017): 366–77.

Buber, Martin. *Eclipse of God*. Translated by Maurice Friedman. New York: Harper, 1954.

Cott, Jonathan, ed. *Bob Dylan: The Essential Interviews*. New York: Wenner Books, 2006.

Curnyn, Sean. "The Pope and the Pop Star." *First Things*. May 10, 2007. https://www.firstthings.com/web-exclusives/2007/05/the-pope-and-the-pop-star.

Dylan, Bob. "Blowin' in the Wind." Warner Bros., Inc. 1962. https://www.bobdylan.com/songs/blowin-wind/.

Dylan, Bob. "Blowin' in the Wind—From Newport Folk Festival 1963." YouTube, 4:04. November 6, 2013, https://www.youtube.com/watch?v=jleLj9Pj1Gw.

Hampton, Timothy. *Bob Dylan's Poetics: How the Songs Work*. New York: Zone Books, 2019.

Heylin, Clinton. *Trouble in Mind: Bob Dylan's Gospel Years—What Really Happened*. New York: Lesser Gods, 2017.

Lamp, Jeffrey S. "The Hal Lindsey Effect: Bob Dylan's Christian Eschatology." *Dylan Review* 3.1 (Summer 2021): 87–111. https://thedylanreview.org/2021/07/25/the-hal-lindsey-effect-bob-dylans-christian-eschatology/.

Leeden, Jenny. *Prophecy in the Christian Era*. St. Louis, MO: Peaceberry Press of Webster Groves, 1995.

Maré, Leonard P. "Ezekiel, Prophet of the Spirit: חור in the Book of Ezekiel." *Old Testament Essays* 31.3 (2018): 553–70.

Marshall, Scott M. *Bob Dylan: A Spiritual Life*. Washington, DC: WND Books, 2017.

Rapp, Allison. "25 Years Ago: Bob Dylan Plays for the Pope." *Ultimate Classic Rock*. September 27, 2022. https://ultimateclassicrock.com/bob-dylan-pope-performance/.

Rotolo, Suze. *A Freewheelin' Time: A Memoir of Greenwich Village in the Sixties*. New York: Crown Publishing Group, 2008.

Woliver, Robbie. *Bringing It All Back Home: Twenty-five Years of American Music at Folk City*. New York: Pantheon, 1986.

Chapter 9

Rivers Underneath

The Spirit in Underground Music

Jeremy Hunt

This chapter envisions music as a two-way path, back and forth to and from the Spirit, focusing specifically on how underground music can open up an embodied dialogue for individuals raised in communities with an impoverished pneumatology. Music gives us something to participate in—the Spirit as articulated by music. The Spirit is a two-way conduit to the infinite divine, not just from God to/upon us, but also from us to/upon God. In order to explore this, I want to put the wisdom of theologians in conversation with the embodied insights of underground music. We will look at art arising from bands that tend to exist on the fringes of mainstream music.

One of the ways that underground music operates is by providing space that can become a clearing ground for meditative and even transcendent experiences. I want to be careful here, as underground music is not the only form of music capable of doing this, but there are certain aspects that make it especially amenable to those experiences. Punk, hardcore, metal, noise rock, indie rap, and so on, are often free to operate outside of traditional art structures, whether in the way that the music is written and constructed, the places in which it's recorded, or the locations where it is performed. This is particularly true for both the earliest phases in which these genres were formed and the beginning days of the bands or artists themselves. They are committed to the wilderness of the underground, without the traditional support structures provided by major labels, touring guarantees, or massive fanbases. They're a modern-day echo of the prophets operating largely in obscurity, Jeremiah or John the Baptist living on the fringes, yelling like individuals possessed by an otherworldly calling, shouting at their respective cultures to open their eyes and ears to actually see and hear what's happening to and around them.[1]

There is a DIY component to these genres that encourages thinking and creating outside centers of power. Whether it's due to financial, time, or space restraints, bands often record quickly and cheaply, performing on generator stages, in coffee shops, or in warehouses—anywhere they can play for free or for a minimal fee, and where setup and teardown are fast and easy in the event that the show gets shut down by local authorities. Now, this is not to say that these bands stay in these (physical/mental) spaces forever. Depending on the genre, there are multiple examples of bands that started out small and scrappy and have grown to have fans all around the globe, making enough of a living off touring, merch sales, and the music itself to turn their art into a career.[2]

But this doesn't happen for every band, nor is it often the end goal. As Stephen Graham, a lecturer in music at Goldsmiths, University of London, proposes,

> The word "underground" connotes a sense of concealment, even of contraband, and this is at the heart of what still defines it as a musical philosophy. The music's general abrasiveness repels the mainstream; the distinct willingness of the general public to either turn away or ignore its existence in the first place is what gives underground its identity.[3]

Hence, my focus here is primarily on the music arising from the underground that doesn't necessarily have a tangible form of success attached to it. The type of music this chapter is interested in doesn't care about the mechanisms of the mainstream. The underground stalks several borders, existing in liminal spaces, one of which is an alternate view of economy and what is worth the investment of time needed to create. It is here that we land on the ideas that will enliven the rest of this exploration: *both the Spirit and these forms of music can be understood as a gift freely given and as a conduit between the messenger and an attentive audience.*

GROUNDING AND POSITIONALITY

As we journey into the sounds of the underground in the ensuing exploration, it will be helpful to kick things off with some background and definitions. My good friend and mentor, Kutter Callaway, often says (echoing Frederick Buechner in *The Alphabet of Grace*[4]), "All theology is biography." I will endeavor to widen my reflections ahead as much as possible, hopefully holding the door open as long as I can for as many as want to enter in. But in the interest of transparency, all of what follows is inevitably filtered through my life's experiences. I have been participating in underground music for decades, first as a fan, next as a writer, interviewing and reviewing bands, and most recently, as a musician creating albums and running a small DIY label. Additionally, due to the nature of the spaces where underground music has arisen, academic coverage can be sporadic. So by necessity, what follows will be a mix of traditional research conversation partners written intentionally with an on-the-ground tone of music writing.

With that said, let us begin here: I come to just about any discussion of the Spirit as an outsider. Or perhaps more accurately, an in-betweener. To glean wisdom from another friend and mentor, artist and speaker Mako Fujimura often talks about fellow artists being border-stalkers, or *"mearcstapas,"* a term taken from *Beowulf* to describe Grendel:

> *Mearcstapa* is not a comfortable role. Life on the borders of a group—and in the space between groups—is prone to dangers literal and figurative, with people both at "home" and among the "other" likely to misunderstand or mistrust the motivations, piety, and loyalty of the border-stalker. But *mearcstapa* can be a role of cultural leadership in a new mode, serving functions including empathy, memory, warning, guidance, mediation, and reconciliation. Those who journey to the borders of their group and beyond will encounter new vistas and knowledge that can enrich the group.[5]

I am a *mearcstapa* when dealing with the Spirit because I wasn't raised in a tradition that embraced the Spirit. While I grew up in the church and was part of various faith communities throughout my childhood and teen years, none of them spoke at length about the Spirit. The teachings during those years amounted to an acknowledgment of the Spirit at best or treating the Spirit as a non-functioning part of the Trinity at worst: an appendage whose time had already come and gone. I remember pastors saying that if the gifts of the Spirit had ever really existed, then they had been present for the early church and that was about it. The Spirit was helpful then but had no real bearing on the here and now.

For those who grew up in faith communities like mine, pastors and teachers often lead with the texts of Scripture, which are traditionally the closest thing we have to making the intangible tangible. Baptism and communion are two other key sacraments that have physical form. Scripture can be printed, repeated, memorized, and codified. God is given a multitude of descriptors and poetic language within Scripture to personalize God's identity to us. Likewise, Jesus the Son is literally incarnate, so while we don't have actual physical characteristics to rely on, the annals of church history are lined with icons, sculptures, paintings, films, and other representations of his presence. But what of the Spirit? The movement of the Spirit, the Spirit's working in our lives and in our hearts, is a largely invisible thing until that work takes on physical manifestation, like a change of one's behavior or habits. For those who grew up in a Christian tradition lacking a well-developed pneumatology, understanding and perceiving the Spirit can often feel like a fool's errand.

It can come across as an attempt to give definition and edges to something unformed and ephemeral to the extreme. Is it possible that music can open us up to that working and give us something to participate in? Can the shared experience of music bring about a communal existence that replicates what can happen in a community united by the Spirit?

SPIRIT/UNDERGROUND MUSIC AS A GIFT

While they might differ on other aspects in their approach to pneumatology, theologians Clark Pinnock and Eugene F. Rogers Jr. both express a view of the Spirit as the outpouring of God's love, presence, and essence of being. For Pinnock, the Spirit is the creative motivator and enactor of God's plans: "Spirit is essentially the serendipitous power of creativity, which flings out a world in ecstasy and simulates within it an echo of the inner divine relationships, ever seeking to move God's plans forward."[6] Furthermore, Pinnock envisions the Spirit as the host of a great celebration, setting the table for everyone to join: "I hear the Spirit saying: let the party begin, let the banquet be set, let us enter into the play of new creation! The Spirit choreographs the dance of God and also directs the steps of creatures entering God's dance."[7] Thus, it is through the Spirit that we are all able to enter in and commune with God.

The Spirit offers the presence of God and expressions of God's love in joyful, welcoming ways. The Spirit is both the invitation and the means by which the invitation is sent. Rogers' exploration harkens back to the Patristics but arrives at a similar place:

> The Son *bids* the Father to *grant* human beings the Spirit, as the Son had bid the Father grant him a body. The body is a gift to the Son; the Spirit is a gift to the body; but each gift is free, not mandated, following in a pattern that reveals character rather than automation. . . . Athanasius displays a moment of interval of gratitude by the Son for the gift of a human body; an interval of pleasure by the Father at the Son's stewardship of the gift; an interval of prayer by the Son that the Father give the gift of the Spirit even unto others in characteristic or musical response.[8]

Notice specifically how Rogers calls out the musicality inherent in the gift of the Spirit. The interplay between the Son, the Father, and the Spirit is compared to a "musical response." This is reminiscent of the back and forth, the call and response of many punk or hardcore shows, where the crowd is engaged in the music, the band is locked in, everyone is in it together, and there is almost no separation between the audience and the musicians. It's an experience I've partaken in and witnessed at some worship services I've been a part of, spaces where the musical response of the congregation is in sync with the band performing worship music. These are instances where we lose ourselves in our individuality and rediscover ourselves in a communal way.

I recall a specific one-time performance that I witnessed at Cornerstone, an influential Christian music festival that took place mostly in Illinois from 1984 to 2012. I was able to attend in the summer of 2003. A group of musicians from other bands (Ghoti Hook, Vroom, and others) came together on one of the smaller stages to perform as "Grayson." They played in matching outfits, wearing all white shirts and pants while wearing angel wings, and performed a set based on an Old Testament story. To this day, I feel a potent sense of gratitude for being able to partake in that performance as an audience member. I knew, even then, that what we were experiencing was something special. It was fleeting and moving, a gift that has since taken on epic proportions in my memory. As Albert Camus wisely stated, "any authentic creation is a gift to the future."[9] Bands like this are playing for cheap, perhaps making a little money off merch sales, but by and large, it is the love of the music that is driving them, and it is offered up to the listener as such.

SPIRIT/UNDERGROUND MUSIC AS A CONDUIT

These sorts of experiences at underground shows reveal a conduit, by way of the Spirit, between the infinite and the finite, God and God's creation. The Spirit moves and surges between us and God. This is also where underground music can open us up to be receptive to that movement of the Spirit. We *are* the music and the music *is* us. It would be a step too far and too much of a sweeping statement to say that music is *always* tuned to the same station as the Spirit, but perhaps it's in the same frequency range. When all things are aligned, the transmitter and receiver are in tune in transcendent ways. As Pinnock puts it, "Spirit opens God up to what is nondivine, as the divine ecstasy directed toward the creature."[10]

This is one of the crucial aspects of underground music that often gets lost in other arenas (literally and figuratively). The space between a band and the audience (transmitter and receivers) at an underground show is often permeable. Audience members jump on and off the stage, and vocalists often share mics with the audience for their chants and shoutings at crucial moments in the songs—sometimes the stage itself is barely a stage. In some venues, it's simply a slightly heightened portion of the floor, a 4- or 5-inch step up from the surrounding areas. This contrasts drastically with the multi-million-dollar productions often experienced at arena rock or pop concerts.

All that tech and stagecraft serve to keep the audience at an arm's-length from the music and performance. The production is a simulacrum. The band is at a distance, removed. The sweat and energy off the musicians' bodies are not being directly transmitted to the audience. There is a certain proximity granted, often gated by crowd barriers and security guards, without the direct connection offered by underground shows, and at prices that make tickets inaccessible for anyone who doesn't have large amounts of discretionary income at their disposal. It is a musical experience presented through the lens of an economy of scarcity. It's a stark contrast to Rogers' assessment of how the market of the Spirit works, saying,

> It is an economy of excess and an ethic of always. This is why the Holy Spirit is not a finite thing but a person: because the language of ending and enoughness is one of competitive economy, whereas the Trinity and, by grace, the creation bound for it are an everlasting community.[11]

Once again, the importance of the gift of the Spirit and the gift of underground music surfaces. It calls to mind monastic traditions wherein the participant gives up something traditionally clung to in basic human existence in order to gain a deeper relationship with the divine. In the case of certain underground bands, the forfeiture of the pursuit of success opens up the opportunity to connect with audiences on a deeper level. The D.C. punk band Fugazi had a legendary reputation for their commitment to keeping shows affordable ($5–$15 per ticket) and not even making merch items. As Michael Iafrate explains,

> They have have continually turned down major label offers and, unlike most bands, Fugazi does not make and sell band merchandise such a T-shirts, nor do they sell their recordings at shows, in part to emphasize that the shared experience of music is not about buying and selling but the experience itself.[12]

More recently, mewithoutYou gained a reputation for a commitment to creative and artistic freedom through financial austerity. They toured in a van that had been converted to run on fryer oil gleaned from restaurants and fed themselves by dumpster diving for discarded, uneaten food, all while holding potlucks for their fans before their shows.[13] They were modern monks and committed to ascetic practices within the band's existence that allowed them to give continuously to their audiences while on tour.

According to Rogers, the Spirit enables the occasion for us to spend time with God: "The Holy Spirit allows God to take time for human beings. Or if 'allows' sounds too strong, the Holy Spirit is the divine person *in whom* God takes time for human beings."[14] The conduit of the Spirit flows in both directions. It is in the day of Pentecost, descending upon humanity, and again present as a translator of the saints' prayers, sighing and groaning in intercession for us to God. But the Spirit is also present in the ordinariness of human expressions, the stuff of quotidian life. The Spirit grants permission to us for our activities of joy, passion, and creativity to be pleasurable and worthwhile pursuits in and of themselves. This too is a conduit back to God, a mapping of creation's worth back to the Creator:

> The "necessity" of the Spirit is 'only' so that God should not be without beauty, without celebration, creation, and (grace upon grace) even human beings. The Spirit has the non-necessity of things that take and delight in time, like music and liturgy and sex.[15]

There is an overflow, an abundance to the nature of the Spirit that is reflected in the best of these underground bands, the Fugazis and the mewithoutYous of these scenes. And perhaps most ironic of all, by foregoing the traditional routes of musical success, their commitment to their artistic paths, existing as conduits for the music being transmitted through them, can lead to a fervent level of love from their audiences.

RIVERS UNDERNEATH: THE ARTISTRY OF STAVESACRE

Up until now, I've kept this exploration somewhat in the realm of the theoretical. I've used a few concrete examples from bands and communities that I know, speaking out of years of attending shows, supporting artists directly through buying music and merch, and hearing the stories told on message boards and via social media of friends who've done the same. But to give these ideas a specific skin, I'd like to focus on a band who exemplifies much of what I've been attempting to outline up to this point. This band wrote the song "Rivers Underneath," which provided the inspiration for this chapter's title and many of its themes.

Founded in Southern California, Stavesacre is a heavy rock band with alternative, metal, and hardcore influences that has been in existence in a couple of different iterations since 1995 (including a hiatus during the mid-2000s). In that time, they've earned a fervent following both in the States and abroad, releasing a total of six albums: two studio EPs, a split with Denison Marrs, a live EP, and a compilation album. They spent most of their career on Tooth & Nail Records, a Seattle-based label focusing on underground Christian and Christian-adjacent punk, hardcore, and alternative bands.

Most recently, they crowdfunded their latest record, *MCMXCV*, in 2017. Ironically, even this route blew up in their faces, as the crowdfunding platform they used went belly up soon after their campaign ended. I experienced the roller coaster in real-time as a supporter of the band, and it was fairly heartbreaking to read the updates as they came in, as they faced multiple setbacks getting the album finished and fulfilling the promises of the campaign without the support of the platform itself. It probably didn't feel like much of a gift while in the midst of the trenches, but the finished album stands alongside their classics and, if this ends up being their final record, it will be a passionate close to a discography packed with moving and introspective music.

One of the recurring themes of Stavesacre interviews over the years is a reticence to preach from the stage, but rather to let their tunes do the talking: "All these Christian kids want you to preach at your concerts. It's killing our band."[16] They continued,

> The whole assumption that a Christian band is supposed to be a ministry, I don't know where that came from. To say that "a Christian band should use every opportunity they have to preach the gospel and try to get people saved. . . ." Okay, that sounds perfectly cool. Only problem is that it's never that easy.[17]

While lead singer Mark Salomon doesn't refer to the band's music specifically as a conduit to the divine, it would certainly seem that he views it as something that helps to break down walls and create connections with their listeners. In his book *Simplicity*, he unpacks this more fully with a story about a performance at a church where the Spirit was moving, only to be interrupted by an impatient pastor who insisted on injecting himself into the moment. At this point in their career, Stavesacre's shows often reached a meditative space during the performance of their song, "Gold and Silver." In contrast to the majority of their song catalogue, it starts out in more subdued, contemplative cadence. Salomon's vocals are quieter as he reflects on loss, building to a crescendo in the chorus where he sings about taking shelter "under wings of gold and silver."[18] In this particular instance, he recounts that both the band and the crowd could feel themselves entering into that shared space, even commenting that it felt like prayer was emanating from the room. This next section is worth quoting in full:

> Just as we were about to go into "You Know . . .," the pastor from the church jumped on stage and took the mic. Music stops. Awkward is a word that comes to mind. He then launched into a whole monologue about how he was the pastor of that church and that it was his responsibility to make sure that the Gospel, "goes out from this stage!" Everything else that he said after that is a blur. All I could think at that moment was *Why? Why are you doing this, and this way?* The mood in the room switched from personal to one of total confusion.
>
> If that pastor had been paying attention at all to what was going on in the room, he would have seen that everything was *exactly* how it need to be. "Not broken, do not fix." He could have waited until after the show, maybe gotten to know some of the local kids, maybe show a little down to earth love, or just been available to whomever the Holy Spirit was have been leading.[19]

Unfortunately for Stavesacre, this experience is an excellent summation (positive and negative) of what I'm chasing after here. Their music, presented as a gift, being used as a conduit transmitted from the band to the audience, opening space up for the recognized presence of the Spirit, only to be brought crashing down by someone who thinks they know better or is afraid of a boundary-less space that can't be neatly defined.[20]

SPIRIT/UNDERGROUND MUSIC AS INVITATION INTO THE UNKNOWN

Which brings me to the conclusion of this exploration: Spirit and underground music as centers of the divine unknown. Stated plainly, much of what we think we know about God hinges on tradition, writings handed down through the centuries, and the witness of the Church universal. But at the end of the day, it's all faith. We choose to follow and believe through faith. And I believe that both the Spirit and underground music overlap in their work to provide us with experiences that deepen and broaden our understanding of God.

It's one thing to be presented with a gift via a conduit to the divine, it's another thing entirely to have the openness to receive that which is given, especially when it comes in ways that are not expected. Whether it's the announcement of Jesus' birth to the lowliest of society's members first or the two travelers on the road to Emmaus not recognizing the resurrected Savior (and other stories in between those two bookends), Christians should be accustomed to encountering the presence of God in unlooked-for places. By stretching our ears and hearts to receive new and unexpected sounds, underground music is an excellent companion to the Spirit. Expanding our patience to listen, widening our hearts to love more art, broadening our minds to appreciate other forms of creativity . . . this all maps wonderfully to the work of the Spirit in helping us to more deeply love our neighbors as ourselves.

The unknown, whether it's within our own hearts or as exemplified by the lives of our fellow human beings, can be a great source of fear, the divine even more so. But the Spirit/underground music can provide us with greater avenues for dialogue, between one another and between us and God.[21] Passages like Exodus 20, Deuteronomy 4, and 1 Kings 19 include mentions of specific sounds that act as a sort of sonic clearing, calling the listener's attention to God, causing the listener to make room: thunder, a trumpet, a fire, a great wind, an earthquake, rocks breaking, mountains splitting, and more fire.[22] These noises are conduits into God's presence. The connection to the Spirit is made explicit in the New Testament, as Pentecost is recounted with aural and spiritual descriptors:

> When the day of Pentecost had come, they were all together in one place. And suddenly from heaven there came a sound like the rush of a violent wind, and it filled the entire house where they were sitting. Divided tongues, as of fire, appeared among them, and a tongue rested on each of them. All of them were filled with the Holy Spirit and began to speak in other languages, as the Spirit gave them ability. (Acts 2:1-4)

Elsewhere, the Spirit is depicted giving our prayers utterances that are auditory in nature, but beyond language itself:

> Likewise the Spirit helps us in our weakness; for we do not know how to pray as we ought, but that very Spirit intercedes with sighs too deep for words. And God, who searches the heart, knows what is the mind of the Spirit, because the Spirit intercedes for the saints according to the will of God. (Rom. 8:26-27)

The Spirit can meet us in the form of underground music, which in turn can be a hub of learning those new languages, an extension of those first tongues of fire that descended, allowing for greater fluency in communication across the planes of existence. May we dive in deeper still, unafraid of what the divine has to say and unafraid to talk back.

NOTES

1. "When you can assume that your audience holds the same beliefs you do, you can relax a little and use more normal means of talking to it; when you have to assume that it does not, then you have to make your vision apparent by shock—to the hard of hearing you shout, and for the almost-blind you draw large and startling figures" (Flannery O'Connor, *Mystery and Manners: Occasional Prose* [New York: The Noonday Press, 1969], 34).

2. Bands like Cave In, Every Time I Die, Melvins, Mastodon, Thrice, and Thursday exemplify the sort of home-grown success and acclaim that I'm getting at here.

3. Stephen Graham, "Where is the Underground?" (2010), https://journalofmusic.com/focus/where-underground (accessed 1/3/24).

> 4. At its heart, theology, like most fiction, is essentially autobiography. Aquinas, Calvin, Barth, Tillich, working out their systems in their own ways and in their own language, are all telling us the stories of their lives, and if you press them far enough, even at their most cerebral and forbidding, you find an experience of flesh and blood, a human face smiling or frowning or weeping or covering its eyes before something that happened once. (Frederick Buechner, The Alphabet of Grace [San Francisco: HarperCollins, 1970], 3)

5. Makoto Fujimura, *Culture Care: Reconnecting with Beauty for Our Common Life* (Downers Grove: IVP, 2017), 59.

6. Clark Pinnock, *Flame of Love: A Theology of the Holy Spirit* (Downers Grove: IVP Academic, 1996), 21.

7. Pinnock, *Flame of Love*, 37.

8. Eugene F. Rogers Jr., *After the Spirit* (Grand Rapids: Eerdmans, 2005), 32.

9. Albert Camus, *The Myth of Sisyphus: The Artist and His Time* (New York: Vintage Books, 1955), 212.

10. Pinnock, *Flame of Love*, 38.

11. Rogers, *After the Spirit*, 183.

12. Michael J. Iafrate, "More Than Music: Notes on 'Staying Punk' in the Church and in Theology," in *Secular Music and Sacred Theology*, ed. Tom Beaudoin (Collegeville: Liturgical Press, 2013), 44.

13. Relevant, "mewithoutYou Is Over. mewithoutYou Will Live Forever," (2022), https://relevantmagazine.com/culture/music/mewithoutyou-is-over-mewithoutyou-will-live-forever/. (accessed 2/4/24).

14. Rogers, *After the Spirit*, 182.

15. Rogers, *After the Spirit*, 182.

16. Mike Boehm, "Twists of Faith: Christian Punk Bands Struggle to Define Their Evangelical Roles," (1998), https://www.latimes.com/archives/la-xpm-1998-jun-10-ca-58280-story.html. (accessed 1/9/24).

17. Andrew Privett, "Stavesacre: Hardcore Rockers With a Sensitive Side," (1997), https://www.crossrhythms.co.uk/articles/music/Stavesacre_Hardcore_rockers_with_a_sensitive_side/33620/p1/ (accessed 1/9/24).

18. "Gold and Silver," track 6 on Stavesacre, Speakeasy, Tooth & Nail Records TND1140, 1999.

19. Mark Salomon, *Simplicity* (Huntington Beach: Skeleton Key Publishing, 2003), 219–220.

20. We tend to be biased in the direction of reason as the way to know reality, even in the postmodern situation. But music also speaks to us of the richness and depths of reality. Think of the unity, the harmony, the patterns, the delicacy, the surprises, the delight in music . . . It should not surprise us that music thrills us so much, because it draws us to the celestial sounds of the Spirit within us. (Clark Pinnock, *Flame of Love: A Theology of the Holy Spirit* [Downers Grove: IVP Academic, 1996)], 46)

21. There has long been a sense that music, that most pervasive of human creative acts, somehow connects humanity to the divine, however that term is understood. It does not mean, nor does it have to mean, that music is sacred in a traditionally religious sense of that music is a medium for the exploration of particular religious notions. It's much broader than that. To say that music connects humanity to the divine suggests that, whatever else happens in music, something about it creates an inward space for a kind of openness to something other, something more, something beyond the material. Put differently, music guides listeners as they cross boundaries. (Kutter Callaway and Barry Taylor, *The Aesthetics of Atheism: Theology and Imagination in Contemporary Culture* [Minneapolis: Fortress Press, 2019], 147)

22. "When all the people witnessed the thunder and lightning, the sound of the trumpet, and the mountain smoking, they were afraid and trembled and stood at a

distance" (Exod. 20:18). "Then the Lord spoke to you out of the fire. You heard the sound of words but saw no form; there was only a voice" (Deut. 4:12).

> He said, "Go out and stand on the mountain before the Lord, for the Lord is about to pass by." Now there was a great wind, so strong that it was splitting mountains and breaking rocks in pieces before the Lord, but the Lord was not in the wind; and after the wind an earthquake, but the Lord was not in the earthquake; and after the earthquake a fire, but the Lord was not in the fire; and after the fire a sound of sheer silence. (1 Kg. 19:11-12)

All scripture references are NRSV unless otherwise stated.

BIBLIOGRAPHY

Boehm, Mike. "Twists of Faith: Christian Punk Bands Struggle to Define Their Evangelical Roles." (1998). https://www.latimes.com/archives/la-xpm-1998-jun-10-ca-58280-story.html. (Accessed 1/9/24).

Buechner, Frederick. *The Alphabet of Grace*. San Francisco: HarperCollins, 1970.

Callaway, Kutter and Barry Taylor. *The Aesthetics of Atheism: Theology and Imagination in Contemporary Culture*. Minneapolis: Fortress Press, 2019.

Camus, Albert. *The Myth of Sisyphus: The Artist and His Time*. New York: Vintage Books, 1955.

Fujimura, Makoto. *Culture Care: Reconnecting with Beauty for Our Common Life*. Downers Grove: IVP, 2017.

Graham, Stephen. "Where is the Underground?" Published August 1, 2010. https://journalofmusic.com/focus/where-underground. (Accessed 1/9/24).

Iafrate, Michael J. "More Than Music: Notes on 'Staying Punk' in the Church and in Theology." In *Secular Music and Sacred Theology*, edited by Tom Beaudoin (pp. 35–58). Collegeville: Liturgical Press, 2013.

O'Connor, Flannery. *Mystery and Manners: Occasional Prose*. New York: The Noonday Press, 1969.

Pinnock, Clark. *Flame of Love: A Theology of the Holy Spirit*. Downers Grove: IVP Academic, 1996.

Privett, Andrew. "Stavesacre: Hardcore rockers with a sensitive side." (1997). https://www.crossrhythms.co.uk/articles/music/Stavesacre_Hardcore_rockers_with_a_sensitive_side/33620/p1. (Accessed 1/9/24).

Relevant. "mewithoutYou Is Over. mewithoutYou Will Live Forever." *Relevant* (2022). https://relevantmagazine.com/culture/music/mewithoutyou-is-over-mewithoutyou-will-live-forever/. (Accessed 2/4/24).

Rogers Jr., Eugene F. *After the Spirit*. Grand Rapids: Eerdmans, 2005.

Salomon, Mark. *Simplicity*. Huntington Beach: Skeleton Key Publishing, 2003.

Stavesacre. "Gold and Silver." Track 6 on *Speakeasy*. Tooth & Nail Records, 1999.

Part III

MUSIC IN CHRISTIAN WORSHIP AND WITNESS

Chapter 10

"There Is a Cloud"

The Holy Spirit in Contemporary Worship Songs

Shannan K. Baker

Contemporary worship music has often been described as "Jesus music" made by the "Jesus people." The primary reason for this label is that most songs focus on Jesus and are directed to Him. Many scholars have identified this emphasis on the second Person of the Trinity.[1] It is even reflected in the title of one of the first books on the history of contemporary worship, *Lovin' on Jesus*.[2] The starting point for many of these scholars is a broad search for all three Persons of the Trinity within the songs. Their findings are often similar, whether conducted in the 2000s or recent years: the Father and the Spirit are rarely mentioned. Lester Ruth proposes that the emphasis on Jesus could be because "the worshiper can personalize Jesus Christ and think of him physically in a way that is more difficult to do for God the Father and the Holy Spirit."[3] Nelson Cowan specifically explains that "Pentecostal theologies—largely, though not exclusively, subsets of evangelical theologies—focus on the presence of Jesus Christ as the central theme of worship and proclamation."[4] Since many contemporary worship songs emerge from Pentecostal or evangelical spaces, it follows that Jesus would be a primary focus.

While Jesus is the most referenced, scholars of contemporary worship have identified the sacramentality of music.[5] "A theology of music's sacramentality implies that God is literally present when worshipers gather and sing God's praises."[6] With a strong emphasis on God's presence through singing contemporary worship music, the Spirit may be referenced more often than one might initially expect. This chapter identifies and focuses on the references to the Spirit in a select corpus of popular contemporary worship songs to discern what type of pneumatology could be created from those songs alone.

The contemporary worship songs that are most studied are compiled from the Christian Copyright Licensing International (CCLI) Top 100 lists.[7] These lists are created based on church reporting and are often accepted as a reflection of what the Church is singing. However, scholars have questioned the representation of these lists and whether they are a trustworthy primary source for contemporary worship song scholarship.[8] Other scholars have focused their song research on one artist, such as Hillsong.[9] The artist-focused approach is helpful but leaves the findings relatively limited since most churches will sing songs from multiple sources.

The goal of this chapter is to create a pneumatology of contemporary worship songs. Most laypeople create their theology based on Sunday mornings through the sermon and the songs that are sung. With the strong influence of songs, this chapter examines what sort of pneumatology a person would gain from contemporary worship songs. While a full pneumatology is unlikely to be formed from a corpus of songs, the question remains: what would someone know about the Spirit if they listened only to contemporary worship music? The reception of contemporary worship songs has extended beyond the church, and these songs inundate the ears of listeners even beyond a Sunday morning. In these instances, people gravitate toward specific artists that they will follow.

This chapter studies the full song catalog of the four most prominent worship artists in the 2010s decade: Bethel Music, Elevation Worship, Hillsong Worship, and Passion. Worship Leader Research identified these artists as the primary contributors, the "Big 4," of a cross-referenced 2010s song collection from both the CCLI and PraiseCharts top song lists. In a survey, 69.23 percent of worship leaders indicated they find new songs for their congregation by "following specific artists."[10] Many worship leaders will listen to the complete albums released by worship bands they have previously discovered and use their songs in church. While the most-used songs will appear on the top lists among those by other artists, lesser-known songs from their catalogs are used in church and are listened to by fans of their music. While the Big 4 do not represent the whole of contemporary worship, they operate as some of the most prominent voices in the conversation. By moving beyond their top songs, this chapter seeks to understand to what extent a pneumatology can be developed by listeners of the whole albums of these four popular worship artists instead of a select few songs in isolation from the rest of the artist's collection.

Further still, these worship leaders are not specific to one denomination; contemporary worship songs are used across denominations, even though the most used songs are emerging from specific worship bands housed within distinct churches. While the Big 4's songs originate from a Pentecostal/Charismatic or Evangelical context, the songs are used in Catholic, Reformed,

Wesleyan, and among other denominations.[11] This chapter focuses more on the created pneumatology of the listener than the pneumatological and theological context of the artist and their associated church.

The primary source for this study is the song catalog of the "Big 4" from the 2010s decade. Bethel Music released 129 songs across eleven albums. Elevation Worship released 117 songs across nine albums. Hillsong Worship also had nine albums with a total of 113 songs. Passion released an album each year, aligning with their annual conference, for a total of 140 songs across eleven albums. The cumulative total from these four artists is 499 songs. These songs will be mined for various references to the Spirit.

THE FRAMEWORK FOR CREATING A PNEUMATOLOGY

Before creating our contemporary worship song pneumatology, the key search terms will be defined using Trinitarian theology to establish what is specifically attributed to the Spirit. Additionally, Clark Pinnock's pneumatology, which also starts with the Spirit and the Trinity, provides further depth regarding how the Spirit is understood and, therefore, what should be identified as a Spirit reference in the lyrics.

The first search terms are "Spirit" and "Holy Spirit/Ghost." An additional term that will be searched is "presence." Pinnock distinguishes the Spirit this way: "If Father points to the ultimate reality and Son supplies the clue to the divine mystery, Spirit epitomizes the nearness of the power and presence of God."[12] In Trinitarian theology, the concept of God being three-in-one and one-in-three are simultaneous. With this mutual indwelling of the Persons as one Being, Torrance further explains how the other Persons are still present while the Spirit realizes and actualizes God's presence to us:

> It is this unity of Activity, and unity of Being, and the unity of the Trinity, which force themselves upon our faith and understanding when we know God in the Spirit, and know the Spirit himself as the divine Person who in his oneness with the Father and the Son realizes and actualises among us the presence and power of God's eternal Being.[13]

While all three Persons are present, the presence of God is attributed to the Person of the Holy Spirit. For this reason, explicit references to "presence" will be searched, as Holy Spirit mentions.

In addition to God's presence, specific references to the Spirit's indwelling will also be assessed. These mentions will be found through phrases related to God being "in me" or the Spirit "burning inside." Pinnock states, "Spirit indwelling is a mark of a Christian."[14] Therefore, the indwelling of the Holy Spirit will be a theme searched for in the lyrics.

God's presence and the Spirit are connected to fire throughout the Bible. At Pentecost in Acts 2, the Holy Spirit descends on the disciples as tongues of fire. Since fire can also be used as a metaphor for other things, such as trials, each instance will be evaluated individually. Pinnock explains how other elements are connected to the Spirit in the Bible: "The fundamental idea of Spirit in Hebrew and Greek is breath, air, wind, storm—the intensity depending on the context. It may be a gentle breath, a gale-force wind, a cooling breeze."[15] Therefore, other elements will be searched for and evaluated based on their connection to the Spirit. Related to breath is the concept of the Spirit as the giver of life. The Nicene Creed states, "We believe in the Holy Spirit, the Lord, the giver of life."[16] Any references to receiving life or breath will be attributed to the Holy Spirit.

Pinnock states that "The Spirit is God's face turned toward us and God's presence abiding with us, the agency by which God reaches out and draws near, the power that creates and heals."[17] The Spirit is not passive but active. The Spirit acts in other ways in addition to giving life. References to any actions of the Spirit will also be included.

THE BIG 4'S CONTRIBUTIONS

Each artist case study provides a brief background of the artist and then details the frequency with which the Spirit is referenced in their 2010s song catalog. The explicit references to the Spirit, Holy Spirit, and presence are presented, followed by references to the indwelling of the Spirit and the various means by which the Spirit comes and is invited. Each case study ends with a detailed list of the actions of the Holy Spirit, which adds to our contemporary worship song pneumatology. Since the Spirit is active, each case study will conclude with each artist's inclusion of the Spirit's actions.

Bethel Music

Bethel Music is the music artist associated with Bethel Church. Bethel Church is a charismatic church formerly associated with the Assemblies of God (AoG) denomination. Bill Johnson is the current pastor and started the School for Supernatural Ministry under his leadership.[18] Bethel Music released their first album in 2010. Bethel Music's catalog for the 2010s consists of 129 written songs (excluding spontaneous tracks). While spontaneous singing is a significant element of Bethel's worship practices, the lyrics are not pre-written with the song and are also excluded from the song's resources for use in local churches. The focus of this chapter is the content of the songs whose lyrics can be replicated within church practices. Only twenty-nine songs reference the Spirit, with the greatest percentage of Spirit-reference songs on *For the Sake of the World* (2012).

Bethel Music directly references the Spirit in six of the twenty-nine songs. Two of those songs specifically reference the "Holy Spirit" ("Who You Are" and "Prepare the Way"). Three references are simply to the "Spirit." Two songs expand and refer to the Spirit as the "Spirit of God" ("Prepare the Way") or "Spirit of the Living God" ("Fall Afresh"). Bethel's primary way of referencing the Spirit is through "presence" language. Ten songs directly reference the presence of God. All ten references directly address God using the phrase "Your presence."

Closely related to God's presence is the indwelling of the Holy Spirit, which is God's immediate presence in the believer. Bethel implicitly references the Holy Spirit's indwelling in three songs through fire imagery. In "Heaven Come," it states the reality, "There's a stirring in my soul / And a fire here within" ("Heaven Come"). The other two songs reference it by asking the Holy Spirit to dwell within: "burn like a fire in me" ("For the Sake of the World") and "burn within my soul and mind" ("Come Awaken Love"). These references reflect the common practice of describing the indwelling of the Holy Spirit as a fire that burns inside the believer.

Bethel Music's songs have a wide variety of language to invite the Holy Spirit's presence. Two elemental images used are fire and wind. One fire example is "Your whisper makes Your fire fall down" ("There's No Other Name"), and another is in "Prepare the Way," stating, "Fire fall / wind come blow" ("Prepare the Way"). The second example moves into the other elemental image, wind. The Spirit is asked to "come and blow on through" ("Spirit Move"). In "Revival's in the Air," the chorus starts with the phrase "let the wind blow." Beyond these images, the Spirit is directly asked to fall, come, fill, and move. All these requests involve inviting the Spirit into the space. These phrases also reflect the ancient church prayer "Spirit Come."

The Spirit is also described as acting beyond merely appearing. Bethel's songs exclusively mention the Holy Spirit's activity of giving life. The lyrics often describe this life-giving act as breathing. Some examples are "He's breathing life into my soul" ("Hope's Anthem"), "As You breathe / We live and have our being" ("You Don't Miss a Thing"), and "You breathe the breath of life into our lungs" ("Revival's in the Air"). This life-giving breath is even detailed with resurrecting the dead, "Things that we thought were dead / Are breathing in life again" ("Jesus We Love You"). The Holy Spirit's main action beyond moving is "bringing life" ("This is What You Do").

Hillsong Worship

Hillsong Worship is one of the music ministries of Hillsong Church in Australia. Hillsong was formerly a member of the Pentecostal Australian Christian Churches denomination.[19] Hillsong Church has multiple worship artists, including Hillsong United and Hillsong Young & Free. While each of Hillsong's artists made an appearance in the top twenty-five during the 2010s, Worship Leader Research specifically identified Hillsong Worship as one of the Big 4 due to the higher number of songs attributed to that specific artist. Hillsong Worship (formerly Hillsong Live) has been releasing albums since 1992.[20] Hillsong Worship's 2010s catalog consists of 113 songs. Thirty-four of those songs reference the Holy Spirit. The highest percentage of songs was on the last album of the decade, *Awake* (2019), with 54.55 percent.

Hillsong references the Spirit directly more than Bethel. Four songs simply reference the "Spirit," and two of those instances directly relate to a phrase that references the Trinity. In "King of Kings," the chorus states, "Praise the Father, Praise the Son, Praise the Spirit Three in One." On the same album, "I Will Praise You" uses the phrase "Blessed Father Son and Spirit." These references, which direct attention toward all three Persons of the Trinity, are rare. One song uses the extended name "Spirit of the Lord" ("Where the Spirit of the Lord Is"). It is more common for the Spirit to be directly addressed to God as "Your Spirit" in eight songs. "Holy Spirit" or "Holy Ghost" is used in seven occurrences. All references to the Holy Ghost are from the final album of that decade, *Awake* (2019). Lastly, all twelve references to God's presence use the phrase "Your presence," and a few are near named Spirit references.

Hillsong Worship's lyrics also reference the indwelling of the Holy Spirit. One explicit reference is in "Here With You," which states, "Always with You through Your Spirit in me ev'rything's changed" ("Here With You"). The other three songs return to the fire imagery, similar to Bethel's references. The Holy Spirit is described as a friend who is "breathing holy fire within" ("Behold [Then Sings My Soul]"). In one song, the Holy Spirit is explicitly described as a fire: "Holy Spirit fire burn within my soul" ("Open Heaven [River Wild]"). Another describes how God sets people's hearts on fire: "You set our hearts on fire it burns within me" ("Lift You Higher"). All these references describe the reality of the Holy Spirit dwelling within the believer.

While Bethel was more expressive in their invitation and request of the Holy Spirit, Hillsong's songs only reference the Spirit's coming in three songs. One song asks, "Lord let Your presence fall" ("Where the Spirit of the Lord Is"). Another uses elemental imagery; however, instead of fire, it references water: "Holy Spirit rain falling like a flood" ("Open Heaven [River Wild]"). Lastly, the final song indicates the abundance of the Holy Spirit: "Your Spirit overflows." This lyric is surrounded by more water imagery: "You drench my weary soul" and "here I soak in Your love" ("Never Forsaken"). While these references do not explicitly invite the Spirit, they do relate to an abundance of the Spirit's presence.

The Holy Spirit's primary action of giving life is mentioned in six Hillsong songs. Three directly reference life, and three focus on breath. "Thank You Jesus" simply states, "You've given me life" ("Thank You Jesus"). Giving life is described as resurrecting in "All Things New," "bringing life where it has not been." The third song alludes to the Holy Spirit's act of convicting the believer of their sin by stating, "For You take the sinner's heart and bring new life" ("Open My Eyes"). The other life-giving songs focus on breath. All three references are requests: "Oh Holy Spirit breathe in me like Kingdom come" ("Behold [Then Sings My Soul]"), "breathe in us we pray" ("Let There Be Light"), and "fill my lungs with the wind of Your Sprit" ("Every Breath"). This last reference even includes the common reference to the Spirit as wind.

Beyond giving life, Hillsong expands to include four additional acts of the Spirit in our pneumatology. First, the Spirit is acting in the life of the believer. Each of the references directly mentions the Spirit working. The Spirit is described as speaking through the Word: "I will wait in Your word oh Lord / There Your Spirit speaks" ("Depths"). Another song extends this idea to include that the Spirit leads us to worship in response to the Word: "Your Spirit leads my heart to worship / As Your Word reveals the light of Jesus" ("Your Word"). Lastly, the Spirit is described as a sustainer: "Your Spirit is enough to keep me walking" ("In Control") and a place of trust: "Tame my fears as I lean on Your Spirit / Trusting all of my heart unto You" ("Every Breath"). God's presence through the Spirit is described as making one whole: "In Your presence I'm made whole" ("Forever Reign").

The last two acts of the Spirit relate to awakening and miracles. Two songs reference the Spirit's activity in bringing awakening and igniting the church: "Holy Spirit we desire awakening" ("Awakening") and "Then the Spirit lit the flame" ("King of Kings"). The last activity that Hillsong adds to our pneumatology is the Spirit's role in miracles. When the Spirit of the Lord is present, "chains are broken eyes are open" ("Where the Spirit of the Lord Is"). Another song states, "Signs and wonders from above / When You poured out Your Spirit" ("Open Heaven [River Wild]"). The final miracle, Christ's birth, is mentioned in "This I Believe (The Creed)," which takes language from the Apostle's Creed: "Through Your Holy Spirit Conceiving Christ the Son" ("This I Believe [The Creed]").

Passion

Passion is the church band associated with Passion City Church in Atlanta, GA. Passion was founded in 1995 by Pastor Louie Giglio.[21] The people involved with this band and their annual college conference have included artists such as Chris Tomlin, Matt Redman, and Christy Nockels. While these artists have also had solo careers, Passion releases annual albums with songs used at the conference. These albums also often include songs from guest artists at the conference, such as Kari Jobe and Hillsong UNITED. While other artists may be featured on these albums, a fan of Passion will hear these songs when listening to the Passion albums. This means that while songs from outside artists, including Cory Asbury ("Reckless Love") and Sinach ("Way Maker"), are covered by Passion, they are received by the listener as a part of Passion. Since this chapter focuses on the reception of the songs rather than their origin, these covered songs are included in Passion's song catalog because they are included on Passion's released albums. In the 2010s, Passion released 104 songs. The Holy Spirit is referenced in twenty-nine songs. The album with the highest percentage of songs was *Whole Heart* (2018), with 45.45 percent.

Of the twenty-nine songs that mention the Spirit, seven are explicit references. Four songs refer to the Spirit, with two of those directly connecting that Spirit to God as "Your Spirit" ("The Stand") and "His Ghost" ("Ghost"). One song expands the phrase to "Spirit of the Lord" ("Where the Spirit of the Lord Is"). Similarly, three songs use the longer name for the Spirit, "Holy Spirit" ("Awakening," "Spirit Fall," "Remember"). As previously mentioned, the Spirit is considered the giver of life, so "Lord of Life" ("Behold the Lamb") was considered a reference to the Spirit. The Spirit is most frequently referenced as "presence." Nine songs mention God's presence directly as "Your presence" or, in one instance, as the "presence of heaven" ("There's Nothing Our God Can't Do").

Unlike other artists, Passion does not reference the indwelling of the Holy Spirit through requests. However, Passion does align with the other artists in using fire imagery for its references. Two examples of this are "This fire inside of me is burning for Your name" ("Not Ashamed") and "I cannot contain it / this fire inside," which accompanies the chorus lyrics "it's burning in my soul" ("Burning in My Soul"). The chorus gives more context for what is "burning in my soul" by using phrases such as "we're calling for revival / God let your fire fall again" ("Burning in My Soul"). Since fire imagery is often used concerning the indwelling of the Holy Spirit, the phrase "I am ablaze" ("Never Gonna Let Me Go") is also counted as a reference to having the fire of the Holy Spirit inside the believer. The final reference to this internal dwelling is in "Ghost." "Ghost" is a song that focuses on the Holy

Spirit. In verse 3, the lyrics explicitly state, "His Ghost is inside me / holy fire burning wildly / burning through the things that need to be erased" ("Ghost"). These lyrics expand on one of the roles of the Spirit, which is to convict the believer of their sin, "the things that need to be erased" ("Ghost").

While other artists expand their vocabulary about how the Holy Spirit comes, Passion remains true to the Acts 2 illustration of the Holy Spirit falling from above. Only one of these references avoids elemental imagery: "Spirit fall Spirit fall / Holy Spirit fall fall on me" ("Spirit Fall"). The other two use the biblical fire image: "God let Your fire fall down" ("Here for You") and "We're ready for Your fire to fall" ("Ghost"). One song combines the fire imagery with wind. The chorus starts with "whoa hear the sound from heaven / whoa a mighty rushing wind" and concludes with "whoa we're calling for revival / God let your fire fall again." While not explicitly referencing the Spirit, the chorus of this song uses wind and fire to describe what it is like when the Spirit comes. The final element that is used to describe the Spirit's descent is water: "You're falling now like heaven's rain" and later in the bridge, "let your living waters fall on your sons and daughters" ("Welcome the Healer"). Water imagery referring to the Spirit's coming is often rain since it falls from the sky.

The most common Holy Spirit action that Passion references is giving life. The name "Giver of life" ("You Alone Can Rescue," "Shout Hosanna") is used in two songs: "Lord of life" ("Behold the Lamb") in one song, and one song attributes giving life to God in the phrase "You give life" ("Great Are You Lord"). The chorus of "Great Are You Lord" extends the life concept into the chorus that begins with "It's your breath in our lungs" ("Great Are You Lord"). Passion uses many references to giving life through "breath." This breath is described as a past action, "Before I took a breath, You breathed Your life in me" ("Reckless Love"), a present action, "You breathe on me, You revive me" ("You Revive Me") and "Love breathing to awake my bones" ("Never Gonna Let Me Go"), and a future request, "Come and breathe Your breath on me" ("Spirit Fall") and "Let Your breath come from Heaven / fill our hearts with Your life" ("Here for You").

In addition to giving life, Passion references two additional Holy Spirit acts. The Holy Spirit is the initiator of awakening. In "Awakening," the lyrics state, "Holy Spirit we desire awakening," which implies that the Holy Spirit is the one who brings that. Similarly, "Spirit Fall" emphasizes the Spirit as the one who brings revival. Revival means that something that once existed to be revived. The lyrics repeat, "Like a mighty wind light the fire again" ("Spirit Fall"). This phrase uses two familiar images for the Spirit, wind and fire, and the chorus and title of the song both directly reference the Spirit. Lastly, Passion has two songs that reference the work of the Spirit in the believer. The first song describes the state of the believer as being "made whole" in God's presence (Forever Reign), which, as mentioned above, the Holy Spirit is how we experience God's presence. The second song references all God's actions when He is "here," implying God's presence through the Spirit. These actions include "healing" and "mending" hearts and "turning lives around" ("Way Maker"), which implies convicting believers of their sins and turning their lives toward God.

Elevation Worship

Elevation Worship is the worship band from Elevation Church, a multi-campus church based predominantly in North Carolina. Steven Furtick pastors Elevation Church, which was formerly associated with the SBC denomination.[22] Elevation Worship released 117 songs in the 2010s. Thirty-six of those songs reference the Spirit. Pastor Steven Furtick is heavily involved in songwriting for Elevation, with his name credited on every song for the church. With this pastoral oversight, it is not entirely surprising that Elevation Worship is the most explicit regarding the Spirit. For many pastors, their primary mode of communication is a sermon, so it follows that Furtick's involvement would translate into more explicit language than abstract. Of the thirty-six songs referencing the Spirit, 52.8 percent are direct references that include "Spirit."

Only three songs reference the Spirit without any further description, with phrases such as "for the honor of the Spirit" ("For the Honor") and "Sing the praises of the Spirit Son and Father" ("My Testimony"). All the other references give further information about the Spirit. Eleven songs use the phrases "Your Spirit," "His Spirit," or "Spirit of Jesus," attributing the Spirit specifically as the Spirit of the Son. "There is a Cloud" uses the phrase "Spirit of God," and "Here as in Heaven" uses a similar phrase, "Spirit of the Lord." The explicit Spirit references are rounded out with two songs that use "Holy Spirit" ("The King is Among Us" and "Here Again").

In addition to the direct references, fifteen of Elevation's songs mention "presence." Eight songs use the phrase "your presence." One song explicitly states whose presence it is with the words "presence of the Lord" ("Here in the Presence"). The last album in 2020 includes the final three addresses. "The Blessing" and "There is King" both refer to "His presence," and "No One Beside" states, "the presence of my God." Elevation Worship references the Spirit the most directly, both as Spirit and as presence.

Like the other artists, the indwelling of the Holy Spirit is referenced indirectly, often through the image of fire. Some songs elaborate more than others with phrases such as "We need Your revival Holy Spirit fire / Burning ever brighter in our souls" ("The King is Among Us") and "Spirit of Jesus living in us / fire rising in my soul" ("Yahweh"). A more implied reference is in the song "Then He Rose," which states, "all our hope in this same power living in us" ("Then He Rose"). "Sun Stand Still" also asks for the internal Holy Spirit fire: "God most high stir a fire in us."

The Holy Spirit is invited to appear in various ways. Some requests reflect the ancient church prayer, "Spirit Come" ("Fullness") or "Come Holy Spirit" ("Here Again"). Others are simple phrases used in other worship songs, such as "Spirit of God fall fresh on us" ("Here as in Heaven"). As mentioned, elemental imagery is typical when referencing the Holy Spirit's coming. These references can reflect a current reality such as "His fire is falling" ("The King is Among Us"), "a new wind is blowing right now" ("Never Lost"), or "We receive Your rain" ("There is a Cloud"). Another is asking God, "Pour out Your fire and flow through our lives" ("This City is Yours").

Elevation Worship's songs provide a mix of the expected acts of the Spirit, such as giving life, with a few new additions to our pneumatology. Five songs reference the Spirit giving new life, specifically being raised to life. "For the Lamb" states, "By His Spirit we are raised / To the fullness of new life" ("For the Lamb"), and "Here Again" references Ezekiel 37 while inviting the Holy Spirit with the lyrics, "Come Holy Spirit / dry bones awaken." ("Here Again"). Similarly, "Authority" references the Creation story of God breathing life into humans, "The breath that brought the dust to life" ("Authority"). "First and Only" simply states, "In your presence I am alive" ("First and Only"). Other songs merely reference rising in the power of the Spirit: "By Your Spirit I will rise" ("Resurrecting") and "Now we rise by His Spirit" ("Then He Rose").

Like Hillsong, the Spirit is further described as leading the believer, "I'll follow where Your Spirit leads" ("Available"). Two new actions are added to our pneumatology by Elevation Worship. First, the Spirit is described as affecting change. "Here as in Heaven" illustrates that the Spirit of the Lord changes the atmosphere when present, "The atmosphere is changing now / For the Spirit of the Lord is here" ("Here as in Heaven"). "You are on Our Side" extends the change to be something that occurs in us by the Holy Spirit, "You promised Your Spirit / Would change the world through us" ("You are on Our Side"). Lastly, Elevation Worship is the only artist of the Big 4 that mentions that the Holy Spirit directs attention to the Son: "Tongues of fire / testifying of the Son" ("Fullness").

A Contemporary Worship Pneumatology

Each artist's case study has provided something different to our contemporary worship pneumatology. Bethel Music provided the most language for referring to the presence of God, and Elevation Worship provided the most direct language when referring to the Spirit. Passion provided the most language related to the Holy Spirit as the giver of life, specifically through mentioning God's breath. Lastly, Hillsong Worship provided the most acts of the Spirit by expanding beyond those named by the other three artists.

As mentioned previously, the Spirit is active. The following are the cumulative acts of the Spirit from the Big 4. The Holy Spirit gives life, speaks, leads, sustains, makes one whole, is the source of awakening/revival, performs miracles, changes the world, and testifies of the Son. While the references to the Spirit are fewer than the Son, the songs from these four artists combine to create a received contemporary worship song pneumatology rich in language and theology beyond merely stating "Spirit" to check some Trinity box.

CONCLUSION: DOES THIS MEAN THAT PEOPLE HAVE A DEEP PNEUMATOLOGY?

This pneumatology is a starting place for understanding how the listeners of these songs are being formed theologically. The songs sung in church communicate theology and shape the worshiper's understanding of God. To comprehend how the believer will engage with this pneumatology, it is helpful to return to our Trinitarian theological lens where pneumatology is located. Trinitarian theologian Thomas Torrance provides nuance to our knowledge of God by using scientific levels of knowledge.

Collectively, these contemporary worship songs shape the listener's thoughts about the Spirit, developing a pneumatology that articulates who the Spirit is and what the Spirit does, while also shifting focus as the Spirit does by directing attention to the other Persons, the Son and the Father. The ground level of Christian knowledge is that of experience. Torrance describes this level for the believer as "the evangelical and doxological level," which is "the ground level of religious experience and worship in which we have to do with God's revealing and saving activity in the Gospel, and are committed to faith in Jesus Christ whom God in his love has given to the world as its Saviour so that whoever believes I him should not perish but have everlasting life."[23] This first level is where the Christian faith begins and leads to worship. The second level of understanding is where the Christian faith becomes more developed, including understanding God as Trinity and the three different Persons who are distinct in Person yet one in Being.[24] So, while the Christian faith begins with Christ as our way of knowing God, the other Persons of the Trinity become apparent as the believer continues to learn and grow. This is where certain activities are attributed to the Spirit, though the Son and Father are still present.

While a person could sing the songs by these artists and only walk away with a few references made explicitly to the "Spirit" or "Holy Spirit," a

Christian who has learned more about God as Trinity would be able to start identifying the aspects of these songs that refer to the Spirit even if the word "Spirit" is not used. Contemporary worship songs, while only having a few explicit references, provide a rich pneumatology that becomes more apparent as one learns more about the Spirit. Pneumatology informs our reception of the songs, and the songs provide us with new language when referring to the Spirit.

NOTES

1. Lester Ruth, "How Great Is Our God: The Trinity in Contemporary Christian Worship Music," in *The Message in the Music: Studying Contemporary Praise and Worship* (Nashville: Abingdon Press, 2007); Lester Ruth, "Some Similarities and Differences between Historic Evangelical Hymns and Contemporary Worship Songs," *Artistic Theologian* 3 (2015): 68–86; Tanya Riches, "The Evolving Theological Emphasis of Hillsong Worship (1996–2007)," *Australasian Pentecostal Studies* 13 (January 1, 2010): 87; Nelson Cowan, "'Heaven and Earth Collide': Hillsong Music's Evolving Theological Emphases," *Pneuma: The Journal of the Society for Pentecostal Studies* 39, no. 1/2 (March 2017): 78–104, https://doi.org/10.1163/15700747-03901001; Michael A. Tapper, *Canadian Pentecostals, the Trinity, and Contemporary Worship Music: The Things We Sing*, vol. 23, Global Pentecostal and Charismatic Studies (Leiden: Brill, 2017); Shannan Katherine Baker, "The Mystery, Music, and Markets of Contemporary Worship Songs: An Interdisciplinary Comparison of the CCLI Top 25 and Number-One Songs from 2010–2020" (Ph.D., United States—Texas, Baylor University, 2022), https://www.proquest.com/docview/2721647338/abstract/73E24ABB74CF4007PQ/1.

2. Swee-Hong Lim and Lester Ruth, *Lovin' on Jesus: A Concise History of Contemporary Worship* (Nashville: Abingdon Press, 2017).

3. Ruth, "Some Similarities and Differences between Historic Evangelical Hymns and Contemporary Worship Songs," 71.

4. Cowan, "Heaven and Earth Collide," 92.

5. Steven Félix-Jäger, *Renewal Worship: A Theology of Pentecostal Doxology*, Dynamics of Christian Worship (Downers Grove: IVP Academic, 2022); Emily Snider Andrews, "Exploring Evangelical Sacramentality: Modern Worship Music and the Possibility of Divine-Human Encounter" (Ph.D., United States—California, Fuller Theological Seminary, Center for Advanced Theological Study, 2019), http://search.proquest.com/docview/2382057897/abstract/4C60B2BB9F4B4D24PQ/1; Lester Ruth and Swee-Hong Lim, *A History of Contemporary Praise and Worship: Understanding the Ideas That Reshaped the Protestant Church* (Grand Rapids: Baker Academic, 2021).

6. Félix-Jäger, *Renewal Worship: A Theology of Pentecostal Doxology*, 95.

7. These lists were used in Ruth, "How Great Is Our God: The Trinity in Contemporary Christian Worship Music"; Ruth, "Some Similarities and Differences between

Historic Evangelical Hymns and Contemporary Worship Songs"; Tapper, *Canadian Pentecostals, the Trinity, and Contemporary Worship Music*; Baker, "The Mystery, Music, and Markets of Contemporary Worship Songs."

8. R Matthew Sigler, "Not Your Mother's Contemporary Worship: Exploring CCLI's 'top 25' Lists for Changes in Evangelical Contemporary Worship," *Worship* 87, no. 5 (September 2013): 447–49; Shannan Baker, "What Does the Church Sing?," *Sing! The Center For Congregational Song* (blog), October 9, 2023, https://congregationalsong.org/what-does-the-church-sing/; Adam Perez, Shannan Baker, Elias Dummer, Marc Jolicoeur, and Mike Tapper, "'Do It Again': Chart-Topping Worship Songs and the Churches Behind Them," *Liturgy* (forthcoming).

9. Riches, "The Evolving Theological Emphasis of Hillsong Worship (1996–2007)"; Cowan, "Heaven and Earth Collide."

10. Baker, "The Mystery, Music, and Markets of Contemporary Worship Songs," 263.

11. Sarah Kathleen Johnson and Anneli Loepp Thiessen, "Contemporary Worship Music as an Ecumenical Liturgical Movement," *Worship* 97 (July 2023): 207–8.

12. Clark H Pinnock, *Flame of Love: A Theology of the Holy Spirit* (InterVarsity Press, 2022), 10.

13. Thomas F. Torrance, *The Christian Doctrine of God, One Being Three Persons*, Second, Cornerstones (London: T&T Clark, 2016), 149.

14. Clark H Pinnock, *Flame of Love: A Theology of the Holy Spirit* (InterVarsity Press, 2022), 194.

15. Pinnock, *Flame of Love*, 16.

16. Robert Letham, *The Holy Trinity: In Scripture, History, Theology, and Worship*, Revised (Phillipsburg, NJ: P&R Publishing House, 2019), 184.

17. Pinnock, *Flame of Love*, 16.

18. Emily Snider Andrews, "Exploring Evangelical Sacramentality: Modern Worship Music and the Possibility of Divine-Human Encounter" (Ph.D., United States—California, Fuller Theological Seminary, Center for Advanced Theological Study, 2019), 91, http://search.proquest.com/docview/2382057897/abstract/4C60B2BB9F4B4D24PQ/1.

19. Tanya Riches, "The Evolving Theological Emphasis of Hillsong Worship (1996–2007)," *Australasian Pentecostal Studies* 13 (January 1, 2010): 88.

20. "Hillsong Church Fact Sheet," Hillsong, accessed December 16, 2023, https://hillsong.com/fact-sheet/.

21. "Story," Passion Music, accessed December 16, 2023, https://passionmusic.com/story/.

22. Bob Smietana, "Steven Furtick's Elevation Church Leaves the SBC," *Christianity Today*, July 3, 2023, https://www.christianitytoday.com/news/2023/july/elevation-church-steven-furtick-leave-southern-baptist-sbc-.html.

23. Thomas F. Torrance, *The Christian Doctrine of God, One Being Three Persons*, Second, Cornerstones (London: T&T Clark, 2016), 88.

24. Torrance, 92.

BIBLIOGRAPHY

Andrews, Emily Snider. "Exploring Evangelical Sacramentality: Modern Worship Music and the Possibility of Divine-Human Encounter." Ph.D., Fuller Theological Seminary, Center for Advanced Theological Study, 2019. http://search.proquest.com/docview/2382057897/abstract/4C60B2BB9F4B4D24PQ/1.

Baker, Shannan. "What Does the Church Sing?" *Sing! The Center For Congregational Song* (blog), October 9, 2023. https://congregationalsong.org/what-does-the-church-sing/.

Baker, Shannan Katherine. "The Mystery, Music, and Markets of Contemporary Worship Songs: An Interdisciplinary Comparison of the CCLI Top 25 and Number-One Songs from 2010–2020." Ph.D., Baylor University, 2022. https://www.proquest.com/docview/2721647338/abstract/73E24ABB74CF4007PQ/1.

Cowan, Nelson. "'Heaven and Earth Collide': Hillsong Music's Evolving Theological Emphases." *Pneuma: The Journal of the Society for Pentecostal Studies* 39, no. 1/2 (March 2017): 78–104. doi: 10.1163/15700747-03901001

Félix-Jäger, Steven. *Renewal Worship: A Theology of Pentecostal Doxology*. Dynamics of Christian Worship. Downers Grove: IVP Academic, 2022.

Hillsong. "Hillsong Church Fact Sheet." Accessed December 16, 2023. https://hillsong.com/fact-sheet/.

Johnson, Sarah Kathleen, and Anneli Loepp Thiessen. "Contemporary Worship Music as an Ecumenical Liturgical Movement." *Worship* 97 (July 2023).

Letham, Robert. *The Holy Trinity: In Scripture, History, Theology, and Worship*. Revised. Phillipsburg, NJ: P&R Publishing House, 2019.

Lim, Swee-Hong, and Lester Ruth. *Lovin' on Jesus: A Concise History of Contemporary Worship*. Nashville: Abingdon Press, 2017.

Passion Music. "Story." Accessed December 16, 2023. https://passionmusic.com/story/.

Pinnock, Clark H. *Flame of Love: A Theology of the Holy Spirit*. InterVarsity Press, 2022.

Riches, Tanya. "The Evolving Theological Emphasis of Hillsong Worship (1996–2007)." *Australasian Pentecostal Studies* 13 (January 1, 2010): 87.

Ruth, Lester. "How Great Is Our God: The Trinity in Contemporary Christian Worship Music." In *The Message in the Music: Studying Contemporary Praise and Worship*. Abingdon Press, 2007.

———. "Some Similarities and Differences between Historic Evangelical Hymns and Contemporary Worship Songs." *Artistic Theologian* 3 (2015): 68–86.

Ruth, Lester, and Swee-Hong Lim. *A History of Contemporary Praise and Worship: Understanding the Ideas That Reshaped the Protestant Church*. Grand Rapids: Baker Academic, 2021.

Sigler, R Matthew. "Not Your Mother's Contemporary Worship: Exploring CCLI's 'top 25' Lists for Changes in Evangelical Contemporary Worship." *Worship* 87, no. 5 (September 2013): 445–63.

Smietana, Bob. "Steven Furtick's Elevation Church Leaves the SBC." *Christianity Today*, July 3, 2023. https://www.christianitytoday.com/news/2023/july/elevation-church-steven-furtick-leave-southern-baptist-sbc-.html.

Tapper, Michael A. *Canadian Pentecostals, the Trinity, and Contemporary Worship Music: The Things We Sing*. Vol. 23. Global Pentecostal and Charismatic Studies. Leiden: Brill, 2017.

Torrance, Thomas F. *The Christian Doctrine of God, One Being Three Persons*. Second. Cornerstones. London: T&T Clark, 2016.

Chapter 11

When the Spirit Moves

Black Gospel Music as an Embodied Witness

Jennifer Thigpenn

From the time I was young, I have fond memories of hearing gospel music wafting through my home; gospel greats like Mahaila Jackson and modern artists like Kirk Franklin created the soundtrack of my life. I danced with fervor when Fred Hammond and Radical for Christ's "When the Spirit of the Lord" came through my speakers, I sang out with gusto every time Aretha Franklin's ten-minute rendition of "Amazing Grace" started, and I cried the first time I sat with Maverick City Music's "Breathe" after two years of a global pandemic and protests against injustice toward marginalized groups. For me, gospel music has not simply been a connection to my roots as a black American; it has been a lifeline to encounter the Holy Spirit in all the joys and sorrows of my life and my community.

From its inception in the spirituals of enslaved Africans to the present day, black music has consistently navigated the tension between suffering and hope. In *The Spirituals and the Blues*, theologian James Cone offers an interpretation of spirituals and the blues as black musical traditions and cultural expressions united by the experience of black people in the United States. Cone argues, "Black music must be *lived* before it can be understood."[1] In exploring the functional, social, political, and theological implications of black music that were birthed out of black experiences, Cone notes the tensions that black people have held over centuries and how musical expression has functioned as a means of defining identity and a clarion call toward action. He observes,

> Black music is unity music. It unites the joy and sorrow, the love and the hate, the hope and the despair of black people; and it moves the people toward the direction of liberation. It shapes and defines black existence and creates cultural structures for black expression. Black music is unifying because it confronts the

individual with the truth of black existence and affirms that black being is possible only in a communal context.²

Thus, the Spirituals and the Blues—perceived as opposites along the sacred-secular divide of history—and the gamut of black musical expression over the last two centuries has been shaped by the practice of community affirming black "somebodieness" in a society that has regularly tried to disparage and destroy black personhood. In the final chapter of *The Spiritual and the Blues*, Cone discusses how the blues were considered a worldly alternative to the religious themes found in the Spirituals. They were rejected outright by early twentieth-century black Christians because of their scandalous topics and explicit themes. He concludes, however, that pitting the spirituals and the blues against one another is an unhelpful dichotomy. He offers,

> Both the spirituals and the blues are the music of black people. They should not be pitted against each other, as if they are alien or radically different. One does not represent good and the other bad, one sacred and one secular. Both partake in the *same* black experience in the United States . . . Music has been and continues to be the most significant creative art expression of African-Americans. Blacks sing and play music (in their churches and at juke-joint parties) as a way of coping with life's contradictions and of celebrating its triumphs.³

What sets spirituals apart from other black musical expressions, like the blues or jazz, is the affirmation and embodiment of faith. Rooted in the biblical narrative, the spirituals and black gospel music have provided a mirror to the black experience of struggle for justice and freedom while reflecting on it in light of the hope of the gospel message. As spirituals intersected European hymnody in church buildings and American revivalism at tent meetings in the late 19th and early 20th centuries, the spirituals were rearranged and formalized for choirs, quartets, and soloists, making way for the birth of the modern black gospel movement. Burton W. Peretti writes, "black gospel was the product of the complex evolution of nineteenth-century song styles (especially spirituals) in the Jim Crow era, when persistent poverty and bigotry undercut advancements by African Americans."⁴ The rich melodies and resonant truths highlight the resilience and faith of generations of black songwriters and artists who have navigated this ongoing tension, as well as the ever-present redemptive and reconciling work of the Holy Spirit.

The ecstatic nature of Pentecostalism made room for physical expression within worship gatherings, harkening back to the black experience rooted in African song and dance. Gospel's elements of call-and-response patterns, layers of harmonic voicing, and rhythmic cadences create an energetic and expressive demonstration of the gospel's "good news" that calls forth faith, hope, and light in the darkest seasons of human history. In his book *Renewal Worship,* Steven Félix-Jäger comments,

> There is a critical, social quality of gospel music that tends to underscore the notion of liberation from oppression. Indeed, religious studies scholar Ashon Crawley sees the "joyful noise" that is uttered in Black Pentecostal worship as a critique of the theology and social structures of dominant culture that play a part in subjugating black communities. The very act of exuberant worship in Black communities has an implicit, prophetic function. So if lament occurs when people need deliverance from something, then the socially conscious, celebratory worship that comes from Black worshiping communities must be understood in this light. In other words, the joyful declaration of victory in the face of oppression is a prophetic form of lament, even if it appears triumphalistic.[5]

The invitation of gospel music is not merely to contemplate and reflect on the melodies, instrumentation, words, or themes; no, the invitation of gospel music is to move as the Spirit moves—to respond with one's whole self—to the action guided by the Spirit. This action can be within the walls of the church: clapping, singing, dancing, shouting, and praying. This could be action outside the walls of the church: marching, protesting, dismantling unjust systems, liberating the captives, and freeing the oppressed. This embodied notion to move as the Spirit moves invites participants to bear witness to the work that God is doing in and among the people now, as God has done in ages past.

THE SPIRIT IN THE FIELD

The theological and musical origins of black gospel music in the United States have roots in the spirituals of enslaved Africans in the eighteenth century. Having survived the slave ships crossing the Middle Passage and subsequently being sold to European settlers in North America, these men and women clung to their faith and the musical traditions of their homeland. In many West African traditions, storytelling through music was a significant part of the culture, a way to pass on the histories of people from one generation to another.[6] As the African people began to develop their own cultural identity in North America, an identity in which black people were seen as property rather than as humans, the spirituals became a way of passing on their histories and thus affirming their humanity. Reflecting on the interpretative work of Howard Thurman, Cone notes that "the black spiritual is an expression of the slaves' determination to *be* in a society that seeks to destroy their personhood. It is an affirmation of the dignity of the black slaves, the essential humanity of their spirits."[7] He continues,

> The essence of ante-bellum black religion was the emphasis on the *somebodiness* of black slaves. The content of the preachers' message stressed the essential worth of their person. . . . Because religion defined the *somebodiness* of their being, black slaves could retain a sense of the dignity of their person even though they were treated as things.[8]

I remember the stories of the founding of our nation from my Christian elementary school; my teachers established that the settlers who came to North America did so to be able to worship God freely, which could not be done in their home country of England. I remember being told how the slaveholders took their faith and passed it on to those in their household, including their slaves. The inference was that the faith of the enslaved Africans was merely a carbon copy of the faith of their white masters, who gifted Christianity to them. However, it would seem that the content of the spirituals indicates a contextualized theology of Christianity by enslaved Africans in the United States. The songs of the fields provide an understanding of who enslaved people understood God to be and who they understood themselves to be in light of that understanding. Cone lays it out simply:

> The basic idea of the spirituals is that slavery contradicts God; it is a denial of God's will. To be enslaved is to be declared *nobody*, and that form of existence contradicts God's creation of people to be God's children. Because black people believed that they were God's children, they affirmed their *somebodiness*, refusing to reconcile their servitude with divine revelation.[9]

He contends that for the enslaved Africans of the antebellum South, the understanding of God always pointed toward liberation, not just as an eschatological reality in the life to come but in their present reality of brutality and dehumanization by those who enslaved them.[10] As a result, the embodied sound of a black witness to their deep sorrow and steadfast hope was found in the spirituals.

Eileen Guenther describes the musical beginning of spirituals as "the chants and moans of the field, becoming more subtle and complex over time."[11] The development of what would become spirituals reflects Paul's letter to the Romans, where he writes, "but we ourselves, who have the firstfruits of the Spirit, groan inwardly as we wait eagerly for adoption as sons, the redemption of our bodies."[12] As enslaved Africans waited and hoped for the liberation of their bodies either as the result of escape, release, or even death—as freedom was their birthright as the children of God—the groans of their spirit became the songs of a people. Guenther describes the Spiritual as "not composed in the traditional sense of the word but created, with one person beginning a song and others adding to it, resulting in a song that was 'owned' by the community."[13] Because the development of spirituals was a communal act, the formation of black identity and the pursuit of freedom became communal act as well.

The spirituals not only were a way of encouraging oneself in the Lord or passing on the faith from one person to another, but also became a means of survival, by which codes would be passed from person to person or plantation to plantation to give information or become a signal for those who were attempting to escape to freedom. Utilizing the biblical narrative, the simplicity of the lyrical pattern, and melodies, the spirituals became a vehicle of communication about the truth of the enslaved person's circumstance. Marvin V. Curtis observes,

> Musically, the spiritual used a biblical text, usually but not always the Old Testament. The musical form was similar to the work song in its use of call-and-response. The spiritual served as a social commentary either on treatment by the masters or a means of escape. Many of the songs had hidden meanings known only to the slave community . . . it was, among other things, a way to "sing about somebody, what you could not say to their face."[14]

For example, the Spiritual "Wade in the Water," with its simple melody and simple lyrics, was not just a reflection on biblical allusions or reminiscing about swimming in a cool body of water on a hot day. Eileen Guenther explains,

> The resistance encoded in *Wade in the Water* has multiple facets, perhaps more than any other single song. First, waterways were boundaries between the freedom and enslavement (such as the Ohio River); slaves escaping often walked besides rivers or creeks and move to the water when the dogs were heard barking in the distance to make it harder to track their scent. It references healing (the pool of Bethseda as recorded in the New Testament in John 5), and confidence that God would, indeed, "trouble the waters" and ultimately the slaves would be free when they would be united with their friends (in heaven, or in freedom—*If you get there before I do . . . tell all my friends I'm comin' too* they sang.).[15]

The religion and spirituality of enslaved Africans were deeply entrenched in the affirmation of their humanity and the voice of the community; their hope rested in a God who was on the side of justice and liberation,[16] a crucified yet resurrected Savior who shared in their sorrows[17] and the Spirit who empowered them to move toward freedom.[18] The songs that were developed in the fields of the antebellum South would not only preserve the histories of a people who were in bondage but would also pass on the faith in a liberating, redemptive God who was present to those on the margins of society.

THE SPIRIT IN THE TENT

In the early nineteenth century, the United States experienced a surge of religious revivalism known as the Second Great Awakening. During this time, camp and tent meetings became a part of the religious life in America, leading to an increase in Protestant converts, black and white alike, moved by the passionate preaching and calls to holiness.[19] The Second Great Awakening also led to the founding of the first African American denominations and people moving toward social reform, including abolitionist movements. In the early twentieth century, in the years surrounding the Azusa Street Revival led by African American holiness preacher William J. Seymour, and the acknowledged beginning of the Pentecostal movement in North America, there was an increase in the writing, collection, and distribution of gospel music. Thomas A. Dorsey, known as the "Father of Gospel Music," began writing and distributing gospel music in the 1930s, which infused the musical elements of blues and jazz music with church music and spirituals.[20] Dorsey's most famous song is "Precious Lord, Take My Hand," written following the death of his wife and child, which reflected a more personal relationship with God through song. His work would go on to be popularized by the performances of singers Mahalia Jackson and Willa Mae Ford Smith.[21]

The experiential nature of Pentecostal worship spaces invites participants to engage with the Spirit's movement with a physical response. Whether vocalizing agreement or praise, raising hands, clapping, dancing, or shouting, an encounter with the Holy Spirit in a congregational worship setting makes space for an externalized response. The participatory nature serves as an affirmation of the immediacy of the experience. The emphasis on the gifts of the Spirit, including prophecy, speaking in tongues, and demonstrative worship, deeply influenced the culture of praise and worship within the black church context, giving rise to a musical genre that fused some of the stylistic markers of blues music and the hope from the spirituals to produce gospel music. Gospel music gave new expression to the goodness of good news for black people in the United States. Though they were no longer enslaved, they were still marginalized by segregation, Jim Crow laws, and other forms of systemic racism; gospel music functioned as an expression of the longstanding tension between earthly sorrows and hope for deliverance.

The shift from spiritual to gospel music was noticeable in theme. Curtis observes,

> Whereas spirituals were the community-composed songs of the African-American people, the gospel hymns were compositions of ministers and musicians. Gospel hymns grew out of a personal experience with God. The biblical stories of the Old Testament were replaced with the "I" songs of the gospel.[22]

The authors of *The Black Church in the African American Experience* concur:

> The transition from congregational hymns to songs for specialized soloists and ensembles had important sociological consequences. While the former united worshipers through the collective activity of singing and declaring theological and doctrinal commonalities, the new style required the congregation to assume the role of audience. In essence, worshipers became bystanders who witnessed the preaching and personal testimonies of singers. At best the congregation was to share in those attestations by affirmative "amens," nodding, humming, clapping, swaying, or occasionally by singing along on choruses and vamps. One unexpected consequence was that black worshipers and concertgoers often became the audience to a new homiletical gospel experience.[23]

THE SPIRIT IN THE STREETS

In Luke 4:18-19, Jesus stood before the synagogue in his hometown, reading from the prophet Isaiah, adopting the Spirit-charged prophetic utterance as his own and proclaiming that fulfillment was at hand. The redemptive, liberating work of the Spirit was the introduction to Christ's earthly ministry and continued as a through-line for the duration of the New Testament writings and much of the work of the early church. The Holy Spirit's availability to all—tearing down the walls of gender, class, ethnicity, and language—as exhibited at the event of Pentecost in Acts 2, reinforced Jesus' demonstration of a kingdom that was filled with hope, liberation, and freedom for those who had been bound. For many African Americans in the throes of the Civil Rights Movement of the 1960s, the description of who Jesus had come for—the poor, the oppressed, and the prisoner—reflected their own reality. For many black communities, it was not enough for a movement of the Spirit to simply take place within the four walls of their church buildings; the Spirit's movement was to be the liberating force for those marginalized by racism, sexism, poverty, and more. The declaration of the gospel was not simply good news for their souls but also for their social realities.

The leaders and activists of the Civil Rights Movement were the living embodiment of what the liberating power of the Holy Spirit can look like in the world. Men and women of the movement, like Martin Luther King, Jr., John Lewis, Malcolm X, Fannie Lou Hamer, and countless others, prophetically resisted injustice and called for a world that provided equality, justice, and freedom to all people. The eloquent speeches and hope-filled pleas for unity by these giants of history were accompanied by the voice of the gospel music tradition. In partnership with the Pentecostal ethos that emphasizes the empowerment of all people, the melodies and lyrics of gospel songs found their way out of the church house and into the streets. These songs served as anthems of protest, cries of freedom, and melodies of hope; those whom the Spirit had moved to pursue the love of God and love of neighbor joined the ranks of those who would be beaten, imprisoned, and outcast with a prayer in their heart and a song on their lips. The anthem of the Civil Rights Movement, "We Shall Overcome," was adapted from a Spiritual and an early twentieth century gospel hymn by Charles Tindley; the Spiritual "Wade in the Water" was used in demonstrations to integrate public swimming pools; gospel songs like "If You Miss Me from Praying Down Here" had adapted texts to reflect an issue of the movement.[24]

> The freedom songs did not passively lament the black condition; they made God active in human history day by day with social agitation. African Americans were not just singing about freedom, they were systematically seeking it, and their songs were deliberate instruments tactically utilized in the effort. Freedom songs chronicle the historical events of the various forms of protest, personal reflections, testimonials, and religious responses to the oppressive forces opposing the struggle for freedom.[25]

Following the radical ways of Jesus, who declared that he would bring "good news to the poor . . . proclaim freedom for the prisoners, and recovery of sight for the blind, to set the oppressed free . . ."[26] these men and women moved in the same Spirit that Jesus declared was resting on him to accomplish the good, liberating work of the kingdom of God.

THE SPIRIT ON THE STAGE

As gospel music continued to evolve throughout the twentieth century, the crossover between other genres, such as blues, jazz, and soul, shaped the mainstream American music industry and made way for artists like Aretha Franklin, Sam Cooke, and Mahalia Jackson to popularize the gospel genre globally, where it is lauded for soulful expression and musical innovation. As the music industry made more space for black artists, several left gospel to find success in secular markets; however, their entrenched roots in the black church and the black gospel tradition would find their way into their songs. Gospel music did not stay confined to the black church experience, as the rise of the Christian music industry created an opportunity for church music to be recorded and disseminated to the masses. From traditional hymns to contemporary praise and worship, black gospel has found a market within the industry to appeal more broadly, transcending racial, cultural, and even denominational lines.

Andraé Crouch was one of the most influential gospel artists of the twentieth century. His broad appeal in religious circles and outside of them crossed musical, denominational, and racial lines in a country that was finding its footing in the post-Civil Rights era. Claudrena Harold recounts, "In the late 1960s and throughout the 1970s, Crouch stirred the passions of whites and blacks alike with such gospel classics as "The Blood Will Never Lose Its Power," "Through It All," "Jesus Is the Answer," "My Tribute (To God Be the Glory)," "It Won't Be Long," and "Soon and Very Soon." These songs not only formed the building blocks of his amazing career but also helped establish the sonic and lyrical foundations of Contemporary Christian Music (CCM)."[27] She continues, "Crouch mastered his art form and in the process achieved massive popularity among white and black Christians. More than any religious artist before or since, he helped bridge some of the racial divides within the Christian music world."[28]

Crouch's unique fusion of traditional gospel elements with contemporary musical elements from jazz, rock, pop, and R&B captivated audiences worldwide and earned him widespread acclaim. Influenced by his upbringing in the Church of God in Christ (COGIC), Andraé Crouch's musical journey began at a young age, composing one of his most famous works, "The Blood Will Never Lose Its Power," at fourteen years old.[29] Crouch's success across racial lines can be linked to his engagement with the Jesus Movement in the late 1960s and early 1970s.[30] Crouch's musicianship, as well as his lyricism and spiritual heritage that spoke to the inherent dissatisfaction with the societal mores of the mid-twentieth century, garnered a large following among White "Jesus People" Christians.[31]

In the thematic vein of the spirituals of the antebellum South, the orientation of Crouch's gospel tunes toward the Jesus of Scripture, the tensions of lament and joy as valid expressions of faith, and hope for a liberated future appealed to followers of Jesus across color and denominational lines in the 1970s. However, even Crouch's broad appeal did not negate the fact that the United States was still reacting to the Civil Rights Movement of the 1960s, and the American church was not immune from reconciling its beliefs and practices when it came to engagement across racial lines. Harold observes,

> Tempting as it might be to present Crouch as a musician who transcended the color line, such a representation would be an inaccurate portrait of the complex politics of race, religion, and culture in 1970s America. Even among Jesus movement supporters, tension often surfaced around the issue of race and cultural difference . . . More specifically, some whites had trouble seeing African Americans as coworkers in the kingdom of God. In their view, African Americans "were more properly the object of missionary work than fellow laborers in the vineyard of the Holy Spirit. White Christians' subtle and overt racism did not escape the notice of the perceptive Crouch, who refused to ignore the hardcore reality of racial prejudice within American Protestantism in general and Christian music in particular.[32]

Even as he navigated the waters of racism throughout his career, Andraé Crouch stayed true to a gospel message that was for all people. His influence was significant in how he mentored and sponsored Christian artists, black and white alike. While he was highly respected by his peers and producers across genres, including collaborations with artists like Madonna and Michael Jackson, gospel music purists felt that Crouch was capitulating to Hollywood success and becoming "too worldly" in the way that he lived his life.[33] In an interview with the *Los Angeles Times* in 1982, Crouch responded to the criticism, saying, "Every song I've written takes you through the Scriptures and reinforces the word of God. I give people a beautiful message, but I do it with pop, rock, funk, jazz or disco or anything that will make it appealing."[34] Reflecting on Crouch's legacy, Harold concludes,

> His songwriting and production informed the work of such gospel acts as Richard Smallwood, Fred Hammond, Israel Houghton, Smokie Norful, Donnie McClurkin, and CeCe Winans, along with white contemporary Christian musicians like Amy Grant, Michael W. Smith, and Steven Curtis Chapman. His pioneering work in the world of contemporary Christian music also blazed a path for African American performers like Larnelle Harris, Leon Patillo, and Ron Kenoly, who achieved remarkable success with predominantly white audiences. In addition to integrating the world of CCM, Crouch created a body of work that would become foundational for praise and worship music, a genre that transformed the black gospel sound and continues to do so.[35]

Artists like Andraé Crouch demonstrated that the invitation to participate in the movement of black gospel was no longer confined to the church building on a Sunday morning or to the milieu of a significant moment of social change or upheaval. As gospel music continues to evolve and reflect the diverse experiences of African American communities in the United States and beyond, the invitation to sing of and live out the good news finds its place in more diverse communities, churches, and contexts, as a testimony to the Holy Spirit's presence at work from the stage, in the church, on the streets, and in the fields.

CONCLUSION

The legacy of gospel music bears witness to the enduring power of faith, hope, and resilience of individual and communal trust in the liberating, transformative grace of God. However, it is not without its challenges. In the contemporary era of gospel music, the high-value commercialization of the gospel music industry has demonstrated the increased entertainment value of the black gospel song. As gospel music has moved into other spheres of influence beyond the walls of the church, including the recording studio and concert halls, a resounding critique has been the transformation of the worshiping community into a consumeristic audience.[36] As an aficionado of gospel music and a worship leader at a local church, I navigate this tension regularly. In the summer of 2022, I joined over 10,000 people in the Crypto.com Arena in Los Angeles to see several of my favorite gospel artists perform. In one moment, I was entertained like it was a concert, jumping and dancing and rocking out to the songs I listen to on my commute; in another moment, it felt like a massive worship service as I raised my hands and sang songs that I would include in a Sunday morning worship set; in a different moment, it felt like a highly produced hybrid of communal and consumer engagement. While that gathering was not a "church service," I felt like the artists had taken me to church.

Where contemporary gospel music is having its day in the commercial and cultural *zeitgeist*, it is more difficult to bring the songs of modern gospel artists into the congregational voice of the local church. The "I" song that was established with the creation of the gospel hymn in the early twentieth century is hitting its fever pitch in the twenty-first century, and the communal nature of song creation and singing is less prevalent than in generations past. The melismatic vocalizations, complex instrumentation, verbose lyricism, and tepid theology can often make contemporary gospel less accessible for the congregational voice. In the broader conversation about the American church, including gospel and contemporary worship spaces, many are wrestling with how we are to engage as an embodied community when entertainment value is what many are searching for.

Even with its challenges, the experience of Black gospel music lends itself to embodied engagement with the Holy Spirit. The ecstatic spiritual expressions of Pentecostal worship styles, the movement toward redemptive social change, and the building of a reconciled community affirm the need for the voice and tradition of gospel music to inform our witness as the larger body of Christ. Reflecting on the profound impact of Black gospel music on my life and society at large, one cannot help but consider the transcendence of time, space, and circumstance of these songs that speak to the deepest parts of the soul, inspiring and uplifting with truth-filled lyrics affirming the love, power, and presence of God. This enduring art form, which has become a soundtrack to personal moments and social movements of transformation, is a testament to the evergreen tension between suffering and hope and how that shared experience can be catalyzed for participation in the redemptive nature of the kingdom of God for all of humanity. As long as there are people crying out for justice, as long as there is hope in the midst of sorrow, and as long as we await the redemption of all things, the nature of Spirit-led movement to the margins to bring good news to the poor, set the oppressed free, release the captives, recover sight for the blind, and proclaim the year of the Lord's favor[37] will result in shouts and tears, singing and dancing, and the ushering in of the kingdom of God, on earth as it is in heaven.

NOTES

1. James H. Cone, *The Spirituals and the Blues: An Interpretation* (Maryknoll: Orbis Books, 1991), 3.
2. Cone, *The Spirituals and the Blues*, 5.
3. Cone, *The Spirituals and the Blues*, 129.
4. Burton W. Peretti. *Lift Every Voice: The History of African American Music*. of *The African American History Series* (Lanham: Rowman & Littlefield, 2009), 126.
5. Steven Félix-Jäger, *Renewal Worship: A Theology of Pentecostal Doxology* (Downers Grove: IVP Academic, 2022), 136.
6. Cone, *The Spirituals and the Blues*, 15.
7. Cone, *The Spirituals and the Blues*, 16.
8. Cone, *The Spirituals and the Blues*, 16–17.
9. Cone, *The Spirituals and the Blues*, 33.
10. Cone, *The Spirituals and the Blues*, 83–87, 95.
11. Eileen Guenther, "Music of the Soil and the Soul," *The Choral Journal*, Vol. 57, No. 7 (2017), 66.
12. Romans 8:23. All scripture reference are NIV unless otherwise stated.
13. Guenther, "Music of the Soil and the Soul," 67.
14. Curtis, Marvin V. "African-American Spirituals and the Gospel Music: Historical Similarities and Differences," *The Choral Journal*, Vol. 4, No. 8 (2001), 13.
15. Guenther, "Music of the Soil and the Soul," 75.
16. Cone, *The Spirituals and the Blues*, 32–43.
17. Cone, *The Spirituals and the Blues*, 43–52.
18. Cone, *The Spirituals and the Blues*, 4.
19. Eric C. Lincoln and Lawrence H. Mamiya, *The Black Church in the African American Experience* (Durham: Duke University Press, 1990), 346.
20. Lincoln, *The Black Church in the African American Experience*, 361.
21. Curtis, "African-American Spirituals and the Gospel Music," 19.
22. Curtis, "African-American Spirituals and the Gospel Music," 18.
23. Lincoln, *The Black Church in the African American Experience*, 361–362.
24. Lincoln, *The Black Church in the African American Experience*, 369.
25. Lincoln, *The Black Church in the African American Experience*, 373.
26. Luke 4:18–19.
27. Claudrena N. Harold, *When Sunday Comes: Gospel Music in the Soul and Hip-Hop Eras*. of *Music in American Life* (2020), 43
28. Harold, *When Sunday Comes*, 44.
29. Harold, *When Sunday Comes*, 46.
30. Harold, *When Sunday Comes*, 51.
31. Harold, *When Sunday Comes*, 52.

32. Harold, *When Sunday Comes,* 53.
33. Harold, *When Sunday Comes*, 45.
34. Bruce Weber, "Andraé Crouch, 72, Who Infused Gospel With Soul, Dies," *New York Times*, Jan 9, 2015, https://www.nytimes.com/2015/01/11/arts/music/andra-crouch-72-who-infused-gospel-with-soul-dies.html (accessed 3/9/24).
35. Harold, *When Sunday Comes,* 64.
36. Lincoln, *The Black Church in the African American Experience*, 362.
37. Luke 4:18-19.

BIBLIOGRAPHY

Cone, James H. *The Spirituals and the Blues: An Interpretation.* Maryknoll: Orbis Books, 1991.
Félix-Jäger, Steven. *Renewal Worship: A Theology of Pentecostal Doxology. Dynamics of Christian Worship.* Downers Grove: IVP Academic, 2022.
Harold, Claudrena N. *When Sunday Comes: Gospel Music in the Soul and Hip-Hop Eras.* of *Music in American Life.* Urbana: University of Illinois Press, 2020.
Lincoln, C. Eric, and Mamiya, Lawrence H. *The Black Church in the African American Experience.* Durham: Duke University Press, 1990.
Peretti, Burton W. *Lift Every Voice: The History of African American Music. The African American History Series.* Lanham: Rowman & Littlefield, 2009.
Weber, Bruce. "Andraé Crouch, 72, Who Infused Gospel With Soul, Dies." *New York Times*, January 9 2015, https://www.nytimes.com/2015/01/11/arts/music/andra-crouch-72-who-infused-gospel-with-soul-dies.html (accessed 3/9/24).

Chapter 12

"Oh Happy Day"

The Migration and Reclamation of the Soul of Pentecostal Faith

Kimberly Ervin Alexander

One of the many significant contributions of Ahmir "Questlove" Thompson's 2021 film, "Summer of Soul," is the recovery of video of the Edwin Hawkins Singers' June 1969 performance of "Oh Happy Day" at the Harlem Cultural Festival. While other recordings of performances on popular television programs of the era have been available, this newly uncovered footage reveals the power of the song, the arrangement, and, especially, the vocal lead as the Spirit moves the predominantly African American audience on a Sunday morning in Harlem.[1] One year before, in 1968,[2] a Church of God in Christ (COGIC) youth choir from the Bay Area in California rearranged and recorded Phillip Doddridge's eighteenth-century hymn, "Happy Day"—a song that had been commonly sung in American camp meetings and revivals from the mid-nineteenth century. When the youth choir's record was played by a San Francisco DJ, it was quickly picked up by others, leading to a record deal for the group renamed the Edwin Hawkins Singers. By 1969, the single, "Oh Happy Day," had reached number four on Billboard's pop chart, number two in Great Britain, and number two on Billboard's R&B chart. The single won a Grammy in 1970 for Best Soul Gospel Performance. Eventually selling over 1.5 million copies, lauded as the biggest-selling gospel album of all time, in 2005, its significance was recognized as it was added to the Library of Congress National Recording Registry.[3]

Musicologists and historians of African American music agree that the breakout of this song was a turning point in the history of Black gospel music.[4] Mellonee V. Burnim states unequivocally, "The release of the recording 'Oh Happy Day' by the Edwin Hawkins Singers in 1969 ushered in the contemporary gospel era."[5] Analysts take note of its musical innovation—the addition of Latin-influenced rhythms, jazz as well as conga drum and bass.[6]

But most scholars, as well as journalists, musicians, and singers, cannot but focus on the lead vocal of Dorothy Combs Morrison.

Just as black Pentecostal women singers of the early Pentecostal revival, such as Jenny Moore Seymour at Azusa St., had lifted hearers out of earthly spaces into heavenly ones, so the vocal lead by Morrison carried the song and its black Pentecostal fire into the turbulent late-sixties cultural mainstream, putting "Pentecostal exaltation on the pop charts."[7] Influencing the music of George Harrison,[8] Joan Baez,[9] and other pop/rock artists, as well as country artists, such as Glen Campbell,[10] the song became an anthem of hope after a decade of war, unrest, and assassinations. But Morrison also revived the essential African and feminine roots of Pentecostalism itself, as the Hawkins' version gained popularity among white Pentecostal youth choirs and was sung—then and now—in still-segregated Pentecostal spaces.

This chapter explores how a church basement recording of a sung Pentecostal testimony, and the Spirit-infused and driven vocals of a young Pentecostal woman migrated a spirituality into popular culture. More importantly, it argues that this African feminine root crossed back into what were even less-porous borders—those of the white Pentecostal tradition in America— where high walls had been built by leaders bowing to the cultural norms of the Jim Crow South, who, in spite of their holiness convictions and claims to holiness experience, had resisted civil rights legislation.

A SPIRIT-INFUSED RECORD CROSSES THE BORDER INTO THE TURBULENT SIXTIES

Edwin Hawkins (1943–2018) grew up in a musical family, as one of six children, living in the projects in Oakland, California. His father was a porter and longshoreman who worked the Oakland docks to provide for his large family.[11] Edwin began playing piano at the age of five and, by seven, was the keyboard player for his family's gospel group.[12] Hawkins recalls, "Practically every Sunday afternoon at 3:00 pm we were on a program to sing somewhere in the San Francisco Bay Area."[13] They were faithful and active members of the Good Samaritan COGIC,[14] then the Ephesians COGIC. In May of 1967, Hawkins and Betty Watson organized the Northern California State Youth Choir (NCSYC), under the First Jurisdiction of the Northern California COGIC. Hawkins and Watson had as their goal forming a choir that would sing in state and national conventions within the COGIC denomination. In order to raise funding, the choir recorded an album, *Let Us Go Into the House of the Lord* in 1968 in the basement of the Oakland's Ephesian COGIC.[15]

Watson's liner notes on the back of the album are helpful not only because they provide titles of the eight songs but also information about some of the choir personnel, as well as the choir's understanding of its purpose. She identifies herself as "Directoress" and soloist on the song "Early in the Morning;" Hawkins is identified as "director and pianist," as well as "talented arranger." Watson writes of the choir, "The choir was organized to inspire youth everywhere to live and do a greater work for God." She concludes, "Each member of the choir is a singer in his or her own right as shown in this album; and, as life requires harmony among individuals, so does this choir set an example with precision in harmonies—tenderly yet daringly performed."[16] Notably, seven of the nine soloists listed are female. Also noteworthy is the listing of COGIC state youth department president, the "state chairlady," "state mother," and "state bishop"—demonstrating that this choir was, at this point, firmly situated in the COGIC *habitus* of Northern California.

Like several of the eight songs on the album, "Oh Happy Day" was a new arrangement of a traditional song.[17] The 1755 hymn, "Oh Happy Day" was composed by a white English Baptist clergyman and had made its way through numerous revisions as it was sung in the nineteenth century camp meeting circuit in the United States.[18] The Hawkins version followed closely a 1957 one by another black gospel singer, A. Kenneth Morris.[19] But, according to Thomas Dorsey, the prolific gospel songwriter who could recall singing the Morris version, Hawkins' arrangement was marked as a work of the Spirit: "I guess he was inspired from on high, and he put a beat into it. Not only beat, but the curves, the rhythmic curves, and the harmony. It creates a new style in gospel music, and I think he did a wonderful job."[20] Acknowledging the Spirit's role in the arrangement's origin, Hawkins himself used the term "inspired." In an interview published in the Oakland Tribune in May 1969, he described his arranging process: "Usually I am inspired in church. I work out the arrangements in my head."[21] Important for this study is a brief assessment of this process: In the community formed by the Spirit, a Spirit-gifted musician is in*spir*ed to rearrange a song composed under the in*spir*ation over two hundred years before and anointed by the Spirit in Holiness and Pentecostal camp meetings over the century leading up to the moment of Hawkins' own in*spir*ation.

The next stage of the song's journey might also be understood as driven by the Spirit, and certainly it was understood that way by the singers themselves. The choir initially had 500 copies of the album pressed for its fundraising venture—with the goal of selling them to church folk at five dollars each.[22] Months later, in March 1969, a rock promoter named John Lingel "stumbled onto" the album and passed it along to an underground radio DJ, Abe "Voco" Kesh, in San Francisco. SKAN-FM began playing the "Oh Happy Day" cut—the first song on the B side of the album.[23] Within a day, Lingel's employer, a music distributor, had orders for 1,300 copies of the single. Buddha Records re-released the album, with orders for 250,000 albums and 350,000 singles.[24] Within two months, the single was being played on various Bay Area stations: Top thirty, jazz, "middle of the road," "'progressive rock'" as well as soul.[25] Gaining nationwide, and eventually global, airplay, it climbed to the top of the charts in both the United States and the United Kingdom.[26] Immediately embarking on a national tour, now under the name "The Edwin Hawkins Singers," by June 29, they were appearing on the opposite coast, at the Harlem Cultural Festival, to an audience of 50,000.[27] That summer, they appeared at music festivals on both coasts, alongside their COGIC-traditioned Bay Area neighbors, Sly and the Family Stone, as well as Jimi Hendrix, Led Zeppelin, and other rock and R&B headliners.[28] They appeared on American Bandstand on September 5[29] on television talk[30] and variety shows.[31] In 1970, "Oh Happy Day" won a Grammy for Best Soul Gospel Performance.[32] Sales eventually reached 1.5 million.[33]

The nature of this meteoric rise has been called "serendipitous" by Burnim,[34] "an unfathomable coincidence" by Robert Darden,[35] and has recently been labeled a "one hit wonder."[36] But the "wonder" of it wasn't lost on Hawkins and others at the time. In an interview with San Francisco's KTVU television station in 1969, Hawkins addresses the timing of the hit:

> What happened because I felt it was time to happen—especially with the situation of the world today—problems people are having. They don't believe in God anymore. A lot of people, they don't go to church and especially our youth. This generation today is really messed up, confused. They don't know who to turn to, which way to go, so they're trying this and that and they're not finding satisfaction. And I felt with young people such as our group, we can show them that God yet lives and instead of us trying to take the gospel to them, maybe by preaching to them, take it to them in song maybe and with contemporary sounds.[37]

For Hawkins, this was what his Pentecostal sisters and brothers understood as "steps ordered by the Lord," the "timing of the Lord," or, in Acts 2 vernacular, a "suddenly" moment. Given both the *temporal* and *spatial* contexts of the song's popularity, it's easy to make the case. The NCSYC formed in 1967, in the San Francisco Bay Area during what might be seen as the peak—both in temporal and spatial terms—of the "Sixties." This was both the scene and season of the Summer of Love and the Monterey Pop Festival. By the time the song had reached the top of the charts and they were appearing at the Harlem Cultural Festival, the choir had lived through the despair of the assassinations of the leader of their dreams of racial harmony and civil rights, Martin Luther King, Jr., as well as presidential hopeful Robert F. Kennedy. No doubt they had known family members and friends killed or wounded in Vietnam. And when a seventeen-year-old member of the Black

Panthers, Bobby Hutton, was killed by Oakland police in April of 1968, their pastor, Rev. E. E. Cleveland, opened the doors of the Ephesian COGIC for the funeral service[38]—the same *space* where they recorded *Let Us Go Up to the House of the Lord*, that same *year*. This was the context which Hawkins addressed in the KTVU interview.

The juxtaposition of the message of the song—the testimony sung by Dorothy Combs Morrison and the choir—"Oh Happy Day"—and the social unrest of the late 1960s is made visible in Questlove's "Summer of Soul." Carol Cooper of National Public Radio described the event in an opinion piece when the film was released:

> Each weekend from June 29 to August 24 in 1969, thousands of Harlem residents flocked to what is now Marcus Garvey Park. The stage featured extraordinary artists from the sisterly harmonies of The Staple Singers to headlining sets by B.B. King and Steve Wonder. Unlike Woodstock, these concerts were no sybaritic celebration of hippie counterculture, but a direct response to the profound losses and violence endured by Black activists and progressives that preceded that summer.[39]

In fact, it was one of the intentions of the festival organizers, headed by Tony Lawrence, in cooperation with Mayor John Lindsay, to celebrate the growing awareness of the beauty of blackness and to instill hope during the long, hot summers in Harlem.[40] The young Sanctified choir—celebrating the beauty of their blackness, in the beauty of holiness, dressed in vibrant choir robes—swayed in the Spirit, toward a hopeful and optimistic Pentecostal version of King's dream. *Rolling Stone* called the song a "Pop Godsend."[41] Soloist Dorothy Combs Morrison, who *Rolling Stone* noted as a "devoted churchgoer," called the ascent of the song "a miracle."[42]

SINGING THE LORD'S SONG IN FAMILIAR AND STRANGE SPACES

Singing enabled by the Spirit—singing that speaks prophetically and proleptically—was not exclusive to the Northern California COGIC youth who recorded what became the best-selling gospel song in history. "Spirited singing," "singing in the Spirit," "singing in the heavenly choir," and singing "new songs" given by the Spirit were all part and parcel of the Pentecostal experience from its inception.[43] This spiritual phenomenon was described on the first page of the first issue of *The Apostolic Faith*, the periodical documenting the Azusa Street Revival that began in Los Angeles in Spring 1906:

> Many have received the gift of singing as well as speaking in the inspiration of the Spirit. The Lord is giving new voices, he translates old songs into new songs, he gives the music that is being sung by the angels and has a heavenly choir all singing the same heavenly song in harmony. It is beautiful music, no instruments are needed in the meetings.[44]

When the youth choir met in 1968 to record the eight songs arranged by Hawkins, they were embodying a tradition at least sixty years old: communal singing of old songs in new ways inspired by the Holy Spirit.

Steve Sullivan described the choir and these eight recordings on the album this way: "A forty-six member Sanctified choir from the emotion-packed and deeply musical Holiness Church tradition, it was young and totally contemporary in style, approaching gospel from a soul/R&B perspective, including instruments such as the Fender bass, bongos, and horns that had not typically been used in previous gospel recordings."[45] Sullivan notes what he calls the "emotion" of the Holiness and Sanctified church tradition. What he may miss, however, is that even the instrumentation he describes was a hallmark of the "Holiness-Pentecostal style" found in the transitional period of gospel music history, beginning in the urban storefront churches of the 1930s, a style that had moved north in the Great Migration. Mellonee V. Burnim locates this introduction of instrumentation previously banned in Baptist and Methodist churches within the Holiness-Pentecostal tradition, specifically in COGIC.[46]

This COGIC distinction is traced to its founder and bishop, Charles H. Mason, whose own Pentecostal experience at the Azusa Street Revival in 1906 resulted not only in *glossolalic* speech, but in singing new songs in the Spirit.[47] Mason, the son of enslaved people, a Baptist convert to the Holiness, and then Pentecostal movements, would embrace his and his church's roots in African slave religion. L. F. Thuston summarizes what this embrace meant for the worship of the church:

> Worship was holistic and often physically animated. Spontaneous, dancing, enthusiastic, singing, and shouting, drums, visions and dreams, call and response preaching, epiphanies from natures, enigmas in roots and branches, and divine healing were among the features of the slave, religious practice.... Mason intuitively connected these ancient modalities as legitimate vehicles of the authentic and normative Christian expressions for individual devotional or corporate worship settings.[48]

Walter J. Hollenweger identified what Thuston describes as the African, or black oral, root of Pentecostalism.[49] As the Pentecostal revival spread globally, that root—was trafficked, at least partially, through "spirit singing."

Six decades later, the Pentecostal African root was being trafficked not just into familiar spaces such as COGIC congregations or conventions, but into less-familiar ones, such as those that were decidedly *not* Pentecostal and, in many cases, not majority African American. From its first airing by white underground radio DJs to the Harlem Cultural Festival in the Summer of 1969, to television variety shows in both the United States and England hosted by Anglo celebrities, and to global venues in Europe and Japan, Holy Spirit-infused prophetic singing lifted audiences out of the turbulence and despair of the late 1960s, to a "Happy Day" and a proleptic vision of walking around heaven in "golden shoes."

Ron Thompson, a tenor in Hawkins' gospel group, the Hebrew Boys, and an original member of the youth choir, reflected on what it was like to sing this distinctively black Pentecostal testimony in venues dominated by white and/or secular audiences around the world. In an interview, Thompson reflected on what it was like to come into a rehearsal on a Monday night at the Roosevelt Junior High School in Oakland. He noted that he and all the singers came in with "baggage" from their life experiences. He described what happened as these young singers with "concerns that were troubling" rehearsed:

> While I was there learning those songs the Holy Spirit would come upon me. And sometimes it was hard to sing for the tears that would be rolling down my face while I'm performing or rehearsing these songs, because they were so relative to what I was going through in my daily life. And it was uplifting and strengthening me. Just as it blessed me while I'm learning the songs and practicing the songs, the same thing occurred when we would be performing the songs, whether before a COGIC audience, a Baptist audience, a secular audience, the same thing occurred. The Holy Spirit would—how should I say—overwhelm me. And, I'm sure it did others in the choir. And we were projecting what the Holy Spirit was giving to us and sharing with the hearers. . . . That's how you respond to God. That's how you respond to the Spirit's moving when you sing, no matter where you are.[50]

Speaking of the song's continuing relevance, in 2012, soloist Dorothy Combs Morrison reflected, "Audience reactions are always strong. People want to have a happy day and that song helps them do it. My delivery is still innocent and real, but sometimes I get so caught up that I have to stop and cry. Hey, the song gets to me too."[51]

This optimistic vision, resulting from the theological DNA of the Wesleyan-Holiness-Pentecostal movement's "optimism of grace,"[52] was embraced by the larger culture, especially those most impacted by the grief and fear of the times. Journalist Kathy Orloff commented on the surprising resonance of the gospel message of the song with radio audiences of 1969:

When a song straight out of church, without commercial hyping, becomes the most requested song on a top 30 station, something is happening. Somehow it seems almost sacrilegious to call such a heavy gospel hymn a "hit." What [sic] it seems to imply is that the listener's (and record buyers [sic]) ears (and heads) are open to anything. "Oh Happy Day" is a song that is full—it is full of love, full of very beautiful voices and harmony, full of a message. And the message is nonsectarian. It is the music that is important, the sound the voices make and the feeling that one gets listening to Dorothy Morrison's delivery.[53]

Reflecting on the porous borders found in 1960s popular music, there was now opportunity for real honesty and creativity. She concludes, "'Oh Happy Day' couldn't be closer to the truth."[54] It seems that Orloff sensed the Spirit's prophetic witness through these young black Pentecostal voices: a witness of the Spirit of grace and truth, delivered again through the voice and body of a young black woman.

DELIVERING THE PROPHETIC WORD THROUGH A BLACK FEMALE VOICE

While the idea of receiving truth, a "word in season," or a "prophetic word" through a female voice may have seemed impossible even to most Christians in the mid-twentieth century, it wouldn't have been quite as unlikely in the spaces inhabited by Pentecostals—especially if that message came through a song or testimony. And Dorothy Combs Morrison utilized both vehicles. While much has been written about the African root of Pentecostalism, less acknowledged is the *feminine root*. What is clear is that the significance of the prophetic voice of women, and the authority their spiritual experience carries in Pentecostal congregations have not always been recognized, even by scholars and historians. However, utilizing a womanist-black feminist methodology, Keri Day has recently asserted that "women guided and birthed [William] Seymour's religious experience of the Spirit, making them cofounders of Azusa with him."[55] Note that it is their ability to nurture spiritual experience that qualifies them as founders and leaders.[56]

This section of the chapter will explore just *how* this young woman's voice conveyed a message of hope and healing to a generation, even as it was conveyed *via* a recording made in the earthy space of a church basement, with limited engineering technology. While Morrison chose not to continue with the Edwin Hawkins Singers after they signed with Buddha Records, and, therefore, did not tour with them, it was her recorded voice that permeated the soundscape of the era.[57] Kernodle credits Morrison's voice with the pivotal transition from traditional gospel to contemporary, as well as this new gospel style's permeation of larger pop culture: One of the first voices of contemporary gospel was not Edwin Hawkins, although he is often thought to have been the architect of the sound, but Dorothy Combs Morrison, the soloist on "Oh Happy Day."[58]

Like a good Pentecostal, choir member Thompson explains that it didn't really matter who was leading the song—"It's the Spirit that's singing there, whether it's Dorothy or Ed or Betty . . . it's the Spirit that's leading."[59] That perspective is important given the fact that "Oh Happy Day" was one song among eight recorded—and among many more in their repertoire. However, it was Morrison's vocal that was nearly always remarked upon in the secular press. Orloff, above, refers to the "feeling one gets when listening to Morrison's delivery." She goes so far as to attempt to describe it: "her voice is one that makes you sigh a big one and say, 'now that's what I call soul.'"[60] Another journalist from the Bay Area, expressed a similar experience in listening to Morrison at the time, "It makes a lot of people happy, warm, closer to that soul feeling which they only be felt, and sometimes sung, but not described."[61] Graeme Boone analyzes the song and Morrison's vocal:

> "Oh Happy Day" remains compelling from beginning to end thanks to its catchy rhythmic, melodic, and harmonic patterns, the extra excitement of its verse and conclusion, the fine singing of its choir, and perhaps above all the stunning solo voice of Dorothy Morrison. Her lines are always rather brief, alternating as they do with the choral lines, but they are marked by rich, sometimes rough tone, a full and consistent vibrato, remarkably wide vocal range, a fine sense of swing, and a power that easily matches the chorus at full tilt.[62]

Earlier in his essay, Boone describes her voice as "commanding." In short, Morrison's voice *stuns*, it *commands,* it *convicts.*

It was the texture of Morrison's voice—what Boone hears as "rich" and "rough"—Ed Pavlíc argues, that drew James Baldwin to the song, while he may have rejected the idea of a "happy day." Still, he identified in Morrison's textured voice a *". . . sound,"* which, for Baldwin, "offered a complex and powerful link between words and what they meant in experience, in black American experience first, and, after that, in encounters with human experience radiating around the world."[63]

That so much could be heard—could be felt—in Dorothy Morrison's vocal points to its *sign*ificance as a conveyor of the Spirit. Like many marginalized women who find themselves leading others into the presence of God, Morrison herself may have, at first, been as surprised as any of her audience. In interviews, she described the "process" of penning the revised lyrics for the recording:

> Edwin Hawkins asked me if I would like to sing in the choir so that's how I got in. He told me he had a song for me and the title was, "Oh Happy Day" And he said, "Now I need you to get some verses." So I went home [and] talked to my brothers—Jerry Combs who is now deceased, and my brother Bill Combs—and I asked them for verses . . . but the verses that they gave me were like preaching. . . . I didn't want to do any preaching. On the way [to the recording session], my husband at the time, Mr. Isadore Morrison, said, "Why don't you just say, 'When I get to heaven I'm going to jump and shout, be nobody there to put me out." So l used that. I wrote that down on my hand and when I got to the recording session, I read it off my hand.[64]

In a 2012 interview with Marc Myers for *The Wall Street Journal*, later published in *Anatomy of a Song* (2016), Morrison elaborates on this story, adding, "During the recording, I put up my hands, with my palms facing me. Everyone thought I was feeling the spirit. I was—but I also was reading the lyrics [laughs]."[65]

Morrison's own awareness of the Spirit's leading—"feeling the spirit"—is more striking, given its context: the COGIC tradition, which forbade women preachers.[66] So, like many women in Pentecostal traditions, she navigated around the obstacles and negotiated a space in which she could fulfill the mission she'd been given. Morrison sang in her family's gospel group throughout her life and was a "PK" [preacher's kid]; therefore, she knew her place.[67] Her family story itself reveals the contradictions found in the experiences of Pentecostal women. Just a few months after her birth in 1944, the ministry-oriented family moved from her birthplace of Longview, Texas, to Richmond, California, where they were steeped in the culture of Bay Area COGIC. In 2005, Dorothy reflected on her mother, Irene—later a COGIC missionary—and her influence: "'She used to gather all of us around on the living room floor and told us Bible stories from memory while she braided our hair. . . . She would teach us songs and organized us into a singing group. That's how we became The Combs Family Gospel Singers.'"[68] Though not allowed to preach, she was a teacher and leader in her own family and, later, a missionary for the church. Like her mother, Dorothy, followed the leading of the Spirit, following opportunities to minister. She emulated singers like Mahalia Jackson, admiring

> how, when they sang, they would give their all. They didn't hold back . . . You would feel it. So that's why I always wanted to sing like Mahalia Jackson and those people. I wanted to sing songs that I could feel and I wouldn't sing anything I couldn't feel.[69]

Following these role models—women leading in the *Spirit*—Morrison penned the words, ad-libbed others, and sang them with power and authority.

This was *her* story; this was *her* song. Though she may have been trying to avoid "preaching," that is exactly what she did—from the opening chorus as she led the choir through the African American "call and response." When they follow her lead, they burst into a communal testimony and shout, "He taught me how. . . ." to which Morrison responds. And in response to the times in which they prophesied, Morrison and the choir revise the original Doddridge lyrics, "He taught me how to watch and pray," adding the appropriate exercise for not only the black experience, but the human experience in a time of chaos and despair, "He taught me how to watch, *fight,* and pray!" Then, they resume with the original lyrics, "And live rejoicing every day!" *That* is Pentecostal spirituality: proleptic watching, spiritual warfare, and daily praise. Despite the COGIC semantics, her *testimony* morphed into Pentecostal prophetic preaching.[70] As Morrison ad-libs, she begins to anticipate a new future—"When I get to heaven"—where she'll walk and talk with Jesus, wearing new shoes, likely a recall of Mahalia Jackson's rendition of the spiritual, "Walk All Over God's Heaven."[71] In a time marked by the assassination of the leader of the Poor People's Campaign, it is the hope of the age to come, when every tear will be wiped away, that is empowering and healing.

With her "earthy" voice, *via* the Spirit, Dorothy Morrison is lifted into a transformed space, where she leads the other singers as well as audiences around the world. In perhaps an even more surprising turn, she helped to move her white Pentecostal sisters and brothers back to their roots—and a sanctifying re-embrace of their African-rooted tradition—whether they realized it or not.

REVIVING THE EXTENDED FAMILY

While the Pentecostal movement was catalyzed by a revival in an African American church, under the pastoral leadership of African Americans—women and men[72]—it's accommodation to a racist (and misogynist) culture in America has been well-documented.[73] William Seymour witnessed this devolution within a few short years of the Azusa Street Revival's beginning. His experiences of racial division within the burgeoning tradition, in part, contributed to his theological reconstruction of the significance of Spirit baptism. While not denying that speaking in tongues would accompany the infilling or baptism of the Holy Spirit, he did qualify or revision his understanding of what Steven J. Land has called the essential nature of spiritual fullness.[74] From the onset of the revival, those being baptized in the Spirit testified to it as being a "baptism of divine love," language resonant with the Wesleyan roots of the revival.[75] But in the quest for "evidence," along the way, running parallel with the accommodation to culture, the essential sign of love had been displaced. As a result, Seymour began to boldly assert that "Divine love, which is charity," is the "real evidence" that one has been filled with the Spirit.[76]

By the time that the NCSYC, Betty Watson, Edwin Hawkins, Dorothy Combs Morrison, and Ron Thompson were singing "Oh Happy Day," Pentecostalism in North America was clearly racially segregated and, for the most part, reflected the dominant culture; in fact, the congregations, jurisdictions, and denominations lagged behind a culture that was beginning its quest for civil rights. Into that charged ethos came a testimony of sins being washed away.

Dodderidge's hymn had been a staple in Pentecostal songbooks for decades[77] and was sung by congregations converging for national denominational gatherings.[78] But by 1970, Hawkins' arrangement was being sung by youth choirs in predominantly, if not exclusively, white congregations. Two recordings of these performances have been located and will be examined. It should also be noted that several other arrangements of traditional songs found on the original NCSYC recording were widely adopted by white Pentecostal (and Evangelical) ensembles. Notable among these are the recordings by an Assemblies of God trio, made up of three white male ministers, The Couriers. In 1969, the year that "Oh Happy Day" topped the charts, the trio recorded the Hawkins arrangement of "Joy, Joy" on their album "Coming and Going."[79] That same year, they recorded an album including the song "I Heard the Voice of Jesus Say."[80] Another influential Southern gospel group that was crossing over to contemporary gospel music, The Imperials—the first group to integrate with an African American lead singer, Sherman Andrus (1971)[81]—recorded "Oh Happy Day" in 1970, with the vocal solo by Joe Moscheo and, again, on a live recording in 1973, where Andrus picks up the lead.[82] Like the NCSYC, The Imperials testify of being taught to "watch, fight, and pray." The Imperials toured Christian college campuses, including Pentecostal ones such as Lee College (now University), during this period.[83]

Within a year of its release, the Hawkins version of "Oh Happy Day," was being replicated by Pentecostal young people in their ensembles, family groups, and choirs.[84] The arrangement had been adopted by a Tomlinson College choir, "The Church of God of Prophecy Youth Aflame Choir," on a 1970 album.[85] The choir, as pictured on the album, is made up of forty white youth, male and female. The lead, sung by a male vocalist, follows the "call and response" pattern of the Black choir, though the adlibs aren't strictly duplicated. Notably, the choir does add the additional phrase "fight and pray."

While the Church of God of Prophecy (CGP) was a much more racially inclusive Pentecostal denomination from its beginnings in 1923, and its educational institutions, including Tomlinson College, had always been integrated,[86] in 1970 a racially mixed touring choir would have found difficulties in travel arrangements—especially as they attempted to find housing in church members' homes while on tour.[87] According to David E. Harrell, the CGP was the first to break the Jim Crow laws in Alabama and, as he noted, between 1945 and the mid-1960s, was the most integrated denomination in the South.[88] Perhaps it is that tension that is responsible for the choir's comfort with the lyrics that the result of having one's sins washed away was being taught how to "watch, *fight*, and pray."

In the year of the nation's centennial, the Bethalto CG (Bethalto, Illinois) recorded "Oh Happy Day" on their album, "On Tour."[89] Pictured on the album cover are forty-three youth, male and female, and all white. The director, J. T. Kelly, is a white male. The song begins with a lengthy organ introduction in a Black gospel style but quickly moves into a full choir rendition. There is no vocal solo; the lead is carried by the sopranos. It is striking that there is no reference to being taught to "watch, fight, and pray" as they opt for the original lyric "watch and pray." Additionally, there is no anticipation of heaven or the age to come.

The social location of these young people is important to take into consideration when considering their replication of an African American song that, as has been argued, trafficked spirituality. Bethalto Village, Illinois, in 1980, had a population of 8,630, with only nineteen of those being Black, 0.002 percent of the population.[90] Madison County's diversity was marginally better at 0.057 percent reporting as Black.[91] The yearbook of the village's Civic High School, from the same year as the recording, reveals the startling lack of diversity.[92] It is also important to note that the Bethalto COG claims a history tied to the Azusa Street Revival.[93] While it is not possible, without further investigation, to trace a direct link between the 1976 recording and the present congregation's self-understanding, it is notable that in a still predominantly white[94] village and county, the associate pastor, up through the end of 2023, was a Black minister of Jamaican descent.[95] It is highly likely that there are still members of this rural congregation who sang on that 1976 recording that echoed its African roots.

It is striking that in all these—admittedly few—instances within the larger world of later Pentecostal gospel singing—whether interracial, African American, or white—only in the COGIC original was the prophetic testimony being carried *via* the voice of a woman. Given the decidedly masculine turn in American Pentecostalism since its more egalitarian beginnings, that eclipsing of female prophetic leadership is not unexpected, but is seemingly incongruent with the movement's feminine root.

CONCLUSIONS

The explosive growth of Pentecostalism has long been documented and traced to many contributing factors: its portability, its democratization, and its miracles. But perhaps this brief study has raised the important issue of how a core part of its spirituality—Spirit-driven singing—has been an essential part of that expansion. Through one youth choir's recording, people have been captivated by the essence of that spirituality—where the Spirit is poured out on daughters and sons who testify and prophesy, bringing the hope of healing and reconciliation. A half-century later, when we face a similar situation where there is increasing violence, racial division, violence against women, and despair, the Spirit may be calling us to sing again.

NOTES

1. The song's continuing relevance and power were witnessed as a group of young musicians and singers, four black and one white, watched the film for the first time in a viewing at my home on December 15, 2023. They were moved by the "raw emotion," the "sanctified part of it," which differentiated them from the secular performers at the festival; "they were on a mission." They noted how Shirley Miller, singing the lead vocal, was "singing from a place" when people needed a "word from the Lord." Group members: Marcel Gore, Isaac Hammontree, Heaven and Jonathan Fortson, and George Walker.

2. The year 1968 is the most-often cited year of the recording, but Marc Myers lists the date as 1967 on the introductory page to a chapter on "Oh Happy Day," though, on the next page, he reproduces an interview with Hawkins in which the choir director states, "In 1968, I hired Century Records, a local vanity label to record an album of songs by the choir." [Marc Myers, *Anatomy of a Song: The Oral History of 45 Iconic Hits That Changed Rock, R&B and Pop* (New York: Grove Press, 2016), 150–151]. This interview appears to be a transcription of an interview of Hawkins and lead singer Dorothy Combs Morrison conducted by Bay Area television station KTVU in 1969. "Edwin Hawkins Singers (1969) https://diva.sfsu.edu/collections/sfbatv/bundles/217357 [Accessed December 20, 2023].

3. Library of Congress National Recording Registry. https://www.loc.gov/programs/national-recording-preservation-board/recording-registry/complete-national-recording-registry-listing/ [Accessed January 1, 2024].

4. See Tammy L. Kernodle, "Work the Works: The Role of African-American Women in the Development of Contemporary Gospel," *Black Music Research Journal* Vol. 26, No. 1 (Spring 2006), pp. 89–109. https://www.jstor.org/stable/25433763 [Accessed May 12, 2023]; Mellonee V. Burnin, "Crossing Musical Borders: Agency and Process in the Gospel Music Industry," in *Issues in African American Music: Power, Gender, Race, Representation* Portia K. Maultsby and Mellonee V. Burnim, eds. (New York: Routledge, 2017), 81.

5. Mellonee V. Burnim and Portia K. Maultsby, eds., *African American Music—An Introduction* (New York: Routledge, 2015), 205.

6. See Graeme M. Boone, "Twelve Key Recordings," in *The Cambridge Companion to Blues and Gospel Music* (Cambridge: Cambridge University Press, 2002), 86–88. See also Burnim, 205.

7. David Hajdu, "What the Harlem Cultural Festival Represented," *The Nation* (July 29, 2021). https://www.thenation.com/article/culture/summer-of-soul-review/ [Accessed January 7, 2024].

8. Stan Soocher, *Baby You're a Rich Man: Suing the Beatles for Fun and Profit* (University Press of New England, 2015), 179. https://www.jstor.org/stable/j.ctv1xx-9hbf.26 [Accessed May 12, 2023].

9. Jerry Hopkins, "Big Sur," *Rolling Stone* No. 44 (October 18, 1969). https://web.archive.org/web/20101006054306/http://www.suitelorraine.com/suitelorraine/Pages/rncsny69.html [Accessed January 1, 2024.] For a video of the performance of Baez singing "Oh Happy Day" with original soloist Dorothy Combs Morrison see the film, "Celebration at Big Sur," available on YouTube. https://www.youtube.com/watch?v=gPdrkJWotcU.

10. https://www.glencampbell.com/releases-archive/oh-happy-day/ [Accessed January 1, 2024].

11. Claudrena N. Harold, *When Sunday Comes:Gospel Music in the Soul and Hip Hop Eras.* (Champaign, IL: University of Illinois Press, 2020), 90. https://www.jstor.org/stable/10.5406/j.ctv19wx7mj.8 [Accessed May 12, 2023].

12. Bil Carpenter, *Uncloudy Days: The Gospel Music Encyclopedia* (San Francisco: Backbeat Books, 2005), 180.

13. Edwin Hawkins, "Foreword," in Carpenter, v.

14. Marc Myers, 150.

15. Burnim, 205.

16. NCSYC, "Let Us Go Into the House of the Lord," https://youtu.be/6tSyz-TIJ82g?si=EGR6FW4YPj_d9igp [Accessed December 21, 2023].

17. Other rearrangements of traditional hymns on the album included "Jesus Lover of My Soul" by Charles Wesley, composed in 1740; "I Heard the Voice of Jesus Say" by Horatio Bonar, composed in 1846; "I'm Going Through" by Herbert Buffam, composed in the late nineteenth/early twentieth century.

18. See "O happy day that fix-d my choice," *Hymnology Archive*. https://www.hymnologyarchive.com/o-happy-day-that-fixed-my-choice [Accessed January 7, 2024.] and "O happy day, that fixed my choice." *The Canterbury Dictionary of Hymnology.* Canterbury Press, accessed January 7, 2024. http://www.hymnology.co.uk/o/o-happy-day,-that-fixed-my-choice.

19. "Oh Happy Day. (1969)—Edwin Hawkins Singers," *Encyclopedia of Great Popular Song Recordings*, Vol. 1, Steve Sullivan, ed. (Lanham, MD: The Scarecrow Press, 2013), 409. https://web.s.ebscohost.com/ehost/ebookviewer/ebook?sid=5ecce3e5-e335-4032-80cd-94629dcb73db%40redis&ppid=pp_410&vid=0&format=EB [Accessed December 21, 2023].

20. Dorsey cited by Mellonee V. Burnin, "Crossing Musical Borders," 81. Cited by *Sullivan*, 409.

21. Peggy King, "Happy Day for Teen Age!," *Oakland Tribune* (May 17, 1969), 11. https://www.newspapers.com/image/38659132/?terms=%22Dorothy%20Morrison%22&match=1 [Accessed 20 December 2023].

22. Myers, 151.

23. Ben Fong-Torres, "'Oh Happy Day': A Pop Godsend," *Rolling Stone* (May 17, 1969). https://www.rollingstone.com/music/music-news/oh-happy-day-a-pop-godsend-183652/ [Accessed December 21, 2023.]

24. Burnin, 81. This record deal with Buddha was a source of conflict within the choir itself and between its directors. According to Ron Thompson, an original choir member who also toured with the Singers following the song's success in 1969–1970, the fact of the oversight by the First Jurisdiction and its bishop, Rev. E. B. Stewart, became an issue in the negotiations with Buddha Records in 1969 and resulted in the division between Watson and Hawkins. Buddha wanted to sign Hawkins, hence the new group name, "Edwin Hawkins Singers"—the name under which they now recorded and toured. Interview with Ron Thompson, original choir member. Interview conducted via Zoom, December 30, 2023. See also King.

25. Fong-Torres.

26. The single reached "No.4 on the US pop singles chart and No. 2 on the UK pop singles survey." For two weeks, it held its spot at "No. 2 on the American R&B singles chart (Carpenter, 181).

27. "Music on 'Harlem Festival,'" *Democrat and Chronicle* (Rochester, NY: July 27, 1969), 30. https://www.newspapers.com/image/136788470 [Accessed December 18, 2023].

28. Concert Archives https://www.concertarchives.org/bands/edwin-hawkins-singers [Accessed January 1, 2024]; Festivial. https://www.festivival.com/festivals/tag/artist/edwin-hawkins-singers [Accessed January 1, 2024]

29. "Sentinel Television Log," *Santa Cruz Sentinel* (5 September 1969), 10. https://www.newspapers.com/image/67679472/?terms=Edwin%20Hawkins%20Singers%2C%20TV&match=1 [Accessed January 1, 2024].

30. "TV Hour by Hour," *Chicago Tribune* (July 4, 1969), 35. https://www.newspapers.com/image/67679472/?terms=Edwin%20Hawkins%20Singers%2C%20TV&match=1; "Tuesday Morning," *Bellingham Herald* (12 December 1969), 6. https://www.newspapers.com/image/769366713/?terms=%22Edwin%20Hawkins%20Singers%22%20David%20Frost&match=1[Both accessed January 1, 2024].

31. Among others, they appeared on the weekly show hosted by Englebert Humperdink ["TV Key Previews," *Portland Press Herald* (11 March 1979), 21. https://www.newspapers.com/image/849049175/?terms=Edwin%20Hawkins%20Singers%2C%20TV%2C%20Humperdinck&match=1] [Accessed 1 January 2024] and Andy Williams ["Television Highlights," *Sidney Daily News* (1 November 1969), 2. https://www.newspapers.com/image/880111754/?terms=Edwin%20Hawkins%20Singers%2C%20TV&match=1] [Accessed January 1, 2024].

32. Ibid.

33. Burnim, 81.

34. Burnim, in Burnim and Maultsby, 205.

35. Robert Darden, *People Get Ready: A New History of Black Gospel Music* (New York: Bloomsbury Academic, 2004), 275.

36. Brett Milano, "The 25 Greatest One-Hit Wonders of All Time," Udiscovermusic (January 14, 2023). https://www.udiscovermusic.com/stories/one-hit-wonders/ [Accessed January 18, 2024].

37. "Edwin Hawkins Singers," KTVU News Report (1969). SFBATV Archives. https://diva.sfsu.edu/collections/sfbatv/bundles/217357 [Accessed December 21, 2023].

38. "1200 at Funeral of Black Panther," *San Francisco Examiner* (April 13, 1968), 3. https://www.newspapers.com/image/458507310/?terms=Black%20Panther%2C%20Ephesian%20Church%20of%20God%20in%20Christ&match=1 [Accessed January 17, 2024.] See also Paul Jacobs, "Letter from Oakland," *the New York Review* (May 23, 1968). https://www.nybooks.com/articles/1968/05/23/letter-from-oakland/ [Accessed January 17, 2024].

39. Carol Cooper, "After A Violent Winter, The 'Summer of Soul' Was A Musical Moment of Healing," NPR (July 13, 2021). https://www.npr.org/2021/07/13/1015347905/summer-of-soul-questlove-1969-harlem-cultural-festival [Accessed December 21, 2023].

40. See Wesley Morris, 'Summer of Soul' Review: In 1969 Harlem, a Music Festival Stuns," *New York Times* (June 4, 2021). https://www.nytimes.com/2021/06/24/movies/summer-of-soul-review.html [Accessed January 7, 2024.] On May 24, 2022, the US Congress recognized the cultural significance of the festival. See S.Res. 647. https://www.congress.gov/bill/117th-congress/senate-resolution/647/text [Accessed January 7, 2024].

41. Fong-Torres.

42. Ibid.

43. See Kimberly Ervin Alexander, "Singing Heavenly Music: R. Hollis Gause's Theology of Worship and Pentecostal Experience" in *Toward a Pentecostal Theology of Worship*, Lee Roy Martin, ed. (Cleveland, TN: CPT Press, 2016), and "Heavenly Choirs in Earthy Spaces: The Significance of Corporate Spiritual Singing in Early Pentecostal Experience." *Journal of Pentecostal Theology*, 25 (2016): 254–268.

44. *The Apostolic Faith* 1.1 (September 1906), p. 1.

45. Sullivan.

46. Burnim, 192–193.

47. C. H. Mason, "Tennessee Evangelist Witnesses," *The Apostolic Faith* Vol. 1, No. 6 (February-March 1907), 7.

48. L. H. Thuston, "C. H. Mason: Sanctified Reformer" in *From Aldersgate to Azusa Street: Wesleyan, Holiness, and Pentecostal Visions of the New Creation*, ed. by Henry H. Knight III (Eugene, OR: Pickwick Publications, 2010), 232.

49. Walter J. Hollenweger, *Pentecostalism: Origins and Developments Worldwide* (Peabody, MA: Hendrickson, 1997), Hollenweger delineates five aspects of this Black oral root: the oral nature of the movement's liturgy, its use of narrative (including dependence on narrative sections of the biblical text as well as the narrative testimony of believers in evangelization), significance given to visions and dreams (in

both public and private worship), communal participation in worship and decision-making, and an integrated view of the body-mind relationship (most notable in prayer for the sick) [Hollenweger, 18–19].

50. Thompson.

51. Marc Myers, "When He Washed My Sins Away," *The Wall Street Journal* (November 22, 2012). https://www.wsj.com/articles/SB10001424127887324556304578123332598062540 [Accessed May 17, 2023].

52. See Henry H. Knight, III, *Anticipating Heaven Below: Optimism of Grace from Wesley to the Pentecostals* (Eugene, OR: Cascade Books, 2014).

53. Kathy Orloff, "Association Cops the Loew's Awards," *The Akron Beacon Journal* (27 April 1969), 101.

54. Orloff.

55. Keri Day, *Azusa Reimagined: A Radical Vision of Religious and Democratic Belonging* (Stanford: Stanford University Press, 2022), 6.

56. See also Cheryl Townsend Gilkes, *If It Wasn't for the Women* (Maryknoll, NY: Orbis Books, 2004); Anthea D. Butler, *Women in the Church of God in Christ: Making a Sanctified World* (Chapel Hill, NC: University of North Carolina Press, 2007).

57. Soloist Shirley King Miller followed Morrison, performing the solo on tour. Most, if not all, video recordings available of the performance by the Edwin Hawkins Singers—including "Summer of Soul"—are of the song being led by Miller, though she is sometimes mistakenly identified as Morrison.

58. Kernodle, 93.

59. Thompson.

60. Orloff.

61. Keith Harmon, "Bright Future for Lovely Lady—Local Singer Rings Up Hit," *Berkeley Daily Gazette* (April 19, 1969), 4. https://www.newspapers.com/image/995115606 [Accessed December 18, 2023.]

62. Boone, 87–88.

63. Ed Pavlić, *Who Can Afford to Improvise?—James Baldwin and Black Music, the Lyric and the Listeners* (New York: Fordham University Press, 2016), 5.

64. Malcolm Marshall, "Q&A: Richmond Gospel Legend Dorothy Morrison on Music, Faith and Home," *Richmond Pulse*. file:///Users/kimberlyalexander/Desktop/Writing%20Projects/Oh%20Happy%20Day/Q&A_%20Richmond%20Gospel%20Legend%20Dorothy%20Morrison%20on%20Music,%20Faith%20and%20Home%20_%20Richmond%20Pulse.html [Accessed January 1, 2024].

65. Marc Myers, "When He Washed My Sins Away." Though the arrangement belonged to Hawkins, Morrison, in essence, wrote many of the new lyrics. The acquisition of the album master by Buddha Records is outlined by Carpenter, 181. Details about the division in the choir itself, and between Betty Watson and Hawkins, are less straightforward. See "Recordings Back to God," *Time* (May 23, 1969). https://content.time.com/time/subscriber/article/0,33009,900873,00.html [Accessed January 1, 2024]. Forty-five years after the recording, she told Myers, "I wasn't paid for the record, but that doesn't matter. I was singing in church, singing for the Lord" [Myers].

66. For a discussion of women in COGIC, see Butler. For examinations of the "mixed messaging" and cognitive dissonance experienced by women in Pentecostal denominations, see Joy E. A. Qualls, *God Forgive Us for Being Women: Rhetoric, Theology, and the Pentecostal Tradition.* (Eugene, OR: Pickwick Publications, 2018); Estrelda Y. Alexander, *Limited Liberty: The Legacy of Four Female Women Pioneers* (Cleveland, OH: Pilgrim Press, 2008); Kimberly Ervin Alexander and James Philemon Bowers, *What Women Want: Pentecostal Women Ministers Speak for Themselves* (Eugene, OR: Wipf and Stock, 2018).

67. See Marshall.

68. Opal Louis Nations, "Oh Happy Day," *Big City Blues* (December 2005-January 2006). https://opalnations.com/files/Dorothy_Morrison_Oh_Happy_Day_Big _City_Blues_Dec.05-Jan.06.pdf [Accessed December 28, 2023].

69. Marshall.

70. See Lee Roy Martin, "Fire in the Bones: Pentecostal Prophetic Preaching" in *Theology of Preaching*, Lee Roy Martin, ed. (Cleveland, TN: CPT Press, 2015), 34–63; see also Antoinette G. Alvarado, "A Hermeneutic of Empowerment: The African American Women's Preaching Tradition," in Martin, 154–180.

71. Mahalia Jackson, "Walk All Over God's Heaven" (1958). https://www.youtube.com/watch?v=vH0Sqpjkb3w [Accessed January 2, 2024].

72. See Cecil M. Robeck, Jr., *The Azusa Street Mission and Revival: The Birth of the Global Pentecostal Movement* (Nashville, TN: Nelson Reference and Electronic, 2006). See also Estrelda Y. Alexander, *Black Fire: One Hundred Years of African American Pentecostalism* (Downer's Grove: IVP Academic, 2011).

73. See Estrelda Y. Alexander and Amos Yong, eds., *Afro-Pentecostalism: Black Pentecostal and Charismatic Christianity in History and Culture* (New York: New York University Press, 2011); Clifton R. Clarke and Wayne C. Solomon, eds., *Skin Deep: Pentecostalism, Racism and the Church* (Lanham, MD: Seymour Press, 2021). See especially Kimberly Ervin Alexander and James Philemon Bowers, "Race and Gender Equality in a Classical Pentecostal Denomination: How Godly Love Flourished and Foundered," in Clarke and Solomon, 155–183.

74. Steven J. Land, "Be Filled With the Spirit: The Nature and Evidence of Spiritual Fullness," *Ex Auditu* 12 (1996), 108–120.

75. See Kimberly Ervin Alexander, "Boundless Love Divine: A Re-Evaluation of Early Understandings of the Experience of Spirit Baptism," in *Passover, Pentecost & Parousia: Studies in Celebration of the Life and Ministry of R. Hollis Gause*, JPTS 35, S. J. Land, R. D. Moore, and J. C. Thomas, eds. (Blandford Forum: Deo Publishing, 2010), 145–170.

76. William J. Seymour, "Questions Answered," *The Apostolic Faith* Vol. 1, No. 11 (1908–1909), 2. In his *Doctrines and Disciplines of the Azusa Street Mission,* he states, "the baptism of the Holy Ghost means to be flooded with the love of God and power for service, and a love for the truth as it is in God's Word." [William J. Seymour, *Doctrines and Disciplines of the Azusa Street Mission of Los Angeles, CA,* (1915), 92.]

77. See, for instance, "O Happy Day," in *Pentecostal Revivalist,* Thoro Harris, ed. (Los Angeles, CA: Aimee Semple McPherson, n.d.), 235. "O Happy Day,"

in *Church Hymnal* (Cleveland, TN: Tennessee Music and Printing, 1951), 86; "O Happy Day," in *Songs of Praise* (Springfield, MO: Gospel Publishing House, 1935), 143.

78. For example, see *Minutes of the Twenty-Ninth Annual Assembly of the Church of God* (Cleveland, TN: Church of God Publishing House, 1934), 11; *Minutes of the Ninth General Conference of the Pentecostal Holiness Church* (Franklin Springs, GA, 1941), 6.

79. The Couriers, "Joy, Joy." https://www.youtube.com/watch?v=a1H4RpMOo2w [Accessed January 2, 2024].

80. "I Heard the Voice of Jesus Say." The Couriers.com. http://thecouriers.com/recordings2.htm [Accessed January 1, 2024]. See James R. Goff, Jr., "Southern Gospel's Preacher Boys," *Assemblies of God Heritage* Vol. 27 (2007), 4–13.

81. Red O'Donnell, "1972: The World Begins to Realize," *Record World* (October 21, 1972), 28. https://www.worldradiohistory.com/Archive-All-Music/Record-World/70s/72/RW-1972-10-21.pdf [Accessed January 2, 2024.] For Andrus' own reflection on "breaking the color barrier" in gospel music, see his interview with Jake Feinberg. https://www.youtube.com/watch?v=5pRe1Dp6a-c [Accessed January 2, 2024].

82. Live With . . . Solid Rock 2LP Set—The Imperials (1973).
https://www.youtube.com/watch?v=KfyC9gxBLgw [Accessed January 2, 2024].

83. Two of the college's "Service Clubs"—Alpha Gamma Chi and Delta Zeta Tau—sponsored a concert featuring the Imperials and Andre Crouch and the Disciples in Spring 1972. [*Vindauga 72—The Yearbook of Lee College* Vol. 31, 134 and 141]. https://archive.org/details/vindagua1972leeu/page/140/mode/2up?view=theater&q=Imperials [Accessed January 2, 2024].

84. See Ginger Hames, "Youth and His Family Harmony," *The Lighted Pathway* Vol. 41, No. 9; and *The 54th General Assembly of the Church of God—1972 Minutes* (Cleveland, TN: The Church of God Publishing House, 1972), 21.

85. Oh Happy Day—The Church of God of Prophecy Youth Aflame Choir (1970). https://www.youtube.com/watch?v=hrdoRx6psi0 [Accessed May 17, 2023].

86. Harold D. Hunter, "A Journey Toward Racial Reconciliation: Race Mixing in the Church of God of Prophecy," in *The Azusa Street Revival and Its Legacy* (Cleveland, TN: Pathway Press, 2006), 277–296. See also Estrelda Alexander, 266–269.

87. Email from Harold D. Hunter, December 21, 2023. Hunter was part of the charter class of Tomlinson College (1966–1968).

88. Hunter email; Hunter, 277.

89. "Oh Happy Day,"—Bethalto Church of God 1976 Youth Choir. https://www.youtube.com/watch?v=EadCP5ISfVI [Accessed May 17, 2023].

90. "Table 15: Persons by Race," "General Population Characteristics--Illinois," *1980 Population of Census*. https://www2.census.gov/library/publications/decennial/1980/volume-1/illinois/1980a_ilab-03.pdf [Accessed January 7, 2024].

91. Ibid.

92. 1976 Civic Memorial High School. https://www.classmates.com/yearbooks/Civic-Memorial-High-School/4182730028?page=1 [Accessed January 7, 2024].
93. "About Us," Bethalto Church of God. https://www.bcog.cc/about-us [Accessed January 7, 2024].
94. See "Bethalto, Illinois Population 2024," *World Population Review*. https://worldpopulationreview.com/us-cities/bethalto-il-population [Accessed January 2, 2024].
95. Ibid.

BIBLIOGRAPHY

"1200 at Funeral of Black Panther," *San Francisco Examiner*, April 13, 1968. https://www.newspapers.com/image/458507310/?terms=Black%20Panther%2C%20Ephesian%20Church%20of%20God%20in%20Christ&match=1

1976 Civic Memorial High School. https://www.classmates.com/yearbooks/Civic-Memorial-High-School/4182730028?page=1

"About Us." Bethalto Church of God https://www.bcog.cc/about-us.

Alexander, Estrelda Y. *Black Fire: One Hundred Years of African American Pentecostalism* Downer's Grove: IVP Academic, 2011.

Alexander, Estrelda Y. and Amos Yong, eds. *Afro-Pentecostalism: Black Pentecostal and Charismatic Christianity in History and Culture*. New York: New York University Press, 2011.

Alexander, Kimberly Ervin "Boundless Love Divine: A Re-Evaluation of Early Understandings of the Experience of Spirit Baptism." In *Passover, Pentecost & Parousia: Studies in Celebration of the Life and Ministry of R. Hollis Gause*, JPTS 35, edited by S. J. Land, R. D. Moore, and J. C. Thomas (pp. 145–170). Blandford Forum: Deo Publishing, 2010.

Alexander, Kimberly Ervin. "Singing Heavenly Music: R. Hollis Gause's Theology of Worship and Pentecostal Experience". In *Toward a Pentecostal Theology of Worship*, edited by Lee Roy Martin. Cleveland, TN: CPT Press, 2016.

Alexander, Kimberly Ervin. "Heavenly Choirs in Earthy Spaces: The Significance of Corporate Spiritual Singing in Early Pentecostal Experience." *Journal of Pentecostal Theology*, 25 (2016): 254–268.

Alexander, Kimberly Ervin and James Philemon Bowers. "Race and Gender Equality in a Classical Pentecostal Denomination: How Godly Love Flourished and Foundered." In *Skin Deep: Pentecostalism, Racism and the Church,* edited by Clifton R. Clarke and Wayne C. Solomon (pp. 155–183). Lanham, MD: Seymour Press, 2021.

Alvarado, Antoinette G. "A Hermeneutic of Empowerment: The African American Women's Preaching Tradition." In *Theology of Preaching*, edited by Lee Roy Martin (pp. 154–180). Cleveland, TN: CPT Press, 2015.

"Bethalto, Illinois Population 2024." *World Population Review* https://worldpopulationreview.com/us-cities/bethalto-il-population

Clarke, Clifton R. and Wayne C. Solomon, eds., *Skin Deep: Pentecostalism, Racism and the Church.* Lanham, MD: Seymour Press, 2021.

Cooper, Cooper. "After A Violent Winter, The 'Summer of Soul' Was A Musical Moment of Healing." NPR, July 13, 2021. https://www.npr.org/2021/07/13/1015347905/summer-of-soul-questlove-1969-harlem-cultural-festival

Boone, Graeme M. "Twelve Key Recordings." In *The Cambridge Companion to Blues and Gospel Music*, edited by Allan Moore (pp. 86–88). Cambridge: Cambridge University Press, 2002.

Burnin, Mellonee V. "Crossing Musical Borders: Agency and Process in the Gospel Music Industry." In *Issues in African American Music: Power, Gender, Race, Representation,* edited by Portia K. Maultsby and Mellonee V. Burnim (pp. 79–89). New York: Routledge, 2017.

Burnim, Mellonee V. and Portia K. Maultsby, eds., *African American Music—An Introduction.* New York: Routledge, 2015.

Carpenter, Bil. *Uncloudy Days: The Gospel Music Encyclopedia.* San Francisco: Backbeat Books, 2005.

Darden, Robert. *People Get Ready: A New History of Black Gospel Music.* New York: Bloomsbury Academic, 2004.

Day, Keri. *Azusa Reimagined: A Radical Vision of Religious and Democratic Belonging.* Stanford: Stanford University Press, 2022

"Edwin Hawkins Singers." KTVU News Report (1969). SFBATV Archives. https://diva.sfsu.edu/collections/sfbatv/bundles/217357

Fong-Torres, Ben. "'Oh Happy Day': A Pop Godsend." *Rolling Stone.* May 17, 1969. https://www.rollingstone.com/music/music-news/oh-happy-day-a-pop-godsend-183652/

Hajdu, David. "What the Harlem Cultural Festival Represented." *The Nation.* July 29, 2021. https://www.thenation.com/article/culture/summer-of-soul-review/

Harold, Claudrena N. *When Sunday Comes: Gospel Music in the Soul and Hip Hop Eras.* Champaign, IL: University of Illinois Press, 2020.

Harmon, Keith. "Bright Future for Lovely Lady—Local Singer Rings Up Hit." *Berkeley Daily Gazette,* April 19, 1969. https://www.newspapers.com/image/995115606

Hollenweger, Walter J. *Pentecostalism: Origins and Developments Worldwide.* Peabody, MA: Hendrickson, 1997.

Hopkins, Jerry. "Big Sur." *Rolling Stone* No. 44, October 18, 1969. https://web.archive.org/web/20101006054306/http://www.suitelorraine.com/suitelorraine/Pages/rncsny69.html

Hunter, Harold D. "A Journey Toward Racial Reconciliation: Race Mixing in the Church of God of Prophecy." In *The Azusa Street Revival and Its Legacy,* edited by Harold D. Hunter and Cecil M. Robeck (pp. 277–296). Cleveland, TN: Pathway Press, 2006.

Hunter, Harold D. Email to author. December 21, 2023.

"I Heard the Voice of Jesus Say." The Couriers.com. http://thecouriers.com/recordings2.htm

Jackson, Mahalia. "Walk All Over God's Heaven" (1958). https://www.youtube.com/watch?v=vH0Sqpjkb3w

Kernodle, Tammy L. "Work the Works: The Role of African-American Women in the Development of Contemporary Gospel." *Black Music Research Journal* Vol. 26, No. 1 (Spring 2006): 89–109. https://www.jstor.org/stable/25433763

King, Peggy. "Happy Day for Teen Age!" *Oakland Tribune*, May 17, 1969. https://www.newspapers.com/image/38659132/?terms=%22Dorothy%20Morrison%22&match=1

Knight, III, Henry H. *Anticipating Heaven Below: Optimism of Grace from Wesley to the Pentecostals*. Eugene, OR: Cascade Books, 2014.

Library of Congress National Recording Registry. https://www.loc.gov/programs/national-recording-preservation-board/recording-registry/complete-national-recording-registry-listing/

Live With...Solid Rock 2LP Set—The Imperials (1973) https://www.youtube.com/watch?v=KfyC9gxBLgw

Marshall, Marshall. "Q&A: Richmond Gospel Legend Dorothy Morrison on Music, Faith and Home," *Richmond Pulse* file:///Users/kimberlyalexander/Desktop/Writing%20Projects/Oh%20Happy%20Day/Q&A_%20Richmond%20Gospel%20Legend%20Dorothy%20Morrison%20on%20Music,%20Faith%20and%20Home%20_%20Richmond%20Pulse.html

Martin, Lee Roy. "Fire in the Bones: Pentecostal Prophetic Preaching." In *Theology of Preaching*, edited by Lee Roy Martin (pp. 34–63). Cleveland, TN: CPT Press, 2015.

Mason, C. H. "Tennessee Evangelist Witnesses." *The Apostolic Faith* Vol. 1, No. 6 (February–March 1907): 7.

Milano, Brett. "The 25 Greatest One-Hit Wonders of All Time," Udiscovermusic, January 14, 2023. https://www.udiscovermusic.com/stories/one-hit-wonders/

Morris, Wesley. "'Summer of Soul' Review: In 1969 Harlem, a Music Festival Stuns." *New York Times,* June 4, 2021. https://www.nytimes.com/2021/06/24/movies/summer-of-soul-review.html

"Music on 'Harlem Festival." *Democrat and Chronicle*, Rochester, NY: July 27, 1969. https://www.newspapers.com/image/136788470

Myers, Marc. *Anatomy of a Song: The Oral History of 45 Iconic Hits That Changed Rock, R&B and Pop*. New York: Grove Press, 2016.

Myers, Marc. "When He Washed My Sins Away." *The Wall Street Journal*, November 22, 2012. https://www.wsj.com/articles/SB10001424127887324556304578123332598062540

Nations, Opal Louis. "Oh Happy Day," *Big City Blues*, December 2005-January 2006. https://opalnations.com/files/Dorothy_Morrison_Oh_Happy_Day_Big_City_Blues_Dec.05-Jan.06.pdf

NCSYC, "Let Us Go Into the House of the Lord." https://youtu.be/6tSyzTIJ82g?si=EGR6FW4YPj_d9igp

"O happy day that fix-d my choice." *Hymnology Archive. https://www.hymnologyarchive.com/o-happy-day-that-fixed-my-choice*

O'Donnell, Red. "1972: The World Begins to Realize." *Record World,* October 21, 1972. https://www.worldradiohistory.com/Archive-All-Music/Record-World/70s/72/RW-1972-10-21.pdf

"Oh Happy Day. (1969)—Edwin Hawkins Singers." *Encyclopedia of Great Popular Song Recordings,* Vol. 1, edited by Steve Sullivan. Lanham, MD: The Scarecrow Press, 2013, pp. 409–410. https://web.s.ebscohost.com/ehost/ebookviewer/ebook?sid=5ecce3e5-e335-4032-80cd-94629dcb73db%40redis&ppid=pp_410&vid=0&format=EB

"Oh Happy Day,"—Bethalto Church of God 1976 Youth Choir. https://www.youtube.com/watch?v=EadCP5ISfVI

Oh Happy Day—The Church of God of Prophecy Youth Aflame Choir (1970). https://www.youtube.com/watch?v=hrdoRx6psi0

Orloff, Kathy. "Association Cops the Loew's Awards." *The Akron Beacon Journal,* 27 April 1969.

Pavlíc, Ed. *Who Can Afford to Improvise?—James Baldwin and Black Music, the Lyric and the Listeners.* New York: Fordham University Press, 2016.

"Recordings Back to God" *Time,* May 23, 1969. https://content.time.com/time/subscriber/article/0,33009,900873,00.html

Robeck, Jr., Cecil M. *The Azusa Street Mission and Revival: The Birth of the Global Pentecostal Movement.* Nashville, TN: Nelson Reference and Electronic, 2006.

"Sentinel Television Log." *Santa Cruz Sentinel,* 5 September 1969. https://www.newspapers.com/image/67679472/?terms=Edwin%20Hawkins%20Singers%2C%20TV&match=1

Seymour, William J. "Questions Answered," *The Apostolic Faith* Vol. 1, No. 11 (1908–1909): 2.

Soocher, Stan. *Baby You're a Rich Man: Suing the Beatles for Fun and Profit.* Lebanon, NH: University Press of New England, 2015. https://www.jstor.org/stable/10.5406/j.ctv19wx7mj.8

"Table 15: Persons by Race." In "General Population Characteristics–Illinois," *1980 Population of Census.* https://www2.census.gov/library/publications/decennial/1980/volume-1/illinois/1980a_ilab-03.pdf

"Television Highlights." *Sidney Daily News,* 1 November 1969. https://www.newspapers.com/image/880111754/?terms=Edwin%20Hawkins%20Singers%2C%20TV&match=1

The Apostolic Faith Vol. 1, No. 1 (September 1906): 1.

The Couriers, "Joy, Joy." https://www.youtube.com/watch?v=a1H4RpMOo2w

Thuston, L. H. "C. H. Mason: Sanctified Reformer." In *From Aldersgate to Azusa Street: Wesleyan, Holiness, and Pentecostal Visions of the New Creation,* edited by Henry H. Knight III. Eugene, OR: Pickwick Publications, 2010.

"Tuesday Morning," *Bellingham Herald,* 12 December 1969. https://www.newspapers.com/image/769366713/?terms=%22Edwin%20Hawkins%20Singers%22%20David%20Frost&match=1

"TV Hour by Hour," *Chicago Tribune,* 4 July 1969. https://www.newspapers.com/image/67679472/?terms=Edwin%20Hawkins%20Singers%2C%20TV&match=1

"TV Key Previews." *Portland Press Herald,* 11 March 1979. https://www.newspapers.com/image/849049175/?terms=Edwin%20Hawkins%20Singers%2C%20TV%2C%20Humperdinck&match=1

Chapter 13

Global Spirit and Globalizing Spirits

Worship Song's Role in Turkish Liturgical Identity

Jeremy Perigo

Recent scholarship on contemporary worship songs has emphasized the global economic trends of commoditizing worship music by megachurches and music publishers. These scholars highlight the unifying agents at work to generate profit and expand the powerful reach of worship ministries through conferences and online music through "selling worship."[1] This globalizing of worship occurs as music technology and economic trends are combined to distribute new worship songs, influencing the worship practices of the global Church. For example, in their analysis of the most used songs from 2010–2020 in the United States, Worship Leader Research concludes "that a few megachurches and a small number of affiliated artists have come to shape the song repertoire of a broad swath of Christian congregations" and, without the support of these churches, new songs "would not easily gain widespread popularity in the industry . . . and the church."[2] A new worship song's success is linked with its ability to be globalized.

Similarly, Monique Ingalls' discussion of the "World Edition" video of American Worship Leader Chris Tomlin's "How Great is Our God" reveals another example of globalizing worship.[3] The video features worship leaders from across the globe singing snippets of the song's lyrics in their own languages along with Tomlin and his band, who are leading center stage at Passion 2012 in the Georgia Dome in Atlanta with thousands of college-aged worshipers. Though the video features distinct languages and cultures, Ingalls states, "Pop-rock style contemporary worship music . . . is presented as the one universal musical language sufficient to unite Christians from around the world."[4] She highlights that the video "visually implies that those best equipped to lead the global church in participating in worship are middle-class, twenty-to-forty-year-old men who adhere to the stylistic norms."[5]

Though the video presents linguistic, sonic, and visual diversity, Chris Tomlin and his Western popular worship music stand center stage.

While some scholars continually point to the globalizing of worship music, songwriters and Christian music executives frequently indicate the global work of the Spirit in expanding a worship song's success.[6] Worship music manager and producer Les Moir emphasizes God's activity in taking UK worship songs global. He writes, "This is not my story but our story. Over the past fifty years God has done an amazing thing in the United Kingdom in His church and with worship. As the Holy Spirit was poured out, the British church moved from formality into freedom."[7] He stresses, "I began to realise that God was going to take worship songs from the UK and bless the nations of the world."[8] In the view of some industry insiders, the Spirit is the central agent producing and promoting these songs from local churches to communities across the globe.

In this discussion, the worship industry can be characterized, at worst, as a nefarious colonizing association bent on global liturgical domination through economic and media influences. At best, in their desire to celebrate the work of the Spirit, popular songwriters, worship artists, and their related companies can display a naivety of their own industry, including their own daily job duties and the dedicated work of their music industry colleagues. Can a global Spirit be at work within globalizing trends? At times, could worship music publishers be knowingly and unknowingly utilizing these powerful market forces in contradiction of the work of the Spirit's work in local churches? Can the Spirit be at work amid a spirit of globalization? How can local churches striving to plan biblically faithful and culturally hospitable worship discern between toxic globalizing market forces and the global Spirit working to enable the flourishing of a community's original music?

Evangelical Christians, including Pentecostals and Charismatics, place particular emphasis on the translation of shared hymns and worship songs along with the encouragement of indigenous leaders to write songs in local musical styles. Christian worship music is distinct among musical genres. While music by pop artists, such as Taylor Swift, is distributed all over the globe and then played in English in shopping malls in Cairo suburbs and emotively sung in karaoke bars in Cape Town, the music of Christian artists like Tomlin is translated, adapted, and assimilated into local languages and musical styles. Though sharing economic and distribution channels with other genres of music, Christian congregational worship songs are open to cultural adaptations. "Musical localization," a category proposed by Ingalls, Reigersberg, and Sherinian, is the diverse "process Christian communities worldwide adapt, adopt, create, perform, and share congregational music."[9] Songs that emerge from the West aren't simply translated, but, in the case of minority groups such as the Lisu in southwest China, Aminta Arrington states popular

Evangelical hymns were often "transformed" through localization as unique phrases or abstract theological terms are replaced and local rhythms are employed.[10] Steven Félix-Jäger offers "reproduction," "contextualization," and "indigenization" as three models of global engagement in contemporary worship music.[11] The reproduction model is when Western worship music is "reproduced in global cultures around the world."[12] In Félix-Jäger's view, this approach isn't forced colonization of worship music by larger worship publishers like Hillsong Worship; instead, he asserts that a worship ministry "intentionally seeks out partners that mesh with their vision and culture."[13] The contextualization model seeks to translate Western worship songs, such as Tomlin's "How Great Is Our God," into local languages and musical styles; the indigenization model empowers local songwriters to create their own original worship songs from their own local context.[14] For Evangelicals, implicit within their theology and practice of mission is a desire to utilize any cultural form to proclaim the gospel, while also encouraging local leaders in frontier mission contexts to utilize their own local cultural forms. Worship songs from the West aren't simply imported or exported, but numerous layers of musical, theological, and cultural nuances are translated and transformed.

In the midst of a growing globalized music industry and contextualized evangelism efforts, Christianity continues to take root in new cultural contexts. Within the Turkish Christian minority context, Turkish liturgical identities are deeply rooted in translated versions of contemporary worship songs emerging from megachurches and major publishers.[15] Though the commoditizing of this music may be at play as Turkish Christians stream ad revenue-generating worship songs, the adaptation of these songs by local congregations in minority contexts may also relate to the activity of the Spirit initiating transcultural unity with a global Church. Drawing from liturgical theology, this chapter offers a grounded study of contemporary worship song's role in Turkish liturgical identity alongside a theological reading that incorporates the role of the Spirit in forming ecclesial identity through shared songs.

LITURGICAL IDENTITY IN TURKISH PROTESTANT WORSHIP MUSIC

Geographically positioned between Europe and the Middle East, Turkey has long been a place of cultural fusion and fluidity, particularly in music and the arts. Even before the growth of streaming music, ethnomusicologists highlight Turkish musicians' historic adaptation of Western and Turkish musical styles, creating unique musical fusions.[16] Turkey is a modern secular state with a Muslim majority, and less than 0.1 percent of Turks identify as Protestant

Christians.[17] There are over 150 Protestant churches in Turkey, and scholars estimate five to eight thousand would identify as Protestant Christians.[18] The history of the growth of the Protestant Church has yet to be published, but James Bultema reports that the translations of the New Testament and later the entire Bible into modern Turkish in 1988 and 2000 were crucial to exponential growth through conversion in the Turkish Protestant Church.[19] As Turkish churches began to grow and new churches began to be established, new music from the growing Contemporary Christian movement in the West began to be translated into Turkish. In 2001, *Sonsuzluklar Boyunca*, a joint Turkish and Vineyard CD project, was released featuring Turkish worship leaders singing popular Vineyard worship songs like "Draw Me Close" and "Come, Now Is the Time to Worship." The tracks feature Turkish worship leaders singing on top of the original Vineyard instrumental recordings, like a type of translated worship karaoke. Songs from this album were rapidly adapted and assimilated, becoming foundational worship songs in the small but growing Christian community. As the Turkish church grew in the 1990s and early 2000s, translated songs from Vineyard, Integrity, and Maranatha! Music, based mainly in the United States, were localized to the Turkish context. Today, these songs provide a soundtrack of the revival of the 1990s and continue to be sung and loved by Turks who learned these as they first responded to the gospel.

Within a few years, a follow-up worship album was released featuring all-original Turkish worship songs called *Seninle Babam*. Sonic resonances of the early Vineyard project are present alongside more traditional Turkish percussion instruments, such as the *darbuka,* and Turkish stringed instruments, like the *kanun.* The employment of popular Turkish melodic and harmonic styles is also distinct. This project features some of the same worship leaders involved in the Vineyard-funded project, yet this all-original Turkish project establishes a Turkish Protestant liturgical identity that embraces the localization of Western music alongside local Turkish music. Over the past few decades, the Protestant Church in Turkey has grown alongside the Contemporary Worship movement. Western missionaries have brought their songs and worship preferences along with their message. Along with assimilating the music of missionaries, Turkish believers have also worked to craft their own sound. The modern Turkish worship context presents a unique case to explore the negotiation of globalizing trends and the work of the global Spirit.

TRANSLATING "THE BLESSING" OR CREATING "A SONG FOR A GENERATION"

During the COVID-19 pandemic, when many churches around the world were forced to move online due to national lockdowns, Christian communities in different global contexts recorded videos of translated versions of "The Blessing" written by Elevation Church's Steve Furtick and Chris Brown and well-known worship artists, Kari Jobe and Cody Carnes. The song draws on key portions of the Aaronic blessing from Numbers 6:23–26 along with prayers for intergenerational blessing and reminders of God's continual abiding personal presence. Over twenty-five different language videos of *"The Blessing"* exist. They often feature different worship leaders and musicians in their own homes, spliced together with images of places linked to specific national identities. UK worship leader and project-organizer for the UK-blessing stated, "I think the Spirit of God [is] on it, the sense of unity, the diversity, you know you've got the Coptic Orthodox church, the Catholic church, the Pentecostal, Church of England, you know, AOG, it's just stunning and so I guess I feel God's gonna do with it what he wants to do with it."[20] Reflecting on the transnational links and the UK version of the song, Mark Porter states, "The UK recording fits smoothly into a relatively homogeneous transnational evangelical imaginary enabled by an ascendant and successful multi-national worship music industry."[21] On one hand, Hughes attest to the activity of the global Spirit unifying the Church, while Porter recognizes globalizing factors at work.

As translated versions of the song from communities around the world were rapidly produced and uploaded, Elevation Worship created a video featuring a global choir. Similar to Chris Tomlin's global version of "How Great Our God," the video features Elevation artists center stage spliced with snippets of the song sung by worship leaders from around the world in their own mother tongues. The video intro testifies to how "God has used the song to minister to families and churches all over the world."[22] Reflecting on Global Christianity and the power dynamics within the video, Candance Lukasick and Lena Rose write that "The Blessing":

> brings to the fore the intimate relationship between power and agency. In focusing too closely on how global contexts loop back into U.S. imperial power, other perspectives are frozen into a curious passivity, whereby the only relevant actors of exploration or analysis are the white American evangelicals that produced and exported the song.[23]

Within the Turkish context, the song received a level of engagement, yet a day before the release of the Turkish version of "The Blessing," Umut Kalesi, a Turkish media group, released "Kuşakların Ezgisi" ("A Song for Generations—Blessing Over Turkey"). As of 2023, the YouTube video of this original Turkish song has over 250,000 views, more than ten times as many views as the Turkish-translated version of "The Blessing."[24] Written by a non-Turk who has lived in the country for years, the song utilizes musical modes and melodies unique to Turkey along with similar production and videography utilized in other global translated versions of "The Blessing." Lyrically, "Kuşakların Ezgisi" contains similar verses to "The Blessing" drawn from the Aaronic blessing. Yet the repetitive bridge of the song builds in intensity featuring a declarative prayer for the nation to come to Jesus, which is often characteristic of evangelically oriented believers in the religious minority. The writer of the Turkish song stated:

> At first, it seemed like "The Blessing" might be hard or awkward to sing in Turkish, but we were inspired by all the Blessing videos happening. Then one morning, I woke up with a sense that God wanted to give me a song. He gave me a couple references, and the song was done in an hour. I hadn't planned to write a Blessing-esque song, but it ended up being exactly that.[25]

Unique to the global phenomenon of "The Blessing," the popularity of this original Turkish song reveals potential for discerning agency within local communities in the midst of global market trends. On one hand, "Kuşakların Ezgisi" utilizes YouTube, a primary globalizing media distribution network, with a similar video production style to translated versions of "The Blessing" yet, at the song's origin, the writer attests to discernment in the challenging and awkward Turkish translation and in God's activity in inspiring a distinctive song in the local language.

Daniel Thornton acknowledges, "Contemporary congregational songs are firmly entrenched in both a global industry and in the local church. They straddle the commercial world and the world of ministry."[26] Though global market forces exist and shouldn't be ignored, these cultural pathways and related media platforms are often used by Evangelicals to spread their message and build their ministry, including allowing and encouraging the translation of their songs. Often local churches planted in indigenous contexts are encouraged to write their own music with their own local music by these same Evangelicals. Within Global Christianity, and particularly the Turkish context, local congregations and individual worship-decision makers sit between a movement exporting globalizing forms linked to an "ends of the earth" view of Christianity that simultaneously encourages and empowers "indigenous church" leadership and decision-making principles.[27] Those on the ground planning and leading worship in unique global contexts require discernment between a spirit of globalization being used to promote the sounds of large worship ministries through their powerful platforms and the global Spirit unifying the worship of a diverse body of Christ. Though the commoditizing of this music is at play as Turkish Christians stream ad revenue-generating YouTube clips of worship songs, translate these songs, and imitate aspects of production, the adaptation of these songs by local Turkish congregations also relates to the activity of the Spirit initiating transcultural unity with a global Church. A theological reading of these global worship trends will help expand this dialogue beyond economic influences to incorporate the role of the Spirit in forming ecclesial identity through shared songs.

THE SPIRIT, SONG, AND GLOBAL CHRISTIAN IDENTITY

The Church was born in culturally diverse worship that was simultaneously unifying and diversifying.[28] The outpouring of the Spirit at Pentecost sent the disciples out into the Jerusalem streets praising God in the particular languages of those gathered to celebrate from around the world (Acts 2:4-11). Jesus's final mission to his disciples to be witnesses throughout all the world was being partially fulfilled as the Spirit gifted the disciples to speak in other tongues. The crowd was gathered in Jerusalem from all over the known world, and through the work of the Spirit, each heard the unique and diverse languages from their own contexts. Witherington suggests, "The major point of all this is that the Spirit overcomes all barriers, even of languages, to witness to the various parts of the known world, even to 'the end of the earth.'"[29] Spirit-inspired praise uttered in indigenous languages was a part of the Church from the beginning.

The tongues were released as a response to the filling of the Spirit; therefore, the disciples were not attempting to undergo an experiment in linguistic contextualization—the Spirit was. Bock indicates, "God is using for each group the most familiar linguistic means possible to make sure the message reaches the audience in a form they can appreciate. Thus, the miracle underscores the divine initiative in making possible the mission God has commissioned."[30] The work of the Spirit was manifested in the Galilean disciples, enabling them to "declare the mighty deeds of God" in unique languages and dialects of the "devout men from every nation under heaven' (v. 5). The praise of God heard by those gathered immediately reminded them of their own context. They stated, "And how is it that we each hear them in our own language to which we were born?" (v. 8).

The post-Pentecost church is a unified church of many tongues and cultures. The work of the Spirit ignited a movement sending God's people proclaiming his mighty deeds into all cultures and contexts. Plantinga and Rozeboom write, "The idea, from Pentecost on, is to enable the peoples of the earth—the whole earth—to hear the word of the Lord and to render their thanks to God in a form suited to their own culture."[31] Worship songs framed by the Pentecost event represent a plurality of indigenous cultures and languages. Best writes:

Pentecost tells us that one artistic tongue is only a start and a thousand will never suffice. There is not a single chosen language or artistic or musical style that, better than all others, can capture and repeat back the fullness of the glory of God. One culture has capabilities, nuances, and creative ways that others simply do not possess. This truism cannot be avoided. Cultures are not infinite. No single one can hold the wholeness of praise and worship or the fullness of the counsel of God.[32]

The activity of the Spirit at the same Pentecost event simultaneously initiated a missional movement that did not segregate the indigenous cultures but instead, as Yong reveals, "binds Samaritans, Ethiopians, and other Gentiles together with Jews."[33]

Of the Pentecost event in Acts 2, Yong proposes an "ecumenical prototype" stating that the "pneumatological grounding of ecclesial identity in diversity, and of unity in plurality, is implicit in this passage."[34] Similarly, *Ad Gentes 4* from Vatican II states, "there was presaged that union of all peoples in the catholicity of the faith by means of the Church of the New Covenant, a Church which speaks all tongues, understands and accepts all tongues in her love, and so supersedes the divisiveness of Babel." Bruce sees the uniting experience of the Spirit as "nothing less than the reversal of the curse of Babel,"[35] yet this view seems to overlook the distinct, diverse languages that are being spoken and heard. Instead of one body with one distinct language, the outpouring of the Spirit at Pentecost created one united Church with many languages from many nations. Though most of those gathered in Jerusalem were Jews, the Spirit also began to be poured out on the Samaritans and Gentiles too (Acts 8:17, 10:44-48, 15:8), creating the need for the leaders of the Church to gather and discuss culture and ritual.

As a unifying, global experience of the Spirit began to gather a diverse people, an argument arose about what constituted the people of God. Some Jewish believers thought Gentile believers would be identified as God's people by following Jewish cultural and religious rituals (Acts 15:1, 5). In a sense, these Gentile believers needed to leave their own culture and become Jewish. In Jerusalem, the apostles and elders gathered together and, by the leading of the Spirit, determined that the Gentiles did not have to follow the Jewish cultural and religious rituals.[36] A difficult "yoke" was averted, allowing the mission to the Gentiles to continue from within their own culture.[37]

Though these Gentiles did not have to become culturally Jewish, the ruling of the apostles did critique the Gentile culture, calling the Gentile Christians to leave behind certain aspects of their own culture. Witherington writes of the Gentiles, "They must not give Jews in the Diaspora the opportunity to complain that Gentile Christians were still practicing idolatry and immorality by going to pagan feasts even after beginning to follow Christ."[38] Gentiles were able to live and practice their faith from within their cultural context, yet unwholesome aspects of their culture must be converted. As the council's decision "that seemed good to the Holy Spirit" began to be sent out, the unified but culturally diverse body of Christ began to experience greater growth. Reflecting on the missiological impact of the Jerusalem Council, Seccombe writes, "One of the great strengths of Christianity is in every age has been its adaptability to any culture, the basis of which was hammered out at the Jerusalem Council."[39] By the Spirit, the unified body of Christ expresses diversity and particularity; while at the same time by the same Spirit, the local, diverse members of the body are bound together and identified globally as the people of God.[40]

The pneumatological framework from Pentecost and the Jerusalem Council recognizes that the experience of the Spirit brings forth a unified people of God that radiates both transcultural and local expressions of worship. The body of Christ is not one homogenous cultural manifestation or one culture above another. By the work of the Spirit, the Church is a fusion of both the global and local. Taylor describes the work of the Spirit as both "united" and "universal,"[41] and Yong's Pentecostal ecclesiology contains "unity in diversity."[42] Bergmann highlights, "All natural and human borders are always open to the transcending Spirit."[43] The Nairobi Statement on Worship and Culture declares, "The resurrected Christ whom we worship, and *through the power of the Holy Spirit* we know the grace of the Triune God, transcends and indeed is beyond all cultures" (italics mine).[44] The global Spirit is at work in local cultures and subcultures, among other things, inspiring praise. The same Spirit working within a particular culture is drawing members of that particular culture into a unified, global body. We should not be surprised to see expressions and activities of particular indigenous churches that reflect both a global and local identity.

With a pneumatological framework, the questions of cultural identity and cultural practices move beyond a dichotomy of global vs. local or Western vs. indigenous, and instead recognize the Christian identity of a local congregation may contain a plurality of cultural expressions. Yong believes, "The many find their wholeness in the one, and the one's effectiveness and beauty are to be found in the diversities of its members, including the sons and daughters, men and women, young and old (Acts 2:17-28) from around the world."[45] In a world of increasing globalization and nationalism, the Spirit inspires and enables unique, local cultural expressions of faith without closing off local churches to the global movement of faith or inciting ethnic rivalries or racial prejudices. Ormerod and Clifton highlight this view, "In the multi-layered reality of culture, it is vital that Christian faith opens us up to a larger reality than just our own local culture, even while respecting the value of that local contribution."[46] As the Spirit works in a church that is located in a particular indigenous context, the Christian community may identify itself by expressing local traditions and values while at the same time adapting globalized rituals from churches in other contexts.

Songs enable God's people to define and express cultural identity. Yet the musical identity of a local church may reflect a global identity, finding enormous value and meaning from translocal songs.[47] In fact, translocal songs from the modern Christian worship movement represent, as Gesa Hartje-Döll sees it, music aiding in the construction of an "'imagined community' of evangelicals around the world."[48] Though a shared repertoire of translocal music may help construct a global identity among Christians, is this unity directly the work of the Spirit? Does every translocal worship song truly represent the unifying work of the global Spirit? The adaptation and indigenization of popular worship songs from external cultures could easily come as a result of the commercialization of worship music. Of the effects of mass media, Kim warns, "dominant cultures may unintentionally communicate that one form of musical worship is superior to others."[49] How does one recognize a genuine global or local work of the Spirit?

The Spirit inspires global unity, but not all examples of global unity are inspired by the Spirit. Additionally, not all aspects of local culture are suitable for Christian worship. From the study of Acts 15 above, we see that the Spirit encourages cultural discernment that critiques cultural rituals and values that are sinful, contrary to the Gospel, or cause other members of Christ's body to stumble (vv. 24-29). Framed by this study, those responsible for the leadership of local congregations should critically evaluate musical styles, lyrics, and the meanings of the musical styles in their local context until they can confidently state of their decisions that "it seemed good to the Holy Spirit and to us." Additionally, not all aspects of exported globalized worship are appropriate. The work of local congregations in their context offers Spirit-led, discerning critiques of the theologies and dominant styles in their translation, adaptation, or disregard of Western worship songs. In the case of "The Blessing" in Turkey, the popular original Turkish song offers lyrical resonances around the Aaronic blessing in "The Blessing." However, it expands missionally beyond the U.S. song's individualized lyrics of personal blessing through a declarative prayer for the nation to come to Jesus. The original songwriting and globally resonant production choices of the Turkish song attest to the global Spirit and globalized media forms that, in this case, enable the expression of a Turkish liturgical identity connected to the larger Christian movement while sustaining their own distinction within that movement. A discerned fusion of global and local worship identities reflects the Spirit who inspires worship songs that unify the global body of Christ and encourages local cultural expressions of worship.

STRADDLING GLOBALIZING TRENDS AND LOCAL SOUNDS

The recent work by scholars in identifying globalizing worship trends facilitates deeper discernment in locating centers of economic power and the roots of dominant musical styles. However, researchers and Christian leaders should not be surprised by the shared global repertoire of worship music that is particularized to a local language, such as Turkish. This trend reflects the unifying activity of the Spirit fundamental to Evangelical liturgical identity. Localized Western worship music sits alongside contextual musical expressions of praise drawn from the various ethnic cultures in the Turkish context. Both global and local worship music have immense value in the religious identity and musical expressions of Turkish believers. Within Turkey and beyond, local churches employ worship planning strategies that encourage the composition and use of original local worship songs, recognize the unifying value of translated songs from other cultures, and discern the impact of these songs on their own liturgical identity. The outpouring of the Spirit inspires local and global songs, yet the Spirit also enables cultural discernment that critiques areas of culture that are sinful, harmful, or contrary to the Gospel (Acts 15:24-29). Local churches are invited to operate in prophetic discernment by critically evaluating musical styles, lyrics, and the meanings of the musical styles in their local context. Careful discernment must be exercised through honest dialogue to determine what musical styles are most appropriate for use. Local or global musical styles can and should be encouraged but only after discussion and dialogue by local leaders and members of the congregation.[50]

Finally, worship leaders and service planners in dominant cultural contexts have opportunities to listen to and localize the songs from the body of Christ in global contexts. Rather than simply writing songs to be translated and exported, worship leaders in the West can open their ears to hear the Spirit's activity in local congregations all over the world. What musical gifts are being missed by dominant, homogenous market trends? Are theologies of community, hospitality, mission, suffering, and victory being inspired by the Spirit but left unheard? For example, songs such as GIA's translation of "Abana," a Middle Eastern version of the Lord's Prayer, with its minor musical setting and intense melody crying out for God to "deliver us from evil" remind Christ's Church that experiences of suffering and persecution are not ancient Bible stories but present realities for our sisters and brothers.[51] Or by naming the origins of Nigerian artist Sinach's "Waymaker," opportunities can be provided to recognize and participate in the Spirit's work and the worship of Christ's global body.[52] Beyond musical ethnotourism, where indigenous songs are misappropriated, celebrating the reach of an individual ministry, discerningly incorporating songs from other contexts can widen global Christian perspectives and enable congregations to walk in solidarity with the global church.

Nearly two thousand years after the Jerusalem Council, the Spirit continues to be poured out in local communities and continually works to unite those communities. Though distance and expansive growth may now prevent the opportunity to all gather and discern issues in identity, culture, power, and theology in one space, through globalized connections, we have greater access than ever to see and hear each other, and increased potential to share and receive the gifts that the Spirit is giving to all people.

NOTES

1. See Pete Ward, *Selling Worship: How What We Sing Has Changed the Church* (Milton Keynes: Authentic, 2005); Monique M. Ingalls, "Introduction: Interconnection, Interface, and Identification in Pentecostal-Charismatic Music and Worship," in *The Spirit of Praise: Music and Worship in Global Pentecostal Charismatic Christianity*, Monique M. Ingalls and Amos Yong, eds. (University Park: The Pennsylvania State University Press, 2015), and Adam Perez, Shannan Baker, Elias Dummer, Marc Jolicoeur, and Mike Tapper (2023) "Do It Again": Chart-Topping Worship Songs and the Churches Behind Them, *Liturgy*, 38:4, 31–40.

2. WLR Team, "Almost 100% of the Top 25 Worship Songs Are Associated with Just a Handful of Megachurches," accessed December 20, 2023, https://worshipleaderresearch.com/100-of-the-top-25-worship-songs-are-associated-with-just-a-handful-of-megachurches/.

3. Monique Ingalls, *Singing the Congregation: How Contemporary Worship Music Forms Evangelical Community* (Oxford: Oxford University, Press, 2018), 209–213.

4. Ingalls, *Singing the Congregation*, 212.

5. Ingalls, *Singing the Congregation*, 212.

6. Worship Leader Research states, "For some in the contemporary worship music world, market success is perceived as a sign of God's blessing." WLR Team, "Raising the Invisible Hand: How Brand and Social Proof Shape Our Study Setlists," accessed December 20, 2023, https://worshipleaderresearch.com/raising-the-invisible-hand/#.

7. Les Moir, *Missing Jewel: The Worship Movement that Impacted the Nations* (Colorado Springs, CO: David C. Cook, 2017), 15. For a scholarly appraisal of the growth of British worship music, see Monique Ingalls, "Transnational Connection, Musical Meaning, and the 1990s 'British Invasion' of North American Evangelical Worship Music" in *The Oxford Handbook of Music and World Christianities*, editors Jonathan Dueck and Suzel Ana Reily (Oxford: Oxford Press, 2013), 425–448.

8. Moir, *Missing Jewel*, 15.

9. Ingalls, Reisgersber, and Sherinian, eds., *Making Congregational Music Local in Christian Communities Worldwide* (London: Routledge, 2018), 12.

10. Aminta Arrington, "'Translated' or 'Transformed': The Use of Western Hymns in the Evangelization of the Lisu of Southwest China," *Religions* 12, no. 9: 772. https://doi.org/10.3390/rel12090772.

11. Steven Félix-Jäger, *Renewal Worship: A Theology of Pentecostal Doxology* (Downers Grove: IVP Academic, 2022), 189–208.

12. Félix-Jäger, *Renewal Worship*, 197.

13. Félix-Jäger, *Renewal Worship*, 200.

14. Félix-Jäger, *Renewal Worship*, 204–207.

15. Jeremy Perigo, "Beyond Translated vs. Indigenous: Turkish Protestant Christian Hymnody as Global and Local Identity," *Religions* 12, no. 11 (2021): 905. https://doi.org/10.3390/rel12110905.

16. See Martin Stokes, *The Republic of Love: Cultural Intimacy in Turkish Popular Music* (Chicago: University of Chicago Press, 2011) and Eliot Bates, *Music in Turkey: Experiencing Music, Expressing Culture* (New York: Oxford University Press, 2011).

17. Sue Whitaker states, "The Protestant Church in Turkey of approximately six to seven thousand worshipers is slowly growing, adding to around one hundred thousand Christians belonging to the existing ancient and Orthodox churches in Turkey." Sue Whitaker, *Music and Liturgy, Identity and Formation: A Study of Inculturation in Turkey* (Eugene, OR: Pickwick Publications, 2021), 14.

18. Though these Protestant churches have formal and informal affiliations with Evangelical, Reformed, Pentecostal, and other Protestant streams around the world, scholars and the churches themselves identify as Protestant. They are united through the *Protestan Kiliseler* Derneği (Protestant Church Association). The organization "gained essential momentum toward the end of the 1990s in response to the growth of the Protestant Community and increasing anti-Christian media and propaganda." Today, a large percentage of local Turkish churches are members of this alliance. This group also interfaces with Orthodox, Catholic, and international churches in the region along with publishing yearly human rights violation reports. See "About Us & Purpose of Our Association," Protestan Kiliseler *Derneği, last modified 2024,* https://www.protestankiliseler.org.

19. James Bultema, "Against Wind and Waves: The Countercultural Movement of a Turk and the Turkish Protestant Church." In *Longing for Community: Church, Umma, or Somewhere in Between.* David Greenlee, ed. (Pasadena: William Carey Library, 2013), 28. Bultema's PhD thesis on the history of the Turkish Protestant Church is currently in process.

20. As cited in Mark Porter, "'Where there is unity, God commands a blessing': Power and the Performance of Difference in Irish and UK Blessing Videos," The Christian Nation Project, accessed December 20, 2023, https://thechristiannationproject.net/porter/.

21. Porter, "'Where there is unity, God commands a blessing.'" In this article, Porter highlights how the Irish Blessing video, where Irish artists record "Be Thou My Vision," "helps to make visible one possible alternative to evangelical worship music's frequent erasure of difference, to the uncomplicated coming together of groups and individuals which downplays their distinctive characteristics and the

tensions which difference might serve to create." In my view, the "Irish Blessing" like the "Blessing for Turkey" show a participation in a global Evangelical moment, while offering their own distinct liturgical and musical identities.

22. Elevation Worship, "The Blessings (Global Choir), May 11, 2020, 9:13, https://www.youtube.com/watch?v=y9EK8dAXl6I.

23. Candace Lukasik and Lena Rose, "Economies of Sound and Asymmetries of Global Christianity," The Christian Nation Project, accessed December 20, 2023, https://thechristiannationproject.net/the-blessing-full-introduction/.

24. Preciosa Sangre, "The Blessing-Turkish Version," May 23, 2020, YouTube video, 9:13, https://www.youtube.com/watch?v=spcvfnlP4eE_ and Adrienne Neusch, "A Song for Generations" [Blessings Over Turkey | Christian Worship Song], Umut Kalesi, May 22, 2020, 5:40, https://youtu.be/ICSNVXnkIUQ?si=X8wkcYbtt6m9slWl.

25. Email with songwriter, 10 November 2022.

26. Daniel Thornton, *Meaning-Making in Contemporary Congregational Song Genre* (Cham, Switzerland: Palgrave Macmillian, 2021), 85. Thornton offers helpful analysis of the meaning of congregational songs incorporate discussion on the music industry, songwriters, the songs, and their use.

27. See Allan Anderson, *To the Ends of the Earth: Pentecostalism and the Transformation of World Christianity* (Oxford: Oxford University Press, 2013).

28. Martin states, "The Christian Church was born in song." Ralph P. Martin, *Worship in the Early Church* (Grand Rapids: Eerdmans, 1975), 39.

29. Ben Witherington, III, *The Acts of the Apostles: A Socio-rhetorical Commentary* (Grand Rapids: Eerdmans, 1998), 135.

30. Darrell L. Bock, *Acts*, eds. Robert W. Yarbrough and Robert H. Steins, Baker Exegetical Commentary on the New Testament (Grand Rapids: Baker Academic, 2007), 102.

31. Plantinga and Rozeboom, *Discerning the Spirits: A Guide to Thinking about Christian Worship Today* (Grand Rapids: Eerdmans Publishing, 2003), 76.

32. Harold Best, *Music Through the Eyes of Faith* (San Francisco: HarperCollins, 1993), 67.

33. Amos Yong, *The Spirit Poured Out on All Flesh: Pentecostalism and the Possibility of Global Theology* (Grand Rapids: Baker Academic, 2005), 137.

34. Yong, *Spirit Poured Out on All Flesh,* 171–172.

35. F. F. Bruce, *The Book of the Acts* revised edition (Grand Rapids: Eerdmans, 1988), 59.

36. Bruce states, "So conscious were the church leaders of being possessed and controlled by the Spirit that he was given prior mention as chief author of their decision." Bruce, *Acts*, 298.

37. Seccombe writes, "The implication drawn from this scripture, in the light of the *de facto* existence of 'saved' Gentiles, is that they may seek the Lord as Gentiles from within their own culture, and not by becoming Jews." "Christ's people will number men, women and children of 'all peoples, nations and languages.'" David Seccombe, "The New People of God" in *Witness to the Gospel: The Theology of Acts,*

eds. Howard Marshall and David Peterson (Grand Rapids: Eerdmans, 1998), 386. See also Aaron Kuecker, "Filial Piety and Violence in Luke-Acts and the *Aeneid*: A Comparative Analysis of Two Trans-Ethnic Identities," in *T&T Clark Handbook to Constructing Social Identity in the New Testament*, eds. Brian Tucker and Coleman A. Baker (London: Bloomsbury, 2014).

38. Witherington, *The Acts of the Apostles*, 463.
39. Seccombe, "People of God," 366.
40. Welker writes, "Through the pouring out of the Spirit, God effects a world-encompassing, multilingual, polyindividual testimony to Godself." Michael Welker, *God the Spirit*, trans. John F. Hoffmeyere (Minneapolis: Fortress, 1994), 235.
41. John V. Taylor, *The Go-Between God: the Holy Spirit and the Christian Mission* (London: SCM Press, 1972), 180–181.
42. Yong, *Spirit Poured Out*, 137–145, 172–173.
43. Sigurd Bergmann, "Revisioning Pneumatology in Transcultural Spaces" in *Spirits of Globalization*, ed. Stural J. Stalsett (London: SCM Press, 2006), 186.
44. Lutheran World Federation, *Nairobi Statement on Worship and Culture: Contemporary Challenges and Opportunities*, 1996: n.p. online: http://worship.calvin.edu/resources/resource-library/nairobi-statement-on-worship-and-culture-full-text [14 January 2015].
45. Yong, *Spirit Poured Out*, 173–174.
46. Neil J. Ormerod and Shane Clifton, *Globalization and the Mission of the Church: Ecclesiological Investigations* (London: T&T Clark, 2009), 140–141.
47. *Translocal songs* are songs written by Christians from other cultures that are shared across cultures.
48. Gesa Hartje-Döll, "(Hillsong) United Through Music: Praise and Worship Music and the Evangelical 'Imagined Community'": in *Christian Congregational Music: Performance, Identity and Experience,* eds. Monique Ingalls, Carolyn Landau and Tom Wagner (Surrey: Ashgate, 2013), 150.
49. Jaewoo Kim, "The Whole World Has Gone 'Glocal,'" in *Worship and Mission for the Global Church: An Ethnodoxology Handbook,* ed. James R. Krabill (Pasadena: William Carey Library, 2013), 46.
50. Written for a Western audience, Hawn's work could be a helpful resource for communities to navigate the use of global worship songs in minority contexts, such as Turkey. See C. Michael Hawn, *Gather Into One: Praying and Singing Globally* (Grand Rapids: Eerdmans, 2003).
51. Laila Constantine, Anne Emile Zaki, Emily R. Brink, and Greg Sheer, *Abana: Arabic Lord's Prayer*, ed. Greg Sheer (Grand Rapids: Faith Alive Christian Resources, 2012).
52. Sinach, "Way Maker—Official Video," December 21, 2015, YouTube video, 5:05, https://youtu.be/n4XWfwLHeLM?si=A6alAFifYOtLIUDm.

BIBLIOGRAPHY

Arrington, Aminta. "Translated" or "Transformed: The Use of Western Hymns in the Evangelization of the Lisu of Southwest China." *Religions* 12, no. 9 (2021): 772.

Best, Harold. *Music Through the Eyes of Faith*. San Francisco: HarperCollins, 1993.

Bock, Darrell L. *Acts*. Edited by Robert W. Yarbrough and Robert H. Stein. Baker Exegetical Commentary on the New Testament. Grand Rapids: Baker Academic, 2007.

Bruce, F. F. *The Acts of the Apostles*. Revised edition. Grand Rapids: Eerdmans, 1988.

Bultema, James. "Against Wind and Waves: The Countercultural Movement of a Turk and the Turkish Protestant Church." In *Longing for Community: Church, Umma, or Somewhere in Between,* edited by David Greenlee. Pasedena: William Carey Library, 2013.

Félix-Jäger, Steven. *Renewal Worship: A Theology of Pentecostal Doxology*. Downers Grove: IVP Academic, 2022.

Hartje-Döll, Gesa. "(Hillsong) United Through Music: Praise and Worship Music and the Evangelical 'Imagined Community'." In *Christian Congregational Music: Performance, Identity and Experienece,* edited by Monique Ingalls, Carolyn Landau, and Tom Wagner. Surrey: Ashgate, 2013.

Ingalls, Monique M., Muriel Swijghuisen Reigersber, and Zoe C. Sherinian, eds. 2018. *Making Congregational Music Local in Christian Communities Worldwide*. London: Routledge.

Ingalls, Monique. *Singing the Congregation: How Contemporary Worship Music Forms Evangelical Community*. Oxford: Oxford University, Press, 2018.

Kim, Jaewoo. "The Whole World Has Gone 'Glocal'." In *Worship and Mission or the Glocal Church: An Ethnodoxology Handbook,* edited by James R. Krabill. Pasadena: William Carey Library, 2013.

Lukasik, Candace and Rose, Lena. "Economies of Sound and Asymmetries of Global Christianity." The Christian Nation Project. Accessed December 20, 2023. https://thechristiannationproject.net/the-blessing-full-introduction/.

Lutheran World Federation. *Nairobi Statement on Worship and Culture: Contemporary Challenges and Opportuninties*. 1996: n.p. online: http://worship.calvin.edu/resources/resource-library/nairobi-statement-on-worship-culture-full-text [14 January 2015].

Martin, Ralph P. *Worship in the Early Church*. Grand Rapids: Eerdmans, 1975.

Moir, Les. *Missing Jewel: The Worship Movement that Impacted the Nations*. Colorado Springs, CO: David C. Cook, 2017.

Perigo, Jeremy. "Beyond Translated vs. Indigenous: Turkish Protestant Christian Hymnody as Global and Local Identity." *Religions* 12, no. 11 (2021): 905. doi: 10.3390/rel12110905.

Plantinga, Cornelius, Jr., and Sue A. Rozeboom. *Discerning the Spirits: A Guide to Thinking about Christian Worship Today*. Grand Rapids: Eerdmans Publishing, 2003.

Porter, Mark. "Where There Is Unity, God Commands a Blessing: Power and the Performance of Difference in Irish and UK Blessing Videos." The Christian Nation Project. Accessed December 20, 2023. https://thechristiannationproject.net/porter/.

Seccombe, David. "The New People of God." In *Witness to the Gospel: The Theology of Acts,* edited by Howard Marshall and David Peterson. Grand Rapids: Eerdmans, 1998.

Thornton, Daniel. *Meaning-Making in Contemporary Congregational Song Genre.* Cham, Switzerland: Palgrave Macmillian, 2021.

Whitaker, Sue. *Music and Liturgy, Identity and Formation: A Study of Inculturation in Turkey.* Eugene, OR: Pickwick Publications, 2021.

Witherington, III, Ben. *The Acts of the Apostles: A Socio-rhetorical Commentary.* Grand Rapids: Eerdmans, 1998.

Worship Leader Research Team, "Almost 100% of the Top 25 Worship Songs Are Associated with Just a Handful of Megachurches." Accessed December 20, 2023. https://worshipleaderresearch.com/100-of-the-top-25-worship-songs-are-associated-with-just-a-handful-of-megachurches/.

Worship Leader Research Team. "Raising the Invisible Hand: How Brand and Social Proof Shape Our Study Setlists." Accessed December 20, 2023. https://worshipleaderresearch.com/raising-the-invisible-hand/#.

Yong, Amos. *The Spirit Pour Out on All Flesh: Pentecostalism and the Possibility of Global Theology.* Grand Rapids: Baker Academic, 2005.

Chapter 14

"We Were All Vibing the Same Way"

Luthercostality in South Brazil

Marcell Silva Steuernagel

It is May 2, 2015. On the main stage at Recanto da Paz, a retreat center on the outskirts of Joinville in Santa Catarina, South Brazil, I look out at the approximately 1,400 teenagers and youth gathered for evening worship. Guitar in hand, I join the band's introduction as the massive high-definition screen behind the stage counts the seconds until the beginning of worship. As the countdown comes to an end, the band launches into a Portuguese version of "Mighty Warrior," a worship song popularized worldwide by Elevation Worship.[1] The song builds, and I can see participants warming up to the experience. I cut the band with a discrete gesture as we return to the chorus from the bridge. The band drops, and the gathered congregation picks up the chorus with raised hands, clapping and singing.

As we progress through the set, participants ramp up their bodily engagement. By the time we launch into a translated version of Jeremy Riddle's "Furious," people are jumping up and down, dancing freely in front of the stage. LED lights sweep the venue, and musicians are surrounded in a cloud of dry ice.[2] I am impressed by the volume of the congregation, which not only matches the band but soars over it. Suddenly, the power required to drive amplification and effects overcomes the capacity of the venue's generator, and all lights and sound blank out. Participants cheer, unfazed. I look back at our drummer, who has shifted into a 4/4 backbeat, the only acoustic instrument loud enough to be heard in the crowd, which continues to worship for minutes without interruption, flowing from song to song. After a while, the generators kick back on, and we continue the set.[3]

This particular retreat was organized by the youth ministry branch of *Movimento Encontrão* or *ME* (Gathering Movement), a revival movement within the *Igreja Evangélica de Confissão Luterana no Brasil* (IECLB), known abroad as the Evangelical Church of the Lutheran Confession in Brazil.[4]

IECLB is one of Brazil's main Lutheran denominations, with a core presence in the country's south.[5] Every few years, *ME* organizes a national youth gathering called *Encontrão Jovem Nacional* or *EJN* (National Youth Gathering). In 2015, this event gathered approximately 1,400 youth for three days of worship, outdoor activities, and fellowship. Along with long-time colleagues Fabiane Behling Luckow and Daniel Sell, I was tasked with organizing and leading worship at *EJN 2015*.[6]

As a Brazilian Lutheran, I am often asked, "what does Lutheran worship in Brazil sound and look like?" When that question arises, my mind wanders to experiences such as the one at *EJN 2015*. While the size of production and participants at local Lutheran congregations rarely match that event, the basic pattern of participation is the same. Over the years, my attempts to describe the particular mixture of bodily engagement, formative influences of German immigration, and Brazilians' avid engagement with community singing have coalesced into a response. I tell people that Brazilian Lutherans are, at least in part, "Luthercostals."

This chapter provides a glimpse into the interactions between the European Lutheran heritage brought to Brazil by immigrants in the nineteenth century and the increasingly pentecostalized worship practices that characterize Brazilian Christianity at large, and this denomination in particular. At that intersection, European Lutheran notions of modesty and reverence collide with Brazilian expressions of religious devotion and musicking practices, which tend to be more forcefully expressed in the body and music of devotees. In this chapter, I make a case for Brazilian Luthercostality as a particular manifestation of the interaction between Spirit and song that is the focus of this volume.

My interest in this topic is not merely abstract. As a Lutheran pastor's kid in Brazil, I grew up deeply immersed in the denomination's music and witnessed firsthand the incorporation of songs from North America and elsewhere into the Brazilian Lutheran repertoire, as well as the development of indigenous compositions that reflected how Brazilian Christians localized these influences into their own creations.[7] Moreover, I witnessed the cross-pollination of worship practices between historical Protestant denominations in their traditional and charismatic expressions, Classical Pentecostals and burgeoning Neo-Pentecostal churches, and external influences such as the North American Christian music industry, even as Brazil's burgeoning *gospel* music industry grew exponentially. Brazil's *gospel* phenomenon should not be confused with North American "gospel," a completely distinct and previous expression; I italicize it here in lowercase to distinguish it from the biblical Gospels. The term was adopted by early proponents of Brazil's Christian music industry and serves as an umbrella description of that industry as a whole.[8]

Therefore, this glimpse into Brazilian Lutheran worship occurs through the lens of my own experience and relies on a mixture of methods and sources. I draw from scholarship on church music and Brazilian immigration, including previous research where I introduce topics in Brazilian church music to English-language readers, such as the role of immigration in the history of the Lutheran church and its hymnody in Brazil and current issues of *evangélico* identity and the music industry in that country. Further, I interviewed Daniel Sell and Fabiane Behling Luckow, my collaborators in that particular event, and Soraya Eberle, who served for many years as the National Music Coordinator for IECLB. Finally, I rely on *YouTube* videos of the worship at *EJN 2015* and my own files and records of our planning and rehearsal process leading up to the event. My goal is to demonstrate how Lutheran Christians in South Brazil perform a "Luthercostality" that imbricates Lutheran theologies of worship with Pentecostal worship practices.

In previous ethnographic research, I have written about the "bits and pieces of elements such as the legacy of missionary activity, transnational worship projects, denominational initiatives and resistances, [that] all come together to create distinct worship environments in which American Anglo-Baptists worship in Texas and Lutheran Afro-polkas are sung by congregants in South Brazil."[9] It is a context characterized by intense fluidity in cultural flows between legacies and musicking traditions. Church music in Brazil, I argue, is touched by messiness in ways that favor a variety of mixtures.[10] It is in that spirit that I speak of Brazilian Luthercostality as a quality, a particular flavor of mixture, that can sit in the interstitial spaces occupied by said Anglo-Baptists, Bapto-Catholics, and other compound denominational labels.[11] Here, I do not propose the term "Luthercostality" based on any defining theological markers of Lutheranism or Pentecostalism, but on the worship practices that characterize, at least in part, engagement with congregational song in that context. I propose the term loosely, acknowledging the vast literature on the history of Pentecostalism, the distinctions between Pentecostalisms and myriad charismatic movements, and other crucial nuances of ecclesiology and church history.

Furthermore, it is important to disclose that, broadly speaking, members of IECLB would not position themselves as Pentecostals on the landscape of Brazilian Christianity; in fact, many would take issue with my descriptor.[12] My interview with Fabiane Behling Luckow illustrates how they might push back at my description. When I first used the term in our conversation, Luckow said, "When you speak of Pentecostalism, I think of the *corinhos de fogo* [fire choruses] in the Assemblies of God. I think of Classical Pentecostalism."[13] Nevertheless, as our conversation progressed, we began to identify certain markers of practice that point to Luthercostality as a viable descriptor.

These caveats should not be taken as "glossing over" the nuances and distinctions, both theological and phenomenological, that characterize such typologies. Instead, I attempt to distill Spirit and song from the lived experiences of these worshiping communities in a particular way. Using the notion of Luthercostality, this chapter deconstructs certain notions of Lutheranism and Pentecostalism as projected from North to South and reconstructs them by creating synapses outside of the Anglocentric conceptual ecclesial framework.

While I have mentioned Luthercostality in other scholarship, the term is not widespread.[14] In the editorial to a special edition of the theological journal *Dialog*, which focuses on mutual learning opportunities in Lutheran-Pentecostal relationships, Lutheran theologian Cheryl M. Peterson acknowledges that Pentecostalism "is the fastest growing Christian movement in the world today, perhaps ever in history," especially in the southern hemisphere. For her, it is "past time for Lutherans (and others) to pay attention to this just century-old expression of Christianity."[15] I argue that, especially in the context of the Global South, this recognition is not only a matter of understanding a separate other but, in fact, wading through a complex web of theologies, ecclesiologies and worship practices that constitute a more imbricated reality in which Lutheran theology and Pentecostal piety intermingle to significant extents.

In the same journal, Evangelical Lutheran Church in America (ELCA) pastor Leila Ortiz—who was raised Pentecostal—freely self-identifies as a Luthercostal; one of the few other uses of the term I have encountered. She writes about the Puerto Rican women of Pentecostal background who, "even after years of membership in Lutheran churches . . . do not apply a strictly Lutheran hermeneutic to any biblical text or to their lives."[16] Instead, argues Ortiz, "their embedded and newly explored theologies have merged and are employed from this dual vantage point and perspective. The theological lens is multifaceted and rich with layers of influence."[17] Ortiz's description of Puerto Rican Luthercostal women aligns with my talk of Luthercostal worship practices in Brazil, which are likewise multifaceted and particularly nuanced.

THE CONTEXT: SOUTH BRAZILIAN LUTHERANISM

Movimento Encontrão traces its beginning to the 1960s, when North American missionary John Aamot began working among Brazilian Lutherans. Aamot emphasized personal conversion and spiritual revival. According to Brazilian anthropologist Valdir Pedde, it is important to note that Aamot's work must be viewed within the context of a larger expansion of Pentecostalism in Brazil, which already at that time favored this type of spirituality.[18] For sociologist Paul Freston, as it coalesced into a discreet movement within IECLB, *ME* brought together traditional German Pietism and Latin American Evangelicalism.[19] The movement has focused both on conversionist renewal inside IECLB and on outward evangelization and has become a significant theological force in Brazilian Protestantism.[20,21]

The rise of *ME* within the context of Brazilian Lutheranism fits within a larger trend of Christianity's move to the Global South. Phillip Jenkins argues that this shift has significant implications for how worship is expressed. "When we look at the Pentecostal enthusiasm of present-day Brazil," argues Jenkins, "then quite possibly we are getting a foretaste of the Christianity of the next generation."[22] In *The Future of Lutheranism,* Aageson and Jacobsen describe a similar movement to the South with effects in the North: "As Lutheranism becomes more fully indigenized in the Two-Thirds World, their worship and music will evolve, and their creativity will enrich North American worship and music. Through worship and music, East and West, North and South are inching closer to one another."[23]

Implied in these predictions is an acknowledgment that, due to the spread of Pentecostalism throughout the globe, what were once considered exclusively Pentecostal or charismatic worship practices are now ubiquitous across denominations and traditions. From this perspective, *ME* can be considered a greenhouse for the grafting of these widespread Pentecostal worship practices into IECLB congregations, whose worship was historically shaped by the Teutonic liturgical perspectives of their immigrant forebears. Along with a few other factors, *ME* helped establish a matrix of Luthercostality within IECLB; a matrix that demonstrates, from the Brazilian side, the "inching closer to one another" that Aageson and Jacobsen speak of.

This matrix was solidified further in the 1980s with the rise of *gospel,* Brazil's native Christian music industry. As we prepared to lead worship at *EJN 2015,* Luckow, Sell and I discussed how we wanted to position the repertoire and aesthetics of music at the event both in relation to transnational worship projects such as Hillsong and Elevation Worship, to Brazil's *gospel* industry, and to the hymnic heritage of IECLB. While it was clear to us that we wanted to distinguish our worship from the larger *gospel* phenomenon, my recent conversations with both Sell and Luckow made clear how our own experiences growing up in the Lutheran church inevitably connected us to Pentecostalism and to *gospel.* Luckow shared how "during our teens, we lived this transformation with the rise of Sara Nossa Terra [Heal Our Land], Estevam Hernandes, and how that invaded all churches; not only Pentecostals, but also Protestant. This deeply influenced the way we worshiped."[24] In his interview, Sell repeatedly mentioned the "band experience": in the 1990s, he was involved with the Christian music outreach circuit with his own band, as was I. Within this circuit, we negotiated regional, national and international influences even as we asked ourselves what it might mean to worship as a Lutheran in that musical landscape.

Further, it might be tempting to consider Pentecostalism and *gospel* as discrete influences, especially because of Pentecostalism's early entry into Brazil's phonographic market in the 1960s, vis à vis the latter's development of *gospel* in the late 1980s. Overall, these influences all mix together in Brazilian Lutheranism. While the rise of *gospel* in Brazil sidelined the work of Brazilian composers like Jorge Camargo and Nelson Bomilcar, who were experimenting with Brazilian styles and rhythms instead of the international pop-rock aesthetic that marked early *gospel* music, their influence remained significant in Protestant circles. Perhaps it is more productive to think of these phenomena as correlated expressions of Christian musics that connect to the overall spread of non-Catholic Christianity in Brazil in the aftermath of the Second Vatican Council. Soraya Eberle, who served as the National Music Coordinator for IECLB during many years, spoke about these connections: "I remember in the 80s, when we would organize *louvorzões* (extended song services), which followed the same format. So there seems to be a continuity between these manifestations."[25] The "same format" she references consists of music-centered worship events with significant room for bodily engagement and spontaneous prayer, and continued into the 1990s. As Luckow says, "the strength of the developments in the 90s to shape and reshape our worship practices was very striking. I've reflected about that in my own story."[26] Even today, two of the main "big players" in the transnational Christian music market, Hillsong and Bethel, were born within the Pentecostal Assemblies of God tradition, even if they later disaffiliated from that denomination.[27] They continue to heavily influence worship music across the globe, and the situation is not different in the Brazilian market, where these influences are subsumed into the maelstrom of influences already present. The boundaries between these repertoires and the stylistic traits that travel with them across denominational lines are fluid and porous, as can be demonstrated by the song selection and aesthetics we curated for *EJN* 2015.

CONVERGENCES AND DIVERGENCES AT THE LUTHERCOSTAL INTERSECTION

Worship at *EJN 2015* was the epitome of many years of experimentation. All three worship leaders had extensive experience in their local Lutheran contexts and leading worship at other *encontrões* or gatherings, both regional and national. By the time we gathered to prepare for *EJN 2015,* we had a deep working knowledge of the worship practices in *ME*-aligned congregations.

Sell claims that, in a sense, our experience at *EJN 2015* was powerful because these years of experience culminated in an event that was particularly potent. For him, "2015 was the strongest, because we were all vibing the same way."[28]

Even as we were "vibing the same way," we assumed a pragmatic attitude toward repertoire for the event. We did not necessarily pick songs we liked. We chose what we knew would work, and ended up with a selection that included our own compositions, a few songs by Brazilian composers well-known in the Protestant context in Brazil, and several others by Vineyard, Bethel, Elevation, and other internationally known artists and worship ministries. This selection was well-received by participants, who sang enthusiastically during the retreat. According to Luckow, "Of all the *Encontrões* I participated in, this had the most careful song curatorship and preparation, and it defined many parameters of what people ended up doing at other gatherings and in congregations in relation to repertoire."[29] In fact, almost ten years later, I still encounter the versions we prepared for *EJN 2015* in Lutheran congregations across South Brazil when I preach and teach there.

Perhaps the receptivity of the youth gathered at that event stems from the fact that we were tapping into a worship style to which Lutheran youth were primed to respond. Luckow told me that, from her perspective, the aesthetic and selection we developed for *EJN 2015* were

> part not only of their cultural formation; this was in fact the sonic universe in which [they] relate to God . . . The sounds we were using were the sounds this generation was socialized into relationship with God. This generation, since very early, are listening to worship music on *Spotify* and *YouTube*.[30]

The resonances between the music we prepared and the sonic universe in which these youth lived online, mediated through various channels, fed back into the worship experience itself; worshipers recognized their own sounds in the soundscape we created, which certainly tapped into the pervading worship aesthetics of transnational worship projects even as it drew from Brazilian composer and compositions, creating a mixture that was unique to South Brazilian Lutheran youth culture.[31]

I offer here a series of convergences between our experience at *EJN 2015* and broader notions of Pentecostality. The first is related to context. Speaking of the developments of Lutheran youth music in Brazil, Eberle identifies the importance of spaces of spirituality outside Sunday morning worship. While liturgy inevitably changes over time, many South Brazilian Lutherans staunchly uphold the value of tradition in liturgy, an attitude that generates a resistance to change and necessitates the creation of other spaces of spirituality more hospitable to experimentation. For Eberle, retreats are alternative spaces in which there are specific expectations about the work of the Holy Spirit, distinct from Sunday morning expectations.[32] I argue that contexts such as *EJN 2015* constitute spaces with unique expectations about how the charisma of the Spirit can or will manifest in musicking. In these contexts, musical worship is the container of the Luthercostal experience—the place of epiphany, of revelation, of catharsis. For many young Lutherans who underwent confirmation, learned Luther's Small Catechism, and were instructed about Lutheran liturgy and worship, retreats serve as a convergent space for Spirit and song. Instead of an environment in which discourse (theological or otherwise) narrates experience, retreats become environments of integration similar to concerts. Sell repeatedly mentioned the rock concert experience, with its invitation to catharsis, as correlated to the worship experience at *EJN 2015,* and spoke about the influences of these extra-liturgical experiences in the expectations for liturgical musicking.

Thus, even if only intuitively, the pneumatological expectations of these young Lutherans at *EJN 2015* were uniquely Luthercostal. In that context, charisma, the marker of the work of the Spirit, was expected to manifest particularly in engagement with song, or what Luckow described as "a mixture between the emotional and the Holy Spirit's inexpressible, imponderable qualities."[33] Moreover, their experience fed back into worship at their local congregations.

Such pneumatological expectations align with the integrative nature of Pentecostal worship, which, instead of splicing theological discourse and liturgical experience, integrates them. Sell, Luckow and myself shared this integrative theological ethos at *EJN 2015*. In that event, describes Sell, "spirituality was pumping, the soul was pumping, and the body was pumping. We tried to bring those things together."[34] Luckow goes further, describing the pitfalls of traditional Lutheran dissociations of discourse and practice: "How narrow-minded it is of Lutherans to continue validating worship music through lyrics. That's so colonial, to think that it's the verbal language that validates the experience. Why do we accept a Taizé song and repeat it forty times, but can't accept other repertoires that rely on repetition?"[35]

At *EJN 2015*, we wanted to intentionally imbricate Spirit and song. We positioned ourselves in contraposition to more Reformed pedagogies of music, perhaps somewhat suspicious of the power of music and what happens when we give ourselves over to musical experience. We wanted to push participants toward the intersection between Spirit and song instead of warning participants of the dangers lurking at that crossroads.

That intention resonated with participants' expectations about that space of spirituality outside of traditional Lutheran worship, creating a liminal bubble in which youth could respond enthusiastically to worship. Sell described the experience as cathartic: "'I'm here, in worship, I'm having this emotional, spiritual, cognitive experience.' My impression is that people kind of go crazy."[36] Eberle was not at the event, but told me that, watching footage on *YouTube*, "[The bodily worship practices of Pentecostalism] are replicated in the worship at *EJN*, and that's not something you will find frequently in historical Protestantism, in which worship is characterized much more by the absence of the body in worship." She further identified particular markers, discrete bodily practices, that distinguished that worship from a more traditional Lutheran ethics of the worshiping body: "the closed eyes, standing to sing, raising one's hands . . . these are not markers of historical Protestant traditions. They are markers of Pentecostalism."[37]

Taken together, this combination of pneumatological expectations, soundscape, and bodily engagement created a potent recipe that was, in turn, imported back into local congregations by the very youth groups that participated in the event. For Luckow, at *EJN 0215*

> people participated with their bodies. The experience also modeled something that people took back to their congregations: patterns, songs, and ways of thinking about worship that arose from what we did there.[38]

On the other hand, certain particularities of our experience at *EJN 2015* were, I argue, distinctly Lutheran. Luckow, Sell and I had exchanged worship leading techniques and strategies for years before that event, and developed what we considered a uniquely Lutheran approach to contemporary worship leadership that (we hoped) was distinct from models proposed by both Pentecostal and *gospel* sources. In other words, we developed a particular Lutheran pedagogy of worship leadership for those in our denomination interested in leading contemporary worship.

This particular pedagogy was shaped by a set of foundational strategies. The first was to avoid metacommentary in worship: no testimonies, no "minipreaching," no extended commentary on the meaning of lyrics, no longwinded verbal exhortations for participants to join. Instead, says Sell, "The music was supposed to speak for itself, and any spoken commentary was supposed to be a tool for contemplation, to support the music."[39] At *EJN 2015*, we rarely spoke between songs in each worship set, preferring instead to read directly from Scripture or invite participants to extemporaneous prayer for short periods of time.

This focus on Scripture as a central protagonist in musical worship is a second trait and connects contemporary worship leadership with Lutheran aspirations around the place of the Scripture in liturgy. We interspersed songs with selections from the Bible, using them to contextualize and interpret the songs and create theological transitions that, hopefully, enriched the worship experience. In other words, while personal experience was certainly important to us, we emphasized the collective gathering around the Scripture (sung or spoken) as a phenomenological center of gravity of the Lutheran experience of worship.

Third, we leveraged uniquely Lutheran perspectives on the place of music in creation and in Christian worship. I have written elsewhere about Luther's theology of creation and the high place of music within it, which creates a particular hospitality for music in Lutheran liturgy.[40] The theological DNA of Lutheranism celebrates music with a potency that gives it sacramental qualities. I employ the descriptor "sacramental" here in alignment with Lim and Ruth, who argue that "one of the distinctive elements of contemporary worship, especially in its Pentecostal expressions, has been to develop this idea of divine presence through congregational song into systems of theology and piety, which might be considered *sacramental* if we allow this term to refer to a general notion of encounter with God's presence."[41]

In our conversation, Luckow argued along similar lines: "[Lutherans] have an almost sacramental understanding of music in worship. It's not only music as thanksgiving, but also to confess sins, to proclaim grace, music that will speak of important aspects of our theology, affirm people's value . . . sacramental in that sense. Music constitutes in itself the liturgical elements we find in a more sacramental liturgy."[42] From this perspective, Lutherans in general, and particularly the Luthercostal youth I speak of here, sustain notions of music and the arts that are closer to Pentecostal traditions than their Reformed siblings. In singing, they are searching for sacramental experience, for the "encounter with God's presence" that Lim and Ruth speak of. This search confers a particular Luthercostal flavor to worship experiences that combine Lutheran proclivities toward the celebration of music in worship with Pentecostal worship practices in search of that encounter.

The final worship leadership strategy we employed at *EJN 2015* is connected to preparation. Lutheran liturgiology places a particular emphasis on preparation of and for the liturgy, a notion that heavily informed our lengthy process of planning and rehearsal for the event. Pentecostal worship frequently invites the unplanned and uninvited, the impromptu, into worship as a marker of charisma. Pentecostal theologian Néstor Medina argues that "Latina/o/x Pentecostal spirituality in community displays an implicit (pneumatological) theological discourse in the form of preaching, coritos, testimonies, and offends, all of which are characterized by spontaneity, creativity, and intense participation."[43] At *EJN 2015*, we carefully curated the song selection and rehearsed worship sets and transitions even as we welcomed intense participation, which is also characteristic of Brazilian engagement with music broadly speaking.

Therefore, while the worship at *EJN 2015* relied significantly on the embodiment, pneumatological expectations, and soundscape typical of

Pentecostalism, it was also shaped by distinctly Lutheran conceptualizations of the place of music and Scripture in worship and the preparation required to weave them together. It was, in other words, Luthercostal worship.

Speaking of Latine Pentecostal pneumatology, Medina describes the "interwoven nature of convivencia [fellowship], acompañamiento [mutual support or accompaniment], kenosis/vulnerability" that constitute "the very essence of the triune God."[44] The worship at *EJN 2015* falls squarely into his description. André Kohlrausch, who at the time served as the Youth Ministry Coordinator for *ME,* described the event in a post on *Luteranos.com*, IECLB's main internet portal. Kohlrausch described an evident avidness to sing:

> with or without electricity, everyone wanted to party. People started partying even before the program began on Saturday. And when the electricity went out, I thought, as the event organizer: "Now we're in trouble!" And God surprised me. To watch the chorus of young people that didn't care about any of that, stringing together songs to God, as if God were telling me: "You thought you were controlling something. Let it be, I'll take it from here."[45]

In that sense, the young worshipers at *EJN 2015* not only sang loudly and enthusiastically but also took ownership of the musical experience when the electricity went out and the three of us on stage with the band, supposed worship leaders, were bereft of the paraphernalia on which we relied to lead. The experience evidences mutual support and fellowship, and the "emptying into the experience" constitutive of Pentecostal kenosis is: sing as loud as you can, jump as hard as you can, for as long as you can. Kohlrausch's comment illustrates how this vivacious engagement is narrated as a meeting place with God.

That particular scene resonates with Ortiz's speculation around Puerto Rican Lutheran women when she asks, "Could it be that Luthercostal Latinas have only begun to *appropriate* Lutheran tradition, and yet, have already *re-appropriated* Luther's hermeneutic audacity? If so, in what other rich and significant ways have our Latina sisters appropriated and re-appropriated our Lutheran heritage?"[46] The youth at *EJN 2015* audaciously adopted a Lutheran hospitality toward music and the fervor of Pentecostal musicking, creating a richly-textured soundscape of spirit and song on that Saturday that was not a tug-of-war between Pentecostal and Lutheran theologies. Instead, it was an interwoven tapestry of influences, from classic Pentecostal Brazilian *corinhos* to *gospel* influences and a Brazilian culture of participatory musicking. This Luthercostal tapestry is an embodied theologization that, in the words of Ortiz, "no longer lives according to one *or* the other theology, but rather, by one *and* the other."[47]

Like music at revival camp meetings in the eighteenth and nineteenth centuries, or early Pentecostal music in the United States, the worship at *EJN 2015* portrays unique instances of contextualization in church music. I spoke earlier of how the experience of the worship leaders with the Lutheran church in South Brazil allowed us to make pragmatic decisions about repertoire and style. Describing the experience and our preparation, Sell argued that "church only exists as a function of a context, not only of a universal truth. That's inevitable."[48] Moreover, he told me that at *EJN 2015*, "we were able to read the context really well at the time. It was our context . . . We went through a process of searching for a voice. And that voice was refined as it echoed between the three of us."[49] This "echo between the three of us" that he describes speaks to the long process of planning, preparation, and rehearsal that we underwent for *EJN 2015*. We knew that it was important to acknowledge older and newer liturgical shifts in the Lutheran musical landscape in Brazil. Brazilian Lutheran worship is, of course, inevitably distinct from that of its European counterparts. Luckow argues that "even the most traditional Lutheran church in Brazil, which might consider itself a guardian of the classic Lutheran tradition, is far removed from its German counterparts." Put another way, she said:

> We inculturate even when we don't want to. It's a natural part of the process of planting roots in a new context, relying on new resources . . . even the materials we use for building churches, the glass for stained glass windows is different, the altars are made with other materials. All these elements create transformations even when people insist on keeping everything the same."[50]

In the case of South Brazilian youth at *EJN 2015*, the localization of contemporary worship meant bringing together Pentecostal worship practices with Lutheran theology and liturgy.

Ortiz describes the particular *locus* of Luthercostality as an estuary: a place where different bodies of water from both the ocean and rivers intermingle into a unique, brackish, distinct ecosystem with defined characteristics. In this estuary, Ortiz finds the "lotus flower," which is the Luthercostal Latina experience. That flower is indigenous to its estuary and flourishes there because the estuary "is representative of the historical, social, and spiritual processes through which the Holy Spirit works. The lotus flourishes as a result of the Spirit pulling seeming opposite realities together, destroying that which threatens life, and nurturing the lotus through the decay/mourning process until new life emerges."[51]

CONCLUSION

Many rivers meet the ocean in the estuary of South Brazilian Lutheranism: the European, and particularly Teutonic, Lutheranism that came to Brazil through immigration in the nineteenth and early twentieth centuries; the Catholic underpinnings of Brazilian society as developed under Portuguese colonial rule; the influence of Pentecostal missionary work in the country, especially during the twentieth century; the rise of Brazil's indigenous *gospel* music industry; and the continued influence of the transnational worship projects that continue shaping how contemporary Brazilian *evangélicos* worship. In that estuary, which sustains various ecclesiologies, liturgies, traditions, repertoires, and practices, the Luthercostal flower is one particular expression of how spirit and song intermingle and produce vibrant participation in the song of the church.

NOTES

1. Elevation Worship, *Mighty Warrior* (Essential, 2014).
2. Bethel Music and Jeremy Riddle, *Furious* (Bethel Music/Kingsway Music, 2011).
3. An amateur recording of this performance can be found at *EJN/ENA 2015—Louvor*, 2015, https://www.youtube.com/watch?v=ALN7l-4QF4E. The exact moment when the generator blacks out can be found at *EJN/ENA 2015—Queda de Energia*, 2015, https://www.youtube.com/watch?v=cb4gq0Y8zLw.
4. More information at: https://www.luteranos.com.br/.
5. In English, "Encontrão" translates to "large gathering." All translations from Portuguese in this chapter are my own unless otherwise indicated.
6. I have written about this same gathering in an article that examines translational aspects of transnational worship repertoire. That essay also begins with a vignette describing worship at EJN 2015, but focuses on a specific song. See: Marcell Silva Steuernagel, "Transnational and Translational Aspects of Global Christian Congregational Musicking," *Religions* 12, no. 9 (September 2021): 1–18, https://doi.org/10.3390/rel12090732.
7. My own compositions, for instance, were featured at *EJN 2015* and can be found in the hymnal of IECLB. See: #37, #82, #89, #106, # 321, and #628 in Soraya Heinrich Eberle et al., eds., *Livro de Canto Da IECLB* (São Leopoldo, RS: Editora Sinodal, 2017).
8. For a detailed account of the rise of Brazil's *gospel* industry and its distinctive characteristics, see: Silva Steuernagel, Marcell, "'Além Do Gospel': A History of Brazil's Alternative Christian Music Scene," in *Christian Sacred Music in the Americas*, ed. Andrew Shenton and Joanna Smolko (Lanham, MD: Rowman & Littlefield, 2021), 131–151.
9. Marcell Silva Steuernagel, *Church Music Through the Lens of Performance*, Congregational Music Studies Series (New York: Routledge, 2021), 15–16.
10. Silva Steuernagel, *Church Music Through the Lens of Performance*, 155.
11. These compound labels are not infrequent in the literature, See, for instance: Nathan Nettleton, "Free-Church Bapto-Catholic," *Liturgy (Washington)*, vol. 19, no. 4 (2004): 57–68.

12. The exception here would be the charismatic movement that grew out of the ME context in the early 1990s; for more, see: Valdir Pedde, "apontamentos sobre o surgimento do movimento carismático (movimentos de renovação espiritual) na IECLB," *Estudos Teológicos*, vol. 42, no. 3 (2002): 29–51.

13. Luckow 2024.

14. Silva Steuernagel, "Songs From Other Heartlands: Church Music in the Global South," in *Worship through Latinx Eyes: Interdisciplinary Perspectives on Public Worship Practices* (Eugene: Cascade Books, 2024), fn. 39. Forthcoming.

15. Cheryl M. Peterson, "Theology Between Wittenberg and Azusa," *Dialog*, vol. 55, no. 4 (2016), 295.

16. Leila M. Ortiz, "A Latina Luthercostal Invitation Into an Ecclesial Estuary," *Dialog*, vol. 55, no. 4 (2016), 308.

17. Ortiz, "A Latina Luthercostal Invitation," 308–309.

18. Pedde, "Apontamentos," 31.

19. Paul Freston, "Dilemas de naturalização do protestantismo étnico: a igreja luterana no Brasil," *Revista de Ciências Humanas*, vol. 16, no. 24 (January 1, 1998), 69.

20. Freston, "Dilemas de naturalização," 70–71.

21. For more information on the history of IECLB and its hymnody, see: Marcell Silva Steuernagel, "History and Structure of Hymns of the People of God, Vol. 1," *Vox Scripturae,* vol. XXIV, no. 1 (2016): 181–197.

22. Philip Jenkins, *The next Christendom: The Coming of Global Christianity*, 3rd ed (New York: Oxford University Press, 2011), 134–135.

23. Aageson and Jacobson, "Introduction," in *The Future of Lutheranism in a Global Context*, eds., James W. Aageson and Arland Dean Jacobson (Minneapolis: Augsburg Fortress, 2008), 3.

24. Luckow, interview with author.

25. Eberle, interview with author.

26. Luckow, interview with author.

27. The third, Elevation Worship, has Baptist roots.

28. Sell, interview with author.

29. Luckow, interview with author.

30. Luckow, interview with author.

31. For further insights into the connection between live worship and mediation, see: Anna E. Nekola and Thomas Wagner, eds., *Congregational Music-Making and Community in a Mediated Age*, Congregational Music Studies Series (Farnham, UK: Ashgate, 2015); Monique M. Ingalls, *Singing the Congregation: How Contemporary Worship Music Forms Evangelical Community* (Oxford: Oxford University Press, 2018).

32. Eberle, interview with author.

33. Luckow, interview with author.

34. Sell, interview with author.

35. Luckow, interview with author.

36. Sell, interview with author.

37. Eberle, interview with author.

38. Luckow, interview with author.
39. Sell, interview with author.
40. Silva Steuernagel, Marcell, "Luther's Musical Thought Through Time and Space: Negotiating Tradition Across the Traditional/Contemporary Divide," in *Celebrating Lutheran Music: Scholarly Perspectives at the Quincentenary*, ed. Jonas Lundblad, Mattias Lundberg, and Maria Schildt (Uppsala, SE: Acta Universitatis Upsaliensis, 2019), 351–365.
41. Swee Hong Lim and Lester Ruth, *Lovin' on Jesus: A Concise History of Contemporary Worship* (Nashville: Abingdon Press, 2017), 185.
42. Luckow, interview with author.
43. Néstor Medina, "Theological Musings toward a Latina/o/x Pneumatology," in *The Wiley Blackwell Companion to Latinoax Theology*, ed. Orlando O. Espín, Second edition (John Wiley & Sons, Ltd, 2023), 183.
44. Medina, "Theological Musings," 195.
45. André R. Kohlrausch, "EJN e EM Em Algumas Palavras," Portal Luteranos, May 3, 2015, http://www.luteranos.com.br/noticias/movimento-encontrao-missao-zero/ejn-e-em-em-algumas-palavras.
46. Ortiz, "A Latina Luthercostal Invitation," 313.
47. Ortiz, "A Latina Luthercostal Invitation," 313.
48. Sell, interview with author.
49. Sell, interview with author.
50. Luckow, interview with author.
51. Ortiz, "A Latina Luthercostal Invitation," 313.

BIBLIOGRAPHY

Bethel Music, and Jeremy Riddle. *Furious*. Bethel Music/Kingsway Music, 2011.
Eberle, Soraya Heinrich. 2024. Communication with author. Barranquilla, Colombia. January 26.
Eberle, Soraya Heinrich, Werner Ewald, Silva Steuernagel, Marcell, and et al., eds. *Livro de Canto Da IECLB*. São Leopoldo, RS: Editora Sinodal, 2017.
EJN/ENA 2015—Louvor, 2015. https://www.youtube.com/watch?v=ALN7l-4QF4E.
EJN/ENA 2015—Queda de Energia, 2015. https://www.youtube.com/watch?v=cb4gq0Y8zLw.
Elevation Worship. *Mighty Warrior*. Essential, 2014.
Freston, Paul. "Dilemas de naturalização do protestantismo étnico: a igreja luterana no Brasil." *Revista de Ciências Humanas,* vol. 16, no. 24 (January 1, 1998): 61–73. doi: 10.5007/%x.
Ingalls, Monique M. *Singing the Congregation: How Contemporary Worship Music Forms Evangelical Community*. Oxford: Oxford University Press, 2018.
Kohlrausch, André R. "EJN e EM Em Algumas Palavras." Portal Luteranos, May 3, 2015. http://www.luteranos.com.br/noticias/movimento-encontrao-missao-zero/ejn-e-em-em-algumas-palavras.

Lim, Swee Hong, and Lester Ruth. *Lovin' on Jesus: A Concise History of Contemporary Worship*. Nashville: Abingdon Press, 2017.

Luckow, Fabiane Behling. 2024. Interview with author. Online. January 24.

Medina, Néstor. "Theological Musings toward a Latina/o/x Pneumatology." In *The Wiley Blackwell Companion to Latinoax Theology*, edited by Orlando O. Espín, 2nd edition (pp. 182–204). John Wiley & Sons, Ltd, 2023. doi: 10.1002/9781119870333.ch10.

Nekola, Anna E., and Thomas Wagner, eds. *Congregational Music-Making and Community in a Mediated Age*. Congregational Music Studies Series. Farnham, UK: Ashgate, 2015.

Nettleton, Nathan. "Free-Church Bapto-Catholic." *Liturgy (Washington)*, vol. 19, no. 4 (2004): 57–68. doi: 10.1080/04580630490490530.

Ortiz, Leila M. "A Latina Luthercostal Invitation Into an Ecclesial Estuary." *Dialog*, vol. 55, no. 4 (2016): 308–15. doi: 10.1111/dial.12276.

Pedde, Valdir. "Apontamentos sobre o surgimento do movimento carismático (movimentos de renovação espiritual) na IECLB." *Estudos Teológicos*, vol. 42, no. 3 (2002): 29–51.

Peterson, Cheryl M. "Theology Between Wittenberg and Azusa." *Dialog*, vol. 55, no. 4 (2016): 295–97. doi: 10.1111/dial.12273.

Sell, Daniel. 2024. Interview with author. Online. January 24.

Silva Steuernagel, Marcell. "'Além Do Gospel': A History of Brazil's Alternative Christian Music Scene." In *Christian Sacred Music in the Americas*, edited by Andrew Shenton and Joanna Smolko (pp. 131–51). Lanham, MD: Rowman & Littlefield, 2021.

Silva Steuernagel, Marcell. "Transnational and Translational Aspects of Global Christian Congregational Musicking." *Religions* 12, no. 9 (September 2021): 1–18. doi: 10.3390/rel12090732.

Silva Steuernagel, Marcell. "History and Structure of Hymns of the People of God, Vol. 1." *Vox Scripturae,* vol. XXIV, no. 1 (2016): 181–97.

Silva Steuernagel, Marcell. "Luther's Musical Thought Through Time and Space: Negotiating Tradition Across the Traditional/Contemporary Divide." In *Celebrating Lutheran Music : Scholarly Perspectives at the Quincentenary*, edited by Jonas Lundblad, Mattias Lundberg, and Maria Schildt (pp. 351–65). Uppsala, SE: Acta Universitatis Upsaliensis, 2019. http://urn.kb.se/resolve?urn=urn:nbn:se:uu:diva-396261.

Silva Steuernagel, Marcell. *Church Music Through the Lens of Performance*. Congregational Music Studies Series. New York: Routledge, 2021. doi: 10.4324/9781003080329.

Silva Steuernagel. "Songs From Other Heartlands: Church Music in the Global South." In *Worship through Latinx Eyes: Interdisciplinary Perspectives on Public Worship Practices*. Eugene: Cascade Books, 2024. Forthcoming.

Conclusion
The Classic Fade Out
Steven Félix-Jäger

When a song ends by fading out, listeners are given a sense that the music never really ends. We imagine ourselves walking away from a music venue as the performing band gets quieter and quieter, or turning the dial down even though we're fully aware that the song hasn't resolved. The band's still jamming, but you are quietly exiting the experience. Let's consider this conclusion a classic fade-out—the conversations surrounding music and the Spirit will continue even as we conclude our little contribution to the dialogue.

Together, this collection of essays says a lot about music—it is emotive, cathartic, expressive, inspiring, communal, formational, imminent, and transcendent. It gathers and unites us and tells us something deep about ourselves as bodies-in-community. These essays also say a lot about the Spirit—God is near, present, revelatory, redemptive, reconciling, comforting, and uniting. The Spirit makes knowable things unknown and obscures the things we think we know too well. Throughout this book, we argue that music tells us things about the Spirit we would not have otherwise known because both the Spirit and music operate in the same spaces. They both operate between languages and cultures, between desires and longings, between the visible and invisible, and between the deep and near.

Our conversation began by asking what music can tell us about God's Spiritedness. Somehow music touches the ineffable—it has the ability to transport listeners beyond themselves, both in a lateral direction that helps them feel something true about others and in a vertical direction that helps them know something of God. To this end, part I of this book looks at how music engages both the divine and our affections. Kickstarting this dialogue, Chris E. W. Green sets out to determine in what ways music is immanent and transcendent. Green draws from a variety of sources (Jewish, Christian Orthodox, and mainline Protestant theology) that all see a mystical connection between music and the divine. Green says music is transcendent *because* it is earthly and immanentizing. In other words, music's ability to draw us together toward each other helps draw us up toward God. We are drawn together as songs are sung together facing the same direction, but also over each other, and (at times) against each other. Singing is mystical, therefore, because it transfigures our communion together and, as such, participates in God's communion in Godself. So in a real sense, we "mystically experience God's experience of God" in song.

Carrying on Green's theme of mysticism, Edwin Rodríguez-Gungor utilizes science and metaphysics to understand music's primordial function in the universe, suggesting that what we observe may, in fact, be God. Rodriguez believes that God is speaking to us through the dimensions of song, both through the music of the material world and the music we create. He believes this is the primary way the Spirit speaks to us and leads us, both physically and metaphysically. According to Rodriguez, God's work is art; God sings, and we are confronted by this reality both physically and metaphysically, through both reason and faith. In a mysterious way, then, the music we hear does not only communicate God to us but *is* God in and around us.

Shifting gears a bit to our immanent frame, Steven Félix-Jäger explores the connections between music, affect, and manipulation. He contends that much of the discourse surrounding music and manipulation is based on equivocations between the words manipulation, persuasion, and affect. While music is affective, it is not manipulative in the narrow sense of the word, which implies deceptive control. While artists and presenters bear an ethical responsibility to assure the noncoercive use of an affective medium like music, ultimately, it is their intention that determines if the music is used manipulatively. Félix-Jäger discusses contemporary worship music as a case study to explore when music is used for manipulation or utilized to foster a genuine encounter with God.

Part I concludes with a fascinating chapter by Sophia Magallanes-Tsang, where she puts Qoheleth, Kierkegaard, and songwriter Elliott Smith into a rich dialogue that hovers around the topic of the human feeling of meaninglessness. Magallanes-Tsang demonstrates how the Spirit can utilize a "negative mode" to lead wanderers out of a wilderness. People can experience peace once they negate everything the world has to offer. Magallanes-Tsang argues that Elliott Smith approached these existential themes in his music through a hopeful absurdism that was willing to be led by a good guide. In this way, music plays a pivotal role in reconnecting people to a sense of wholeness in the midst of apprehension.

This book also looks at how the Spirit functions within, and even determines, culture through music. Music, as a profound human expression, can find itself in a rich dialogue with the Spirit. As such, part II of this book looks at how various songwriters and musicians have engaged with pneumatological themes in their music. We see how various regional and cultural expressions shape unique understandings of the Spirit and the Spirit's work in the world. To kick this part off, Amber Benson considers the work of songwriter Jason Isbell, a contemporary Americana artist. Although Isbell doesn't profess to be a Christian, many of his lyrics are "haunted" by a brand of Southern Christian religious life. As a method, Benson utilizes an insistency-based analysis to uncover what religious themes were repeated and proved significant in his corpus. Benson sees that Isbell frequently discusses the presence of the Godhead, convictions of sin and condemnation, and church hypocrisy. Benson likens Isbell to a Southern Gothic author like Flannery O'Connor. Although Isbell does not identify as a Christian artist, he uses theological concepts to look at both the sacred and profane aspects of our human condition.

In their chapter, musician Marc Byrd and theologian Aaron Ross discuss some theological implications of wordless music. They point out that while sung words frame the meaning of songs and musical experiences, wordless music avoids that sort of framing. Singers and spokespersons can reframe music so that it is received in a measured way, but while the experience of wordless music is still framed, it is framed only by the beauty of its expression. Theologically, we can understand the Spirit as operating in this openness—drawing listeners to re-engage and reinterpret their experiences. This re-engagement denies the reductionist illusions of certainty that's often present in verbal music. In this way, wordless music opens up a theo-aesthetic space for us to explore and encounter the divine.

In his chapter titled "Spiritual Longing in the Music of Jimmy Hendrix," Blaine Charette explores the concept of "longing" theologically, demonstrating how it is present in the lyrics and music of Jimi Hendrix. Hendrix was an introverted man who, despite his public persona, dealt with feelings of loneliness and existential emptiness. Yet, his lyrics also demonstrate a hopefulness for something or someone beyond himself that might bring about redemption. Also present in his corpus is a mystical feminine figure that's powerful, wise, and caring. This feminine figure evokes the Spirit and acts as a guide for Hendrix, who rescues him from his longing.

In his chapter, Jeff S. Lamp contrasts two pneumatological readings of Bob Dylan's "Blowin' in the Wind." Lamp argues that when the song was first performed in 1962 and 1963, around the release of his second album, *The Freewheelin' Bob Dylan*, it functioned as a protest song and became an important song of the Civil Rights Movement. Lamp argues that because of Dylan's biblical references and general framework, this song's performance can be seen as demonstrating the "prophetic Spirit." But when the song was performed again in the late 1970s and early 1980s during Dylan's "Born-Again" period, the song was recontextualized both musically and thematically to present the "wind" as concomitant with the "renewing Spirit." This trajectory shows Dylan establishing (with the same song) an eschatological journey of rebuke to renewal by the Spirit.

Jeremy Lee Hunt closes part II with a chapter titled "Rivers Underneath: The Spirit in Underground Music." Using underground music as a case study, Lee argues that both the Spirit and underground music can be viewed as conduits between a messenger and an alternate audience. The Spirit connects us with the infinite divine, and the live underground concert blurs the line between audience and performer, connecting us to the ineffability of music. Underground music is a unifying agent that connects and unites people on the fringes, just as the Spirit connects those who are disenfranchised back to God.

Finally, this book explores music's placement in Christian spiritual traditions, particularly how Christian experiences of the Spirit shape the way they think about music. As such, part III considered music in Christian worship and witness from various global perspectives. This part explored various ways to understand contemporary worship music and also discussed some of the cultural migrations of worship music. In order to highlight prevalent pneumatological themes in contemporary worship music, Shannan Baker considered the song catalog of four of the most prominent worship artists of the 2010s, in particular, Bethel Music, Hillsong Worship, Passion, and Elevation Worship. Since the only theology many people receive comes from the Sunday morning service, Baker's goal was to see what sort of pneumatology presents itself to a trans-denominational audience that's engaging in the Pent-Evangelicalism of the catalog. In her research, Baker found recurring themes that the Spirit gives life, speaks, leads, sustains, redeems, causes revivals, performs miracles, changes the world, and testifies about Christ. Baker contends that these themes point toward an operant pneumatology that sees the Spirit as personal and active in the world.

Jennifer Thigpenn explores the embodied witness of black gospel music. She contends that from its inception, black gospel music has navigated the tensions between suffering and hope, and that black worshipers find confidence in their communal, embodied expressions of worship. When black worshipers lift up and declare a new reality in the midst of oppression, they meet the ever-present Holy Spirit that perpetually works toward redemption and reconciliation. Black gospel music rearticulates a powerful new identity—black people are children of God, pursued and adopted. Gospel music remains a testament to the enduring power of faith, hope, resilience, and the trust that black individuals and communities place in the liberating, transformative grace of God.

In her chapter, Kimberly Ervin Alexander considers the history and reception of the classic gospel hit "Oh Happy Day." In particular, Alexander looks at how this song, originally written by Phillip Doddridge in the eighteenth century, was covered and recontextualized by the Edwin Hawkins Singers in 1969, and became a mainstay in black gospel music. The Edwin Hawkins Singers were a youth choir from the Bay Area in California; the lead vocalist of the song was Dorothy Combs Morrison. Alexander maintains that it was Morrison's powerful, Spirit-filled vocals that made the song so popular to black and white audiences alike. Alexander shows how the song was able to traverse borders beyond black Pentecostalism to white, Evangelical, and mainline congregants—a major feat during the difficult social climate of the 1960s. Alexander shows how this phenomenon echoes the egalitarian spirit of the Azusa Street Revival of 1906.

Jeremy Perigo considers the role distribution and translation play as worship music proliferates around the world. He asks if this movement is merely another venture of global economic commodification, or if the Spirit utilizes these channels of distribution to help unify a shared ecclesial identity around the world through worship music. As a case study, Perigo considers Turkish contextualizations of Western worship music; in particular, he looks at the translations of "The Blessing." Theologically, Perigo looks back at Acts 2 and notices that through the dispersion of tongues, the Spirit was attempting to undergo an experiment in linguistic contextualization. This allowed the post-Pentecost church to become a unified church of many tongues and cultures. Yet, although the Spirit today utilizes translocal worship music to inspire global unity, not all examples of global unity are inspired by the Spirit. What is needed is cultural discernment enabled by the Spirit to see if the song is in line with the Spirit's work today.

Marcell Silva Steuernagel closes out part III by exploring the ways in which South Brazilian Lutheranism has adopted a pentecostalized worship culture where musical worship has become a foundation for the "Luthercostal" experience, revelation, and catharsis. He draws from a variety of scholarly sources, interviews, and his own firsthand experience of leading worship at the national Lutheran youth gathering called *Encontrão Jovem Nacional*. He concludes that the Brazilian youth were searching for a sacramental experience where they could encounter the presence of the Holy Spirit through musical worship. Because this is a distinctively Pentecostal approach to worship, Silva Steuernagel argues that the youth would best be described as Luthercostal.

While this chapter leaves us with myriad ways to consider the Spirit and music, there is yet the possibility for endless more. Because everyone has their own enculturated and embodied experience of music (and God, for that matter), they'll all have their own particular experiences of how music has transported them beyond themselves. Recounting any of these experiences expands our understanding of the shared liminal spaces in which both music and the Spirit operate. Hence, this topic of conversation can continue to expand in any direction. This topic of conversation truly can persist forever . . . and we're here for it!

It is our hope that these essays have inspired you to listen to music with fresh ears. Perhaps in your listening, you'll find God.

Index

affect, 40–46
allusiveness, 87
alternative rock, 39, 108, 135
Americana, 69
artistic intention, 41–42, 44–46, 48–49, 87, 101
Azusa Street Revival, 164, 177–78, 183, 185, 235

beauty, 1, 4, 17–18, 34, 60, 89, 91, 93–95, 98, 135, 177, 205, 233
Bethel Music, 39, 144–48, 153, 220–21
Black church, 160–61, 164–69, 174–75, 178, 185
"Blowin' in the Wind," 115–19, 121–22, 124–25, 233
Blues, 69, 72, 103, 159–60, 164, 166
born-again, 121
Brazil, 215–21, 224–27

camp meetings, 164, 173, 175, 226
chaos, 31, 93, 183
charismatic, 1, 88, 121, 146, 198, 201, 216–19
Christian Copyright Licensing International (CCLI), 144
creation, 4, 15, 17–18, 23–24, 26, 64, 91, 95–96, 104–5, 110, 124, 135, 153, 162, 169; and music, 26–35, 87–88, 133–34, 224; and wisdom, 56
creativity, 17, 23, 135, 137, 180, 219, 224

discernment, 11, 49–50, 202, 206–7, 235
Dylan, Bob, 115–25, 233–34

Ecclesiastes, 54, 56–62, 111
either/or, 54, 60–64
Elevation Worship, 144–45, 152–55, 201, 215, 219, 221
embodiment, 43, 45, 49–50, 59–60, 129, 159–62, 165, 169, 224–25, 234–35
experience, 2–5, 10, 14–19, 23, 30–31, 42–50, 58–60, 70, 75, 77, 88–96, 106–11, 129–38, 154, 159–60, 166–69, 177–83, 204–7, 215–26, 232–36

Francis of Assisi, 33
frequency (music), 26, 30–33, 133, 146

globalization, 197–202, 206–8
gospel music, 9, 69–76, 116, 119, 173–86; black gospel music, 72, 122–23, 159–61, 164–69; Brazilian *gospel* music, 216, 219–20, 223, 225, 227; Holiness-Pentecostal style gospel music, 178; Southern gospel music, 184

hardcore, 92, 129, 132, 135
Hendrix, Jimi, 103–11, 176, 223
Hillsong Worship, 45–46, 144–45, 148–50, 153–54, 199, 219–20, 234
Holy Spirit, 2–5, 17, 23, 30, 33–34, 40, 49–50, 55, 58–61, 64, 76, 88, 90–94, 96–98, 110, 116–17, 119–21, 123–25, 129–31, 133–38, 143–55, 159–69, 173–75, 177–84, 186, 198–208, 216, 218, 222, 226, 231–32; as creative power, 5, 91, 132, 134; as gift, 130, 132, 137; as healer, 1, 96, 152, 178, 183; as ineffable, 95, 100, 137, 231; as presence, 13, 28, 45, 48–49, 75, 93, 109, 132, 137, 143, 145–53, 168–69, 181, 224, 235; as wise, 32, 56–57, 62–63
hymn, 9–10, 17, 34, 40, 71, 160, 164–66, 169, 173, 175, 180, 184, 198–99, 217, 219

Isbell, Jason, 69–81, 233

Jackson, Mahalia, 164, 166, 182–83
jazz, 69, 72, 160, 164, 166–68, 173, 176
Jesus people, 143, 167
job, 29, 54–58
Jubilee, 120

Kierkegaard, Soren, 54–55, 60–64, 232

Lewis, C. S., 27, 105–6
loneliness, 103–4, 106–7, 110
longing, 5, 9, 14, 43, 98, 104–6, 109–11, 231, 233
Luthercostalism, 215–20, 222, 224–27, 235

manipulation, 40–42, 44, 46–49, 232
metaphysics, 23, 27, 232
Muscle Shoals, 69–70, 72

new creation, 4, 15, 32, 121, 132
Newport Folk Festival, 116–17, 120–21, 123

"Oh Happy Day," 173, 175–77, 179–86

Pentecostal, 9–11, 69, 72, 88, 91–93, 143–44, 160, 164–65, 169, 174–86, 198, 201, 205, 216–27, 235; Australian Pentecostalism, 148, 199; Black Pentecostalism, 161, 174, 179–80, 235; and experience, 14; as movement, 10, 70, 164, 183; as preaching, 1, 183; as traditions, 71, 174, 182, 220, 224
physics, 23, 25
pneumatology, 88, 117, 129, 131–32, 143–46, 149, 153–55, 225, 234
punk, 92, 129, 132, 134–35

Qoheleth, 53–54, 56–63, 232

revivals, 123, 147, 150–54, 160, 164, 173–74, 183, 200, 215, 218, 226, 234

Schleiermacher, Friedrich, 90
sin, 32, 74–77, 79, 81, 149, 151, 233
sixties, 103, 111, 115–16, 120–21, 124, 165, 167, 174, 176–77, 179–80, 185, 218, 220, 235
Smith, Elliott, 54–55, 62–64
Smith, James K. A., 45
social control, 41, 46–47
Spirit-filled, 70, 81, 235
spiritual gift, 49, 131, 203, 208
Spirituals, 159–64, 167
The Spirituals and the Blues, 159–60
Stavesacre, 135–37

Taylor, Charles, 47
"The Blessing," 152, 200–202, 206, 235
Tillich, Paul, 90–91
tongues, 10, 45, 93–94, 138, 146, 153, 164, 183, 201, 203–4, 235
Trinity, 16, 28, 75–76, 131, 134, 143, 145, 148, 154–55
Turkish liturgical identity, 199–200, 207

underground music, 129–30, 133–35, 137–38, 234

von Balthasar, Hans Urs, 4, 49, 94–95

Wesleyan, 11, 80, 145, 179, 183
wisdom, 10, 12, 14, 18, 32, 49, 55–59, 62–63, 129–31
wordless, 33, 88–98, 233

worship, 4, 16, 28–29, 72, 92, 165–66, 168–69, 178, 197–207, 215–27, 232, 234–35; Black gospel worship, 161–62, 166; as Christian worship music, 39–42, 44–50, 132–33, 143–46, 148–49, 152–55, 168, 198–99, 202, 206–7; as gathering, 160; as leadership, 223–25; as liturgical, 10, 18; Pentecostal worship, 69–70, 72, 164; as practices, 197, 216–20, 223–24, 226; as style, 169

About the Editors and Contributors

Chris E. W. Green, PhD, is professor of public theology at Southeastern University and director for St. Anthony Institute of Theology, Philosophy, and Liturgics. He is the author, most recently, of *Being Transfigured: A Collection of Lenten Homilies* and *The Fire and the Cloud: A Biblical Christology*—the second volume of a Christological trilogy published by Baylor University Press.

Steven Félix-Jäger, PhD, MFA, is associate professor and chair of the Worship Arts and Media program at Life Pacific University. An exhibiting artist, songwriter, and producer, Félix-Jäger is also the author of several books, including *Renewal Worship*, the co-authored *Renewing Christian Worldview*, and the forthcoming *The Problem and Promise of Freedom* through Baker Academic. He is an ordained minister of the International Church of the Foursquare Gospel and co-hosts the *TikTok Theology* podcast.

Kimberly Ervin Alexander, PhD, is currently a faculty member and Director of Academics and RU Online at Ramp University, after over twenty years of teaching and administrative leadership in graduate-level theological education. She is an honorary research fellow with the Manchester Wesley Research Center. Her publications include *Pentecostal Healing: Models of Theology and Practice* and *Sisters, Mothers, Daughters: Pentecostal Responses to Global Violence Against Women*, as well as numerous articles focusing on the intersection of women and healing, as well as Pentecostal worship and music.

Shannan K. Baker, PhD, ThM, is a postdoctoral research fellow in music and digital humanities at Baylor University. Baker is a scholar and practitioner who has published articles on contemporary worship songs' musical and theological content and their use in practice. She is a founding member of the group Worship Leader Research, which studies the contemporary worship music industry and worship leaders' engagement with it.

Amber Benson, MTS, is an adjunct instructor of strategic communication at the Schieffer School of Communication at Texas Christian University and the former executive in residence at the Temerlin Advertising Institute at Southern Methodist University. At the Perkins School of Theology at Southern Methodist University, she received the Albert C. Outler award for outstanding theological writing. Benson is a songwriter and an artist member of the Americana Music Association.

Marc Byrd is a Grammy-nominated producer, songwriter, and musician. He is the cofounder of the duo Hammock, whose work has been associated with the ambient, post-rock, and neoclassical movements. His music has appeared in multiple feature films, TV series, art installations, and videogames and has been covered by BBC, The Wire, and NPR, among many others. He is the co-author of the Dove Award-winning song "God of Wonders," covered nearly one hundred times.

Blaine Charette, PhD, is Distinguished Professor of Biblical Studies at Northwest University in Kirkland, WA. He has taught biblical studies for over thirty years at colleges, universities, and seminaries in the United States, Canada, Europe, and Asia. He has published two books on Matthew's Gospel, *The Theme of Recompense in Matthew's Gospel* (1992; reprinted in 2015) and *Restoring Presence: The Spirit in Matthew's Gospel* (2000), co-edited a collection of essays, *Spirit and Story: Essays in Honour of John Christopher Thomas* (2020), and published several academic articles on a variety of New Testament topics.

Jeremy Hunt, PhD, is an affiliate assistant professor of theology and culture at Fuller Theological Seminary. He is the author of the forthcoming book *From Chaos to Ambiguity: A Theology of Noise Rock* and a contributor to various journals and publications. His music and video art explore spaces where noise and music, visuals and static, collide in contradiction and synchronicity via the band QOHELETH and a solo project, Aint Pancakes. He also runs Philip K. Discs, a DIY label dedicated to experimental music.

Jeffrey S. Lamp, PhD, is professor of New Testament and an instructor of environmental science at Oral Roberts University. He is the author of several books and articles in the areas of ecological hermeneutics, ecotheology, and popular culture.

About the Editors and Contributors

Sophia A. Magallanes-Tsang, PhD, is a Latina Pentecostal Bible scholar who specializes in Hebrew Wisdom Literature and Old Testament Studies. She is an assistant professor of biblical and theological studies at Fresno Pacific University. One of her current writing projects is *Reading the Word Interculturally* through Baker Academic.

Jeremy Perigo, DWS, is professor of theology and worship arts at Dordt University and is a visiting lecturer and research supervisor at Regent University and the London School of Theology. His research focuses on global evangelical liturgical theology and the contextualization of Christian worship. He hosts *Worship/Theology*, a podcast focused on faith and ministry praxis, and ministers internationally as a saxophonist, worship leader, and theological educator.

Edwin Rodríguez-Gungor, PhD, is a research fellow at the Ronald Reagan Presidential Foundation and Institute and an adjunct professor at Southeastern University, Tulsa University, and St. Anthony Institute of Theology, Philosophy, and Liturgics. He has six published works including *Spirit and Method* and the New York Times Bestseller, *There's More to the Secret.*

Aaron Gabriel Ross, PhD, is Chief of Staff at the Museum of the Bible in Washington, DC. Previously, Ross served as an assistant professor of theology at Southeastern University. He is the creator of the podcast *Everyday Theology*, has published with various outlets, including the United Bible Societies and the World Council of Churches, and has a forthcoming book with T&T Clark on the intersection between pneumatology and faith.

Marcell Silva Steuernagel, PhD, is assistant professor of church music and director of the Master of Sacred Music and Doctor of Pastoral Music Programs at Southern Methodist University's Perkins School of Theology. Marcell writes at the intersection of church music, theology, musicology, and performance theory. He served as minister of Worship, Arts, and Communication at Redeemer Lutheran Church in Curitiba, Brazil, for more than a decade and is an internationally active composer and performer. His most recent monograph is *Church Music Through the Lens of Performance,* published in Routledge's Congregational Music Studies series.

Jennifer Thigpenn, MDiv, is adjunct faculty in the Biblical Studies and Ministry departments at Life Pacific University. She is an ordained minister of the International Church of the Foursquare Gospel. She currently serves as a Multiethnic Ministry Coordinator for the Western District of Foursquare Churches and as an associate pastor at Pasadena Foursquare Church in Pasadena, California.

www.ingramcontent.com/pod-product-compliance
Ingram Content Group UK Ltd.
Pitfield, Milton Keynes, MK11 3LW, UK
UKHW041304160125
4146UKWH00005B/25